Date Due

A History of Victoria

A History of

J.J. Douglas Ltd.
Vancouver

HARRY
GREGSON

Victoria 1842-1970

with
Illustrations
and
Maps

J.J. Douglas Ltd.
1875 Welch Street
North Vancouver, B.C. V7P 1B7

Canadian Shared Cataloguing in Publication Data

Gregson, Harry.
    A history of Victoria 1842-1970

        ISBN 0-88894-141-2 pa.

        1. Victoria, B.C. — History.   I. Title.
FC3846.4.G74   971.1'34
F1089.5.V6G74

Book design by the Morriss Printing Company Ltd.
Printed and bound in Canada by the Hunter Rose Company
Cover design and photograph by Jim Rimmer

To the many worthy citizens whose names
through sheer limitations of space have not been
mentioned in this book

Contents

Maps and Other Illustrations

Photographs

Courtesy of the Provincial Archives and
Travel Bureau, Victoria, B.C.

Foreword

It has been the author's main endeavour in the three years devoted
to this, *A History of Victoria*, to select from the voluminous published material about Victoria of the last 130 years the significant
facts which would give historical perspective to the city's development.

To give all sources of information would be impracticable. They
range from verbal reminiscences by members of old families to
letters to the editors of the local newspapers through the decades,
city trade directories, historical reviews and the diaries of pioneers.
But mention should be made specially of Edgar Fawcett's *Reminiscences of Old Victoria*, Professor Margaret Ormsby's *British Columbia, a History* and James K. Nesbitt's *Victoria Historical Review*.
The author has also drawn freely on material published in *The
Islander* by such well known writers as Cecil Clark, Archie Wills,
T. W. Paterson, Ainslie Helmcken, James K. Nesbitt and others.
Extensive use has been made of the files of Victoria's two daily
newspapers and of land registry records.

My sincere thanks are due to experts in various fields who have
checked pertinent references in this history, notably to W. Berkeley
Monteith, Lieut.-Col. Art Sherwin and Mr. R. H. B. Ker (the two
world wars), Archbishop H. E. Sexton (church affairs), Doug
Peden (sports), City Assessor A. Joyce (buildings and taxes), Herbert Anscomb (prohibition) and to the staffs of the Victoria Public
Library (reference department) and the Provincial Archives.

The author acknowledges his debt to J. Munro who first suggested
three years ago the writing of this history.

Chapter 1

THE EARLIEST YEARS

THE EARLY SPRING OF 1843.

Through the bush on what is now Dallas Road semi-naked, fishblood-smeared Songhees Indians peered excitedly at a "smoking tree" which had appeared offshore. The smoking tree was the lanky funnel of the *Beaver*, first steamship on this coast.

Although they did not realize it, the Indians were witnessing an historic event. In the *Beaver* was the Hudson's Bay Company chief factor James Douglas. He had arrived to survey the area and build Fort Victoria, the beginnings of today's Victoria.

The *Beaver* had come to anchor off Shoal Point, better known to today's Victorians as the site of the former V.M.D. shipyards. Construction of the Fort began on June 4, 1843 and Victoria's history begins at this date. But the story as distinct from the history of this city began many years earlier. Victoria can be said to have been conceived in the friction arising out of American territorial ambitions.

In the second decade of the nineteenth century many American adventurers, most of them honest men, but some fleeing their creditors and a few preying on their fellow men began to trickle into the Pacific Northwest. These were not the later cattle barons driving thousands of animals over the Oregon Trail, but men whose total worldly possessions were a gun, a water canteen and what they could carry in the "turkey" slung over their shoulders. They lived off the land. Some had arrived in sailing ships via Cape Horn, but for the most part they were men who had braved the plains and coastal ranges to branch south into California, or northwest into Oregon which at that time comprised the present Washington and Oregon states.

Until their coming the London-based Hudson's Bay Company, the oldest chartered company in the world, held, but for the short-lived infringement by Jacob Astor who founded Astoria, the virtual monopoly of trade with Indians in the Northwest Pacific area. It had already absorbed its only rival, the Montreal-based North West Company, and carried on a lucrative trade in beaver skins, sea otter fur, and other commodities. The authority of the Company was reinforced with fortified trading posts, among them Fort George which later reverted to its original name of Astoria, and Fort Vancouver, now Vancouver, Washington.

The social, economic and ecological pattern of the territory was disturbed by the American newcomers. They were no respecters of the Indians or the Hudson's Bay Company. Although the slogan "fifty-four forty or fight" was not coined as a nationalist slogan until 1844, they resented the British and began setting up their own communities.

They preached that all men were equal, but practised policies which in the longer term led to the virtual extermination of their Indian fellow men. The short term result, however, was to endanger the livelihood of the Indians and the trading profits of the Hudson's Bay Company.

John McLoughlin, who began his career as a physician in Montreal and now headed the Company's interests in the Pacific Northwest, saw the danger in the new developments. He doubted that Britain would fight the United States for the sake of the Hudson's Bay Company and instructed his chief factor, James Douglas, to seek safer headquarters for the Company.

Douglas first saw what is now Victoria in 1842 and wrote to a friend: "The place itself appears a perfect Eden in the midst of the dreary wilderness of the Northwest coast, and so different is its general aspect from the wooded, rugged regions around that one might be pardoned for supposing it had dropped from the clouds . . ."

Few people who have seen the approaches to Victoria on a calm, summer day will dispute Douglas's praise. The blue sea and numerous islets, inlets, lagoons and sheltered coves could, but for our cooler waters, be located in the West Indies.

Douglas made a report to McLoughlin and a year later was here again to order the building of a fort in the area now bounded by Bastion, Wharf, Government and Broughton Streets to serve as strongpoint and warehouse. The mooring rings for the ships that used to tie up at the Company's wharf can still be seen embedded in concrete next to the H.M.C.S. Malahat Building on Wharf Street.

According to some authorities, the nearest Indians were at that time in Cadboro Bay and knew the Victoria area as Camosun or Camosack ... the latter name now commemorated with the high skyline apartment building near the water tower. Locally the Hudson's Bay Company post was first known as Fort Albert, but in the Company's records it is always referred to as Fort Victoria.

The Hudson's Bay Company fort was built by 53 Company men, mostly French Canadians who had served in other parts of the Pacific Northwest. They were helped by Songhees Indians who cut the 22-foot-long pickets for the pallisade of the enclosure which measured 330 feet by 400 feet and were given one blanket for every 60 pickets cut. The pickets were brought from Mount Douglas which also became known as Cedar Hill.

The first Fort bastion was where now stands the Army, Navy & Air Force Veterans' Club opposite H.M.C.S. Malahat; it had a cannon to return the salute of incoming ships: buried in Pioneer Square is a gunner named Fish who contacted gangrene and died after his arm was blown off by a misfire. Fish was one of those Company servants known as bluecoats who were paid £17 ($85) a year with board and lodging for a 13-hour working day.

The front gate of the Fort was at the foot of Fort Street — Fort and Wharf Streets — and the back gate on Government Street between what are now the Canadian Imperial Bank of Commerce and until recently the Canadian Pacific Railway ticket office. The Fort was enlarged in 1849 and another three-storey bastion added, but as the danger from Indians declined the bastions were demolished, the last in 1864.

James Douglas lived in one of the few dwellings erected inside the Fort, the remaining area being used for storehouses, officers'

3

hall and main hall. Douglas, who was 40 years old when he anchored off Shoal Point, was a broad-shouldered, slightly bow-legged Scot, born in Demerara. His father was a Glasgow merchant. His administrative experience had taught him to insist on respect for his position and he enforced strict discipline and high standards of conduct. Dinner at the Fort was at a set time, the linen clean and the silver brightly polished. Social distinctions were carefully observed and younger officers had to retire from the table after the toast to the Queen — Queen Victoria after whom Victoria is named.

As Governor he insisted on salutes being fired when he paid official visits to Craigflower, the first local school outside the Fort; to H.M. ships or to the Company's farm on San Juan Island. In later years as his financial position improved, he ordered his uniforms from London and clothed his daughters fashionably.

The Hudson's Bay Company came here to trade. The Royal Navy ships stationed here for the settlement's protection, Russian schooners, American whalers and other passing vessels needed fresh fruits, vegetables, provisions and other supplies. The Company imported goods from England, the West Indies and Honolulu and in addition started farms locally. Douglas brought in cattle, horses and seed, and the Company's cows browsed where now the Law Courts stand. The Indians thought the cattle a conveniently docile species of deer until public whippings restrained their hunting ardour.

Some of the farms started were exclusively owned by the Hudson's Bay Company. Others were operated under lease for The Puget's Sound Agricultural Company, an associate of the Hudson's Bay Company. The Hudson's Bay Company also leased land to settlers, such as George Dutnall, whose farm comprised a large part of James Bay. The whole of what is now downtown Victoria was farmed by Company employees for the Company. Other farms were begun at Hillside, the Uplands, Craigflower, Cloverdale, Viewfield, Constance Cove, Colwood, North Dairy and elsewhere. Their produce found a ready market even in distant San Francisco and Sitka, Alaska.

From their store on Wharf Street the Company enjoyed a monopoly of the retail trade and supplied everything from a needle to

4

a cannon ball. A three-pound loaf from the nearby bakery cost 25¢; boots were $3.75 a pair and lasted longer than the wearer's feet; Hudson's Bay blankets used in trade were famous and their quality made them as good as currency. But the cost of living was high ... prices being about three times those in England. It was somewhat alleviated by the Indians who sold clams at 25¢ a bucket, salmon at 25¢ each and venison at 5¢ a pound.

To further the coastal trade the Company brought in the steamers *Labouchere* and *Otter*; it also had ships specially adapted for immigrants, the fur trade and for exports to the Sandwich Islands (Hawaii).

Society consisted of the higher Company officials, mostly Scots; settler families of good standing and officers of H.M. ships at Esquimalt which was three miles away. The sometimes turbulent passage from Esquimalt to Victoria was generally made by canoe and lives were often lost.

All entertainment was of the self-engendered variety. Those excluded from the higher circles ... that is the Company's labouring servants and white workers on the farms, found their entertainment with each other and with the jolly ratings of H.M. ships. Recreation, one imagines, was the more appreciated when the working day began at 5 a.m. and ended at 6 p.m., the use of leisure being less of a problem than it is today.

Victoria in its early years was a very scattered and largely pastoral settlement. The farms were very different from those in crowded Europe; they consisted of a comparatively small area of cultivated land and much waste land over which cattle roamed. Uplands Farm, for instance, which was started in 1851 in what is now part of Oak Bay Municipality, consisted of a few farm buildings while cattle grazed in an area bounded by Cedar Hill Cross Road in the north, Camas Lane in the southeast, above Allenby Street in the south, Richmond Road in the west and the shoreline in the east. What is now the Uplands Golf Club and the Uplands Park were part of the grazing lands. See map page 206.

Cattle Point is so named because cattle were landed there to fatten in the Uplands prior to slaughter in what was then called 10-Mile Point, but is more probably the site of the Royal Victoria

Yacht Club moorings on Beach Drive where, even today, cattle skulls and other relics of a slaughter house are seen in the water.

First manager of the Uplands farms was Charles A. Bailey. William Leigh succeeded Bailey as manager, but like many pioneers he preferred an office job to farming and became the second city clerk of Victoria.

The Hudson's Bay Company was able to operate so many farms because on the face of it, the agreement it reached with the British government was very generous. The Company leased the whole of Vancouver Island from the Crown at a nominal rent of seven shillings ($1.50) per annum, a condition being that they establish within five years a colony on behalf of the Crown. The Company could sell land and minerals and timber, but nine-tenths of the proceeds of such sales were to be spent on roads, education, the Church and other elements of a stable society.

Roads came first, and Government Street, the oldest street this side of the Rockies was built. Boulders were thrown into the mud to give a foundation and six-inch planks laid side by side to form the province's earliest sidewalk. All the heavy labour was done by Indians and Kanakas (Sandwich Islanders), the latter being expert axemen.

Victorians owe a great debt to James, later Sir James, Douglas. His foresight led not only to the location of a settlement here, but he instituted Victoria's first town plan, created its first park at Beacon Hill and prohibited the felling of trees along the shoreline, thus protecting the new settlement from the cold winds of the Olympic Range. Beacon Hill was so called, of course, because the two signals on top of the hill enabled ships to fix their position in relation to Brotchie Ledge and Victoria.

But settlers arrived very slowly in the early years. At the time of the Fraser River gold rush in 1858, the population of 500 could have been comfortably housed in a modern highrise apartment.

The Reverend E. Cridge, later the stormy Dean of Christ Church, whose cottage "Marifield" on Carr Street was recently demolished, recalled that when he arrived in 1854 there were only 200 people in Victoria and not more than five houses on each of the four main streets ... Government, Fort, Yates and Johnson. Many of the

6

earliest immigrants quit almost immediately for Puget's Sound where land was given away and they were free from the autocratic rule of the Hudson's Bay Company system.

But Douglas had his problems and would have been spared many of them if his advice on settlement had been heeded by the British government. He wanted men, not necessarily with capital, but sturdy men with sturdy sons to break the land. The Colonial Office on the other hand wanted the system which had proved itself in Britain even during the stirrings caused by the French Revolution, namely landed aristocrats offering security to their servants in return for loyal service.

It insisted that settlers with capital bring in their own men to open up the land. Douglas was thereby saddled with some rare misfits. The first settler, Captain Walter Colquhoun Grant, was long on charm and wit, but short on farming experience. He had arranged in London that he be appointed the Company's surveyor (in addition to being a gentleman farmer) in part compensation for his pioneering effort and mislaid his surveying instruments en route. When he did start surveying, Douglas rather wished they had been lost forever. His cordial forgetfulness baffled his colleagues. "He was," said one Company official, "flighty to the point of lunacy."

Grant's eight men were champion grumblers and sowers of discontent. They all left him and Grant himself left finally in 1853 after starting a sawmill. The sawmill was about a quarter-mile from where is now the Sooke River Hotel and later became Muir's sawmill. Both the Sooke mill and Millstream (the other pioneer mill) exported to San Francisco.

After Grant came Edward Edwards Langford. Langford arrived in 1851 and Langford is named after him. Langford's farm was a 900-acre strip running northwest from Esquimalt Harbour taking in what has since become a racecourse and Langford Plains (now the Colwood Golf Club).

Captain Langford's agreement with the Puget's Sound Agricultural Company, an associate of the Hudson's Bay Company and for whom he was bailiff, was a farmer's dream. Buildings, staff and grocery bills were to be paid for by the Company. Langford built

7

what was for pioneer standards a fine country home, naming it Colwood after his Sussex estate. He added 11 buildings for servant and farm use. Among the "groceries" he charged up in one year to the Company were 70 gallons of assorted rum, sherry and brandy.

For the Royal Navy officers in Esquimalt the five daughters of Captain Langford were a mariner's equivalent of a farmer's dream. Colwood resounded to dance music, happy laughter and the clinking of glasses.

The happy round of hunts, picnics and dancing brought a lighter note to people accustomed hitherto to Scottish austerity. When Douglas accused Langford of lavishly spending the Company's capital in luxuries, the Captain was annoyed. As a gentleman farmer he attached more importance to being a gentleman than to farming. His wife shared his tastes. Among the "farming aids" she brought out was a piano.

Langford left the Colony in 1861 and his complaints in London caused trouble for Douglas. Some remains of Langford's farm still exist, notably a former dairy shed now in the garden of a home at 440 Goldstream.

A printed statement circulated in Victoria to the effect that Langford was more adept at milking his employers than milking cows and a consequent libel action which he lost and which led to his imprisonment for contempt of court, preceded the Captain's departure.

The lack of farming zeal by the gallant Captain was more than offset by the excessive farming zeal of the Company's chaplain, Reverend Robert Staines, who arrived with Mrs. Staines in 1849. The drawback to Staines from Douglas's point of view was that Staines was hired to raise good citizens, not good pigs. Staines had no previous experience as a clergyman and, some churchmen maintain, was not even regularly ordained.

He bought 46 acres near Mount Tolmie and 400 acres at Metchosin and loved his fine bred pigs more than he did his parishioners. Before long Douglas was accusing Staines of being a fomenter of mischief and preacher of sedition: Staines reciprocated by accusing Douglas of being a profit-hungry autocrat.

Staines was also schoolmaster at the Fort and his bad temper reinforced with frequent use of the cane made school a terror for his pupils. Mrs. Staines, who taught the few young ladies in the settlement was, in contrast, a good teacher. But she didn't like the Scots fur-trading families, including Mrs. Douglas, who was of mixed blood.

Harmony wasn't improved by Mrs. Douglas's evident preference for the company of her children and chickens to that of Mrs. Staines. She considered Mrs. Staines "uppish." Staines was fired after he had signed a petition protesting the appointment of James Douglas as Governor. He was on his way to London with the petition when he was drowned, as happened with distressing frequency those days.

For better or for worse, the beginnings of more representative government are due to these settlers with grievances. Their complaints were heard in London and the first council was set up in 1851 replacing the one-man rule of Douglas. Its members were John Tod, Captain Cooper and James Douglas, Douglas being the senior member. The Council met within the Fort stockade and was the forerunner of provincial government.

Appraisal of some of these early discontented settlers must take into account the unanticipated handicaps under which they laboured, the greatest of which was housing . . . there was none.

The Skinners, who arrived in the *Norman Morison* in January 1853, were rowed ashore at dawn to find the Fort locked tight. They had to wait under a tree surrounded by curious, semi-naked Indians until the gates were opened. Even then there was no accommodation for them in the Fort. With difficulty a blanket-partitioned shack was found for them and their three servants. Within a month of her arrival Mrs. Skinner gave birth to a daughter.

More fortunate, but in degree only, were the Kenneth McKenzies. They were housed with their servants in an unpartitioned loft in the Fort. The Langfords got a small log cabin near the Fort which they shared with their many children. Later they shared the Governor's modest dwelling where Mrs. Langford gave birth to a son George, probably the Colony's first all-white child.

But the settlers' hardships were not caused by Douglas and the Hudson's Bay Company, although many settlers blamed both. They were due to environment and Colonial Office policy. Many officials in London didn't even know the location of Vancouver Island. One could find equal ignorance today. However pleasant Vancouver Island may have seemed to Douglas, he was no farmer and the terrain here, from an agricultural point of view, compared unfavourably with that in most of the British Isles. In fact a settler who left, John Coles, told the Royal Colonial Institute in London that the land was not good enough for potatoes.

Because there were no carpenters the settlers also suffered when house-building — the Indians had never seen a saw or plane. All lumber was rough and handhewn. In fact it paid to bring processed lumber at ruinous prices all the way from San Francisco. Most land had to be drained and cleared by hand labour. Water had to be brought from Spring Ridge, a mile from the Fort. Entertainment except for the self-engendered variety imported with the immigrants was non-existent, letters few and far between.

The settlers wanted roads, bridges, schools and housing and thought the Company should provide them, but the Company's only revenue for financing the Colony was from the sale of land which few people wanted. When Douglas and his council resorted to taxes on liquor, timber cutting and imports to raise revenue the settlers complained. To meet their complaints the franchise was extended in 1859 to small property owners and tenants: in return Douglas was permitted to levy road building and other charges. Between 40 and 50 people were given the vote and seven members elected, namely John Muir, Dr. J. S. Helmcken, Thomas J. Skinner, J. D. Pemberton, James Yates, E. E. Langford and Dr. John Kennedy.

It would be wrong to conclude that the early settlement seethed with discontent. An aggrieved minority always makes more noise than the complacent majority.

Among the earliest pioneers was John Work (or Wark), who combined farming with the raising of 11 children, eight of them daughters.

John Work grew prize pumpkins — one weighed 108½ pounds according to legend — but still more prized were his daughters who were manna from Heaven for a petticoat-starved community. Three were later wedded to prominent citizens ... Jane to W. F. Tolmie from Inverness who founded Cloverdale farm in Saanich and whose son became Premier; Sarah to Roderick Finlayson, who was in charge of the Hudson's Bay Company fort in 1845 and Suzette to E. G. Prior who later became Premier and Lieutenant-Governor.

Old John Work himself got married a week before daughter Jane. His wife Josette Legace of mixed blood could not write her name so made her mark in the marriage register. Work was associated with the Hudson's Bay Company for many years before he arrived in Victoria and was the biggest purchaser of Company lands, owning 1,304 arable acres. He was also the largest potato grower and only the Douglas farm in Fairfield produced more wheat.

There was much merriment at the Work house, or as some of his children preferred to call it, the "Wark" house. Dances and parties were frequent while the daughters were growing up. His farm included lands from Hillside to the Gorge, Cook Street north to Finlayson Road and south to the city side of Kings Road.

Boys sent by their mothers to buy at John Work's farm could get a sackful of vegetables for 20 cents. The old pioneer is buried in Pioneer Square. No trace remains of Work's farmhouse and its exact location is in dispute.

Chapter 2

THE GOLD RUSH

"THE TOWNSPEOPLE WERE JUST LEAVING CHURCH to return to their whitewashed cottages on Sunday morning, April 25, 1858 when the *Commodore*, a wooden sidewheel American steamer brought the first shipload of gold-seekers. From their position on the hillside (Christ Church hill) they watched fascinated as she disembarked a stream of men, most of them wearing red flannel shirts and carrying packs containing blankets, miners' washpans, spades and firearms. The first large "non-British" element had arrived in the Colony.

"Of the 450 men in the party only 60 were British subjects. Some had money, some were penniless. Most carried bowie knives and revolvers."

This is the dramatic description by a witness of the first gold rush.

Victoria with its few hundred settled white residents, its picnics, intimate parties and amateur theatricals, its politicking and Douglas-baiting had to cater to what some authorities estimated at 25,000 gold-seekers.

If today's Victoria had to find temporary accommodation and supplies for 10,000,000 people the problem would be mathematically in proportion. The settlement became a tent town with acute problems of sanitation, food, accommodation and administration. Even before the gold rush, human shelter was at a premium. One resident had solved his problem by building a house out of the upperworks of a wrecked steamer. Another, Captain W. Gosset, the

Colony's first treasurer, brought out a corrugated iron house from England.

With the arrival of the gold-seekers the settlement swarmed with open latrines, tents, lean-to's, negroes, Kanakas, Chinese, Jews, Frenchmen, Englishmen, Germans and other nationalities. Everyone complained of the stench from open drains. There was no running water except when it rained, and then too much of it. Taverns and drunks were soon in too plentiful supply. Roads were rutted, trails often bearing a sign "no bottom obtainable." Drays on Wharf Street sank axle-deep in mud. Cattle roamed in and out of the tents.

The nationalities congregated like birds of a feather . . . the Jews on Johnson Street, the Chinese in nearby "Little Canton," the Kanakas on Kanaka Row (now Humboldt Street) and the negroes wherever they could find room.

Within six months of the arrival of the first gold-seekers, 225 "buildings," nearly all of them with wooden fronts and canvas sides went up in what is now downtown.

The gold-seekers, many of whom were surprised to find that the diggings were not in Victoria, were eager to get to the Mainland. The *Surprise*, a sidewheeler, made 15 return trips to Fort Langley in 1858, sometimes with 500 passengers. But even so, many of the miners tried making it by canoe and in the treacherous tidal waters not all succeeded.

No private corporation designed solely for trade could possibly cope with all the problems the gold rush entailed. The repeat of these problems with the Barkerville gold rush of 1862, and the Leechtown* rush two years later spelt the end of the Hudson's Bay Company's monopoly, and Douglas and the Company were thankful to be relieved of their burden.

Douglas, backed by H.M. warships and aided by good commonsense and the interest of the Colonial Office, maintained British rule. He also kept order.

Douglas foresaw the need for competent and honest civil servants if British rule was to be maintained. The result was a considerable influx of customs men, legal experts, surveyors and others, whose

* Leechtown is the smaller and lesser known gold rush near Sooke.

presence, while contributing to good administration, aroused the jealousy of many easterners and others who had located here and found a living hard to get.

Douglas also intended that Victoria should derive the main benefit from the gold rushes. He deliberately gave preference to Victoria by making it a free port in 1859, thus ensuring that it became also the main supply centre for the Mainland. Goods entering the Fraser River without being routed via Victoria were taxed.

But for the gold rushes Victoria might have continued for decades as a somnolent backwater . . . a community living on fishing and farming with all that makes for greater sophistication conspicuously absent. Indeed when the first three gold rushes were over that is what many local pessimists thought it would become.

The gold rushes injected money into the economy. The money enabled new buildings, better communications and the incorporation of the settlement as a city.

Land which could hardly be given away in 1857 became suddenly valuable. Improved land values helped to finance public works. The new 800-foot long James Bay bridge (on the site of the present Causeway) was built in 1859. Maintenance seems to have been substandard: a piledriver and four men fell through the rotten planking nine years later. Before the bridge was built, passage from Government Street to the three or four houses in James Bay meant walking (in winter wading), or riding the trail skirting the mud flats where the Church of Our Lord now stands on Humboldt Street.

For many years tides came right up to the Church.

The old bridge from Johnson Street to the Indian Reserve was removed in 1860 thus enabling the waterfront mooring area to be extended. Many wharves went in.

The first Parliament Buildings were put up in this period. They have remained an economic mainstay of Victoria ever since. They were not, of course, the present imposing buildings, but a collection of half-timbered cottages. As to architecture, the *Colonist* described the main building as something between a Dutch toy and a Chinese pagoda and they were immediately christened "The Birdcages."

The scene greeting the first legislators was very different from that of today. Odorous tidal waters lapped right across the present

Causeway under the newly constructed James Bay bridge. The outlook seawards was a junky waterfront, discarded water-logged lumber, shacks and garbage of all descriptions.

Douglas originally intended the buildings to be on Government Street between Bastion and Yates. But the land there having become very valuable as a result of the influx, he decided to sell it and use the proceeds for the Parliament Buildings, locating them where land was cheap.

The Legislature and especially Dr. Helmcken and Amor De Cosmos, a newly arrived, vociferous journalist-politician, wished to censure Douglas for using public moneys to build without Parliament's consent. Douglas's short reply to this was: "It wasn't public money." The motion was thereupon withdrawn.

The main Birdcage, one of five buildings, first faced the harbour front on Belleville Street. Four of the five buildings were demolished to make room for the present buildings. The fifth went up in smoke in 1957. Builder was Gideon Hallcrow, a former Scottish crofter and handyman. He built also the nearby Helmcken House in 1852.

Helmcken House is a very modest single-storey structure (30′ x 25′) with about the same living accommodation as would be found in many an English working class home of the period. There was no running water. Small fireplaces provided the heat. It has the horse-hair sofas, fruit under glass and what-nots beloved by those of the Victorian period.

Douglas persuaded Helmcken to build near him because he was nervous of roaming Indians at night. Helmcken regretted afterwards that he had obliged. Lumber cost $40 per 1000 feet in the rough and had to be hand-processed. The doctor had a servant problem because Indians would not live in a house. He complained that he could have built the dwelling for one-third of the cost a few years later. But with an acre of land around it must have commanded very attractive views.

Incorporation of Victoria as a city is partly the result of Dr. Helmcken's pleadings.

This always cheerful, popular doctor, who charged nothing for his services to poor patients, reminded Douglas in 1859 that he had done nothing about a bill for the enfranchisement of Victoria sponsored by J. D. Pemberton two years earlier. The bill was to make Victoria independent of the Hudson's Bay Company. Douglas still prevaricated but the bill eventually became law in 1862.

Pemberton was not totally disinterested in getting the city franchised. With a colleague, B. W. Pearse, he had laid out the townsite and both were considerable lot holders. They could assume that enfranchisement of the city would enhance the value of their holdings.

The visitor to Victoria in 1862 would have found not a city but a shacktown. There were only 2,500 permanent residents. Two years before the population was only 608 with a temporary summer addition of 25,000 or so gold-seekers from outside.

Stepping ashore on Wharf Street the visitor would have seen a dusty open space, littered with cow and horse dung . . . today's Bastion Square. On his right hand were the Hudson's Bay wharf and the Company's administrative buildings.

There were only a few brick buildings in the whole city. He could have walked round the entire built-up area in 20 minutes and even this area included many patches of wasteland. Outside the perimeter formed by Wharf, Courtney, Douglas and Johnson Streets were very few buildings. The city's franchise extended over 1,000 acres and excluded the larger part of James Bay. Beyond the buildings were bush and marsh where deer, grouse, pheasant and duck were plentiful. Most striking was the abundance of saloons and hotels in the city area.

Here and there between them were merchants' stores, the merchants when business was slack playing cards on upturned packing cases on the sidewalk. But for the harbour front, the uniforms of the Royal Marines and the Royal Navy, one could have been in the Wild West. Nothing looked permanent. The drinking facilities would have astonished the visitor. Government and Johnson Streets had most of the hotels and saloons.

Going north along Government from the James Bay bridge there were successively the Australia Hotel,* the John Bull Hotel, the

* The Australia Hotel which stood on piles on the northeast corner of James Bay Bridge (approximately where the Empress Hotel rock garden is) was notable in later years for being the only saloon with an organ. The organ was

Victoria Hotel, the Brown Jug Saloon, until recently the location of "The Crest" handicraft shop, Hotel de France, the Star and Garter, the St. Nicholas Hotel and next to it, the Island Hotel (see map).

The Victoria, since renamed the Windsor, is the city's oldest still standing hotel. When built in 1858 it was one of the community's two brick hotels. It was renamed the Windsor in 1890 when the New Victoria Hotel, since demolished, went up at the northwest corner of Government and Johnson Streets.

The original Victoria was built by George Richardson who arrived here in the *Princess Royal*. It had an accident in 1876. People were not used to the recently installed gas mains, and Richardson, smelling gas in the small hours, searched for the leak with a candle. The blast blew down a four-inch partition brick wall, tore off the wallpaper, wrecked the interior and wrenched a street lamp from its socket on Fort and Government Streets two blocks away.

Richardson, clad only in loose-fitting nightshirt, was extensively singed and a tenant unnecessarily broke a limb when he jumped from an upstairs window.

The St. Nicholas Hotel on Government Street used to advertise a large public restaurant and a "ladies ordinary," its site being now that of the Poodle Dog restaurant. There was also a hotel on View between Broad and Douglas, the St. George, later to become the Driard Hotel and now part of the Eaton Block.

The plank sidewalk ended at Government and Johnson Streets, so the visitor would turn left along Johnson and avoiding the potholes (one could disappear forever in some of them), would see the Pioneer Saloon, the Lager Beer Saloon and the Royal Hotel.

On Yates Street, between Wharf and Government Streets, were the Identical Saloon, the Phoenix Saloon, the Bank Exchange, the Fashion Hotel, a notorious gambling and dance hall operated by the American John Keenan, and many other drinking places.

---

shipped out by Baroness Burdett-Coutts to Christ Church Cathedral, but was badly damaged in the 1869 Cathedral fire. W. Seely, an Englishman who ran the Australia Hotel, an organ builder by trade, repaired the organ and installed it for the benefit of musically inclined guests. The organ was later located in St. Ann's convent, in the Sunday school of St. Andrew's Cathedral and for 40 years in St. Mark's on Cloverdale before being rebuilt and installed recently in Christ Church Cathedral.

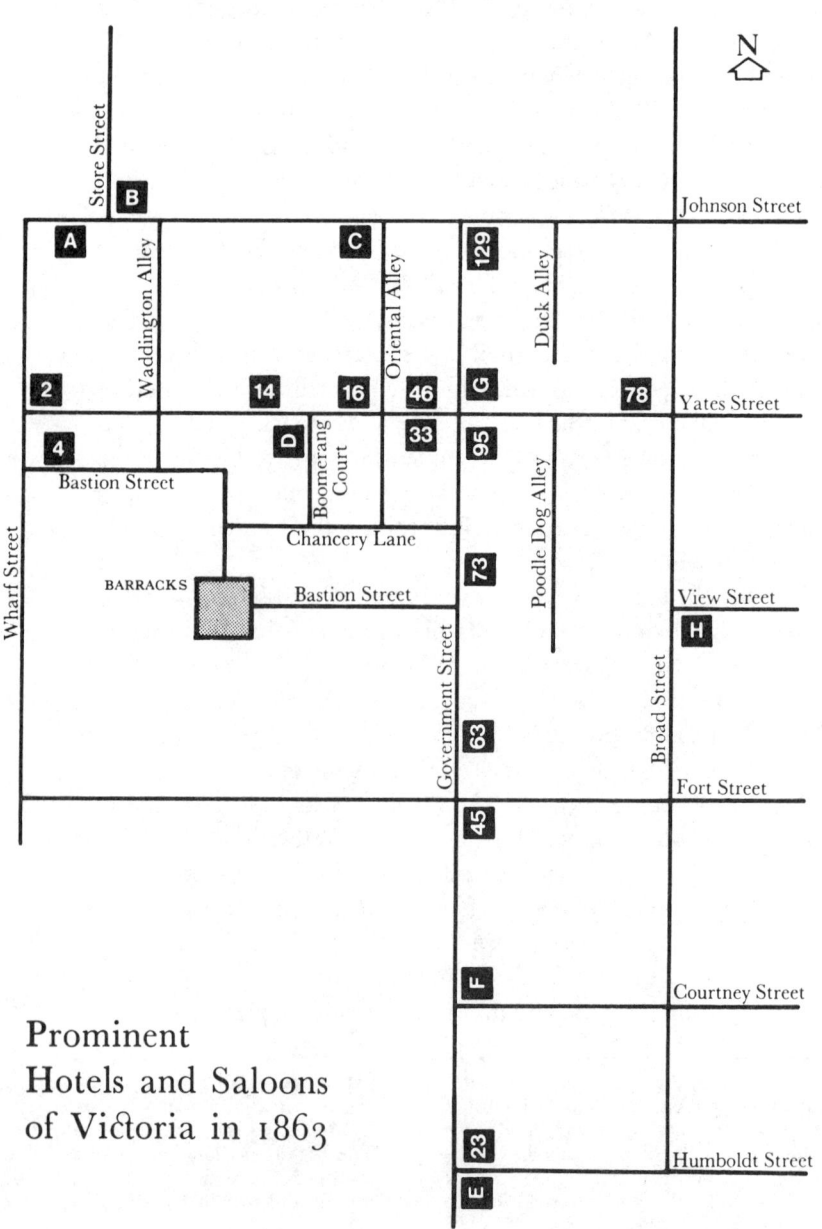

N

Store Street

B

A

C

Waddington Alley

Oriental Alley

129

Duck Alley

Johnson Street

2

14

16

46

G

78

Yates Street

4

D

Boomerang Court

33

95

Bastion Street

Wharf Street

Chancery Lane

BARRACKS

Bastion Street

73

Poodle Dog Alley

View Street

H

Government Street

Broad Street

63

Fort Street

45

F

Courtney Street

Prominent
Hotels and Saloons
of Victoria in 1863

23

Humboldt Street

E

KEY

Where street numbers are not known, approximate locations are designated by letters.

JOHNSON STREET

A   Royal Hotel
B   Lager Beer Saloon
C   Pioneer Saloon

YATES STREET

2   Identical Saloon
14   Albion Saloon
16   Phoenix Saloon
33   Bank Exchange
46   Oriental Hotel
78   Tucker's Saloon

BASTION STREET

4   Steele's Saloon

BOOMERANG COURT

D   Boomerang Saloon

GOVERNMENT STREET

E   Australia Hotel
23   John Bull
F   Victoria Hotel
45   Brown Jug Saloon
63   Hotel de France
73   Star & Garter
95   Colonial Hotel
G   St. Nicholas Hotel
129   Island Hotel

VIEW STREET

H   St. George's Hotel

Eating and lodging houses also abounded. On Government Street opposite the theatre, Mrs. McDonald ran a restaurant and oyster saloon with suppers "all hours of the night." The Royal Hotel and Restaurant built by James Wilcox in 1858 and later renamed the Occidental was at the southeast corner of Wharf and Johnson (now a gas station site).

Ringo, a freed (or runaway) negro slave, ran Ringo's Restaurant on Yates Street. He was an excellent cook and kind to the hard-up. The London Coffee House on Cormorant Street offered breakfast with plate of meat for 25¢, dinner for 37½¢ and coffee with bun 12¢.

One of the better eating places was the Colonial Restaurant at 95 Government Street. It was run by the asthmatic Sosthenes Driard who was later to operate the Driard Hotel, the most famous hotel of its time. Sosthenes' corpulence was a tribute to the quality of his cuisine. Other well-known kitchens were the Regent on Fort Street and the Lord Nelson on Store Street.

Between the saloons on Yates Street was the Metropolitan Lodging house with rooms from $2 to $7 per week per person, or from 50¢ to $1 per night. Board and lodging for $7 a week was the usual charge. The Union Hotel was cheaper. It had 51 beds from 25¢ a night up.

Outside Victoria was Six Mile House at Parsons Bridge, Craigflower. Its opening in 1855 with what an observer described as "a grand spree" was still fresh in memory when the city was franchised and in Saanichton, Henry Simpson from Kent, a former baker for the Hudson's Bay Company, borrowed £83/6/9d in 1858 to build the Prairie Tavern.

The tavern was replaced with the Prairie Inn in 1893 and this building which still stands and serves the public gives a fair idea of the modest nature of much of the accommodation of those days. Some of the "Inns" were smaller than the modern dwelling. "Amenities" in the sixties might include a washstand and ewer and a spittoon; the walls were thin partitions where every conversation and footstep echoed and the lighting, if any, was a lamp or candle.

Victoria was no place for the after-dark stroller. There were no street lights and the dim paraffin lamps in the doorways of saloons and hotels were of little help. Its first gas lights (the gas being produced in the Rock Bay plant) did not appear until 1862 and were then very sparse.

A ravine ran east to west between Johnson and Pandora Streets, debouching into the harbour. It was bridged in three places, at Store, Government and Douglas Streets, but the pedestrian could easily miss the footbridges in the dark with most unpleasant results.

Their social impact apart, it is almost impossible to overestimate the effect of the gold rushes on Victoria's development. Never before or since, to use a current political slogan, had Victoria "had it so good." For one of the few times in her history she was dependent not on local trade supplemented by tourist dollars, but had a captive market landed at her wharves. The Hudson's Bay Company and early settlers in their wildest optimism had never conceived of such a bonanza. Here were scores of thousands of visitors, all of them in need of accommodation, food and drink, clothing, miners' equipment and transportation. People like John Work, Joseph Despard Pemberton, Peter McQuade and many others who later became prominent citizens, previously accustomed to dealing in shillings, found themselves dealing with hundreds of pounds. Hard-pressed householders, glad to trade milk for groceries or after much haggling a horse for a cart, found a ready cash market for anything they could offer.

Anything on four legs that could be used for transportation . . . semi-wild mules, horses fit only for the knackers' yard, even camels were imported and found a ready market. The demand for lumber and carpenters for the construction of hotels and saloons was insatiable and many a man abandoned farming or the Hudson's Bay Company service to satisfy the demand or to seek his fortune in the gold-diggings.

As is still the case today, Americans were first to see the business possibilities in Victoria. They had the experience of the California gold rush to guide them. They came chiefly from San Francisco; Alfred Waddington, a Victoria merchant and later Inspector of Schools, describes them: "an indescribable array of Polish Jews, Italian fishermen, French cooks, jobbers, speculators of every kind, land agents, auctioneers, hangers on at auctions, bummers, bank-rupts and brokers of every description."

Before long Victoria had Wells Fargo, the carriers, the Bank of British North America, the Bank of British Columbia, San Francisco shipping companies and agents of all descriptions. Many of the merchants left when the gold rushes were over, but a lot of their money remained here. Transient or permanent they had to buy or rent land on which to erect their stores and saloons. One-third of the advertising in Mallandaine's first city directory came from San Francisco.*

Whereas in the early months of 1858 the Hudson's Bay surveyor Joseph Despard Pemberton had been pleading cap in hand with few takers for residents to buy downtown lots at $500 up, late in 1858 Donald Fraser, a British journalist, paid $3,100 for a lot at the corner of Government and Yates Streets. Lots 20 feet by 70 feet on Johnson Street near Wharf fetched an average price of $2,000 each in late 1858. A lot at the corner of Store Street near the gas works bought earlier for $700 sold in 1862 for $3,050. Business frontage downtown rented at $2 to $6 per foot per month.

To illustrate further the demand — small log houses built by the Hudson's Bay Company for its men at a cost of $100 fetched 50 and 70 times this price.

The vendors, chiefly French Canadians, in most cases speedily drank their newly acquired fortunes and in two or three years' time if still living were as poor as when they were born.

And who made the money? There were about 30 holders of 10 or

* Around 80 San Francisco firms advertised in Victoria's first city directory. In a preface to the San Francisco section Mallandaine, the publisher eulogised that "California is now and ever will be the only reliable mart from which these colonies can be supplied with necessaries and commodities." Among the adver-tisers were Professor Cooper, "celebrated physician and surgeon who laid the foundation of the 'Pacific Clinical Infirmary Institute widely and deservedly celebrated on Mission St. Some of his cures miraculous';" Grover & Baker — sewing machines; Dewar and Gehricke — Pioneer Line of Packers; F. B. Conro & Co., flour, grain; George W. Chapin, employees office, Kearny St.; New England House, 53 Sansome St.; Metropolitan Hotel; R. S. Ellis & Co., wagon manufacturers; S. W. Moore, seed warehouse, 110 California St.; Union Iron Works; Coffee & Risdon, steamboilers; Sain Sevain Bros., mature California wines; G. W. Bell, assay office; Nathanial Gray, undertaker, and Hocks & Lamberti who claimed that their axle grease prevented the firing of wheels.

JAMES DOUGLAS
Hudson's Bay Chief Factor, marking
location of Fort Victoria. French-
Canadian employees of the Company
did most of the heavy work.

MODEL OF FORT VICTORIA
by a Hudson's Bay Company official.
The view is from the waterfront:
conspicuous is the beacon tower, right
centre, to guide incoming ships. The
centre buildings are two warehouses
and general store: the bastion in far
left background stood at the present
junction of Government Street and
Bastion Square. The three buildings
in front of the bastion are employees'
houses. The small structure, left
centre, is the powder magazine and
in the forefront is the house of
Roderick Finlayson, officer-in-charge.

In background, right, next to
centre buildings are (1) chief factor's
dwelling and mess hall; (2) men's
quarters and school.

Alongside southern palisade (now
Broughton Street) back to front:
warehouse, men's quarters and blacksmith. In right forefront, dwelling
house and second bastion, the site now
occupied by the Army, Navy &
Air Force Veterans' Club. The road
bisecting the enclosure west to east
became the future Fort Street.

GOVERNMENT STREET in the early 1860's, looking north from Brown Jug Saloon at the corner of Government and Fort Streets. Tommy Golden's Brown Jug is in right foreground. The larger building opposite has the sign: *Thomas Searby, Chemist.* Outside the Brown Jug is a horse-drawn water barrel — the usual method of supplying water before mains were built.

DR. JOHN SEBASTIAN HELMCKEN
was popular both as surgeon
and politician. His home near the
new museum still stands.

THE WATERFRONT SHACKS
were indicative of the gold rush
years and posed grave sanitation
problems for the community.

SUZETTE WORK
who became the wife of E. G. Prior,
a future lieutenant-governor.

JOHN WORK
biggest landowner and farmer in
the early days. He owned all the land
around Hillside.

THE FUNERAL
of Sir James Douglas in 1877 at
the Church of Our Lord (Reformed
Episcopal Church). The land around
the Church was mostly open fields.
In the foreground (right) is the
White Horse Inn, which later became
the Glen Court Hotel, the site now
a parking lot for St. Joseph's Hospital
at Humboldt and Blanshard Streets.
On the hill is the old Christ
Church Cathedral.

WHARF STREET IN 1867

more downtown lots in 1858. They included such well-known names as Charles Bayley, the Rev. Modeste Demers, H. G. Dallas, Roderick Finlayson, Donald Fraser, John Helmcken, Wm. Leigh, Alex Mouatt, D. McTavish, Jeremiah Nagle, James Yates and George Pearkes. Some of them held on to their land. The first city assessment in 1862 shows Donald Fraser as owner of land on Wharf, McClure, Collinson, Vancouver, Government and Yates Streets valued at $250,000. Robert Ker (government auditor) was assessed on $20,000, Dr. Helmcken on $32,000 and R. Finlayson on $12,000. Chief Justice Begbie and Bishop Hills of the Anglican Church were both large landholders as also were John Foster McCreight who later became Premier, Selim Franklin, George Hunter Cary, Jeremiah Nagle and H. A. Tuzo, a Hudson's Bay physician.

George Cary, first Attorney-General, who erected "Cary Castle" (Government House), achieved unwelcome notoriety when in the early years of the settlement he tried to corner its water supply by fencing the spring at Spring Ridge and charging admission. Bishop Hills invested in land on behalf of the Church with funds provided by the Burdett-Coutts banker family. He bought not only downtown but also extensively in Saanich.

Land transactions in the first gold rushes are evidence enough that real estate then, as now, was one of Victoria's chief trading commodities. The gold rush was certainly welcome to the Hudson's Bay Company not only because of its commanding trade interests, but also because back in 1850 the Americans were offering 640 acres of land free to every settler, while Douglas was trying to get $5 an acre here. The gold rushes also convinced Victorians that here and not Esquimalt was the logical townsite, and laid the foundations of fortunes the benefits of which are still enjoyed today by descendants of the pioneers.

Among the early merchants were W. & J. Wilson on Government Street founded in 1862; Kent & Frost, hardware merchants on Fort Street and Peter McQuade, ship chandler on Wharf Street, not forgetting of course, the Hudson's Bay Company which dwarfed all competitors. Other prominent merchants of the day included Hibben & Carswell (Willson Stationers are their successors), William Wilson, draper; J. H. Turner & Co., carpet merchants; E. Marvin

& Co., hardware; Guy Hostin, gunsmith; Alfred Fellowes, iron merchant and J. S. Drummond, stoves and hardware, while Fardon and Maynard & Dalby, pioneer photographers, were willing to mail home a picture of the adventurer in full mining garb. Fardon, who was taught photography by his wife, must have made money. He figures later as owner of the Fardon Building on Langley Street.

Wharf Street was dominated by the Hudson's Bay Company, whose retail store was on the west side. Adjacent to their wharf was Englehardt's Wharf on which was the Company's salmon house. In the first weeks of the 1858 gold rush when accommodation was at a premium, men were allowed to sleep here amidst the reek of salmon for $2 a night.

Two Americans opened what was probably Victoria's first restaurant in this old building, which was demolished in 1878.

At the corner of Wharf and Yates stood Treweek's warehouse, pulled down in 1873. N. Treweek paid $6,000 to have the building erected. It sold for $50.

Victoria in its first year of incorporation suffered from an excess of politicians, lawyers, merchants, transients and saloons and a considerable shortage of accommodation, water, women and good roads. So short was human shelter that some transients would cross Puget Sound to get a good night's sleep. The Council could do little about transients, women and bad roads, but it made a start on sanitation and water.

The first City ordinances banned slaughter houses, tanneries, distilleries and other "offensive" trades. Privies had to be emptied between midnight and 6 a.m. Night soil, soap-lees, ammoniacal and "other such offensive matter" could not be moved along a thoroughfare between 6 a.m. and 8 p.m. Horses and cattle had to be kept off sidewalks and footpaths. This bylaw was probably inspired by the bad behaviour of a bull which tossed and badly injured a child on Pandora Avenue. Wandering pigs and goats were to be impounded. The depositing of rubbish, filth, ashes or offal on sidewalks or roads was prohibited.

An odorous early complication was caused by a dead horse on the James Bay side of city limits. Frantic calls for relief from polluted air came from the City's influential James Bay residents, but ownership of the carcass was denied by residents outside the limits. They even maintained (the prevailing southwest wind favouring them at the time) that the horse was Victoria-bred and owned. Finally some unknown benefactor with a strong stomach pushed the carcass one night inside the City boundary enabling the Council to dispose of it.

As a first fund-raising measure the Council imposed taxes on everything that moved on wheels, two or four legs.

Male residents and dogs (the insult was unconscious) were assessed $1 per head per annum. Also taxed were carriages, buggies, saddle horses, milk wagons, liquor, real estate, theatres, circuses. Lawyers narrowly escaped being taxed. They pleaded that it was wrong for the law (the city) to tax the law.

Thomas Harris was a very popular first mayor. He had done well in Victoria. He arrived with the gold-seekers but speedily exchanged the red shirt of the miner for the striped apron of the butcher, opening first of all a slaughter house on Wharf Street, then Vancouver Island's first butcher shop in 1858. His Queen's Market at Government and Johnson Streets was a favourite social rendezvous. Although he became an M.L.A. in 1861, Harris was always proud to class himself as an " 'umble tradesman," but the term became progressively less appropriate as he ascended the ladder of fortune. His residence where now stands the Government Street branch of the Bank of Montreal (Bastion and Government Streets) was the most handsome and best furnished in Victoria, but quite ordinary by today's standards.

It was one of the few brick buildings of the time and he frequently entertained his supporters there. He also raced horses and was a popular figure on the Beacon Hill course, betting being in his blood. Harris arrived here only a year before Victoria's first horse race on May 2, 1859, and a Jockey Club of sorts came into being in 1861.

A jovial Englishman from Hertfordshire, Harris as mayor needed all his good humour. He weighed 300 pounds and the mayoral chair collapsed under him at the first council meeting. There were no council chambers, the City Hall not being built until 1877. The Council had to meet in the police barracks on what is now Bastion Square, which also contained the court room and the lock-up. On one occasion the Council found the court in session. Harris sent a curt notice to the magistrate telling him to quit in 10 minutes. Ten minutes elapsed. Nothing happened. Harris sent a messenger to ask for the magistrate's reply. The magistrate told the messenger that a reply wasn't necessary and went on with his case.

Some of the outraged councillors exploded into murderous threats. Councillor Copland suggested that 20 specials be sworn in to throw the magistrate into the street. But Councillor Copland coveted the mayor's position and Harris knew it, so took no action.

The Council later got temporary quarters at Broad Street and Trounce Alley.

While in office Harris suffered a bad accident. He was driving to his Saanich farm when the shafts came away from the cart. Harris held tight to the reins and was dragged over the dashboard. He was discovered only the next day . . . an indication of the sparse population of the area. During the mayor's illness Councillor Copland appointed himself deputy-mayor. Many viewed this with disfavour and when he attended an official dinner in his self-appointed capacity he was unceremoniously ejected before he had a chance to eat.

Harris, like many others who had spent too generously during the boom years of the gold rushes, fell on lean times later and had to sell his fine home. He died of melancholia. There were many such deaths among Victoria's pioneers and medical opinion today associates them with heavy drinking. Harris Green, on Pandora Avenue in front of the First Church of Christ, Scientist, opened in 1920, bears a tablet to the memory of the first mayor.

But of greater impact on the citizens than incorporation and the establishment of a more representative Assembly was the establishment of a public bathing place next to W. and J. Wilson on Government Street. This venture by an enterprising San Francisco youth was the forerunner of many others. The bathing establishments conferred an inestimable boon on residents and transients. People were for the first time in Victoria in 1862 able to get a hot bath . . . and some had been here since 1843.

Chapter 3

CHURCH, CRIME AND CULTURE

ONE CONSEQUENCE OF THE Fraser River gold rush, as mentioned
earlier, was an influx of officials from the United Kingdom to mid-
wife the two colonies of British Columbia (the Mainland) and
Vancouver Island in their birthpangs.

Culture cannot develop where people's energies are absorbed entirely by the need to earn their daily bread and the newly arrived
officials had assured incomes and the leisure to enjoy them. A contemporary noted sourly that executive salaries were $50,000 in 1862
against nil a year earlier.

Among the newcomers were two men who made a great impact
on Victoria society. Both were tall and handsome. One was Matthew (later Sir Matthew) Baillie Begbie, first judge of British
Columbia and the other Bishop "Beau Brummel" George Hills.

Begbie's bungalow, the grounds of which included two tennis
courts, was on the rise at the intersection of Collinson and Cook
Streets and his property ran north to Collinson, east to Linden and
south to Fairfield Road. Begbie used to walk downtown for official
functions dressed like Sir Walter Raleigh . . . black velvet breeches
and buckled shoes, flowing cape and wide-brimmed hat, wearing a
Van Dyck beard and invariably followed by his half-dozen spaniels.

On Sundays he changed into the cassock and surplice of a Cathedral chorister and often read the lesson. His high-pitched voice when
excited was in contrast with his masculine bearing. Oddly enough
this apparently most eligible bachelor (he was 40 when he came to

the Colony) never married although he was "dear Sir Matthew" to every matron with marriageable daughters.

Begbie shot duck and entertained in his Fairfield surroundings. An invitation to his Tuesday tennis parties or to his Saturday night dinners (two sittings . . . one until 10 p.m. for the clergy and the second after 10 p.m. for cards and men of the world) was the hallmark of acceptance in the upper echelons of society. He was also an enthusiastic rosarian, a fine horseman, tennis player, pianist and whist player. Whist was then as popular as is bridge today.

A power though he was in British Columbia, Begbie did not have a great legal mind. "His judgments," as a member of the Bar Association wrote after his death, "sometimes defied precedent." Indeed he owed his advancement to his proficiency with Gurney's shorthand, which brought him to the attention of prominent Colonial office officials, rather than to legal brilliance. But if his judgments were sometimes unorthodox, so were the conditions under which he worked in the Colony. Travelling on horseback through the rugged Cariboo, accompanied by a manservant, or swinging along in shirtsleeves singing at the top of his voice, he often held court in a tent. He thought the gold-seekers "rough" rather than tough, dealt with them condescendingly and showed his contempt by, on one occasion, emptying the contents of his chamber pot on a group pitched nearby, to whose remarks he took exception. In his early years in the Colony he referred to British Columbia as a "land of Siwashes," but in later years grew to love the country and especially Victoria.

When Begbie died in Victoria in 1894, so great was the throng of mourners that marshalling orders had to be printed and distributed in advance of the funeral.

One of two friends in the chief mourners' carriage was Peter O'Reilly, whose home now over 100 years old, is open to tourists. It is on Pleasant Street and known as Point Ellice House.

O'Reilly, who made Begbie's acquaintance while serving as a gold commissioner, became a member of the Legislative Council (1863-1870) and a judge. He had no legal training and his elevation to the bench was due to whom he knew rather than what he knew. He married Caroline Agnes Trutch, sister of Sir Joseph Trutch, British Columbia's first Lieutenant-Governor.

Begbie is often slanderously referred to as the "hanging judge." There is no proof that he hanged any who did not deserve it and his trials were impartial. He protected the Indians at whom miners used to shoot as though they were ducks and made the Cariboo as safe for travellers as the dominions of Genghis Khan. A receipt for gold nuggets at Barkerville was as good as cash in the bank in Victoria, provided, of course, it was not Macdonald's Bank. The failure of Macdonald's Bank shook Victoria to its foundations and ruined many lives.

In the late 1850's Alexander Macdonald, a handsome young man from Inverness, arrived in Victoria with his attractive bride. They had spent some time in New Orleans where he had relatives in the banking business. He saw the business possibilities in the gold rush and opened a bank and general store at No. 5 Yates, now the site of Dowell's Cartage (Yates and Wharf). Initially great success attended his venture.

Macdonald's Bank issued its own banknotes, and dealt in bills of exchange, brokerage, bullion and general banking business. Macdonald opened a branch in the Cariboo and was also interested in sawmill and steamship companies. He built a fine home called "Springfield" at 633 Michigan Street at a cost of $12,000 (about $120,000 today) which was the scene of many splendid dances, dinners and other social gatherings. Everybody wanted to be "in" with the young Scot and his bride, and many lent him capital.

When customers went to draw money on the morning of September 23, 1864 they found only a distraught cashier. In the night the bank had been burgled and $25,000 in gold, plus several thousand dollars' worth of silver, dust and currency stolen. Macdonald was away at the time. The bank was in charge of John Waddell, a good-looking and business-like man of 60. Investigations showed that on the night of the burglary the safe had not been fully secured and Waddell had the key in his pocket. Entry had been secured through a skylight and the ladder used was exactly the length of skylight to floor.

Urgent messages for Macdonald to return were sent immediately but although he was continually reported to be on his way back, the panic-stricken and angry depositors had to wait two months before he was again in Victoria. Meanwhile the city seethed with suspicion, people were arrested and released, the police were criticized, slanderous theories were circulating.

When Macdonald did arrive he held a meeting of creditors. This proved to be a prelude to bankruptcy proceedings. A few days before the proceedings were to have been held in December, Macdonald got his manager Waddell to row him to Race Rocks (the harbour was watched) and boarded a ship bound for San Francisco.

His home and everything in it was seized and sold up. People argued for months and still argue as to the extent of Macdonald's guilt.

He left here with nothing, had to look for a job in San Francisco and as a "rogue" banker had great difficulty in getting one. Had he remained to face his creditors in Victoria he would have been imprisoned for debt or worse and indeed his life was in danger.

But why did he delay so long in returning to Victoria after the crime was discovered? Was it not a fact that the outlook for his bank was not very promising with the introduction of new laws restricting private banks? Also had he not encountered fierce competition with the establishment of the Bank of British North America and the Bank of British Columbia at the same time as the gold rush was tapering off?

As years went by, suspicion fell increasingly on his manager, John Waddell. John Waddell's son was arrested in the East some years after the robbery on a charge of murdering his father by throwing him overboard from a sailboat. He murdered his father, it was alleged, to possess himself of several thousand dollars which the parent had acquired through an act of piracy in scuttling a schooner to get the insurance money. A man capable of such a fraud would not think twice of robbing a bank. Macdonald always maintained that Waddell was the culprit.

A year before the Macdonald Bank robbery, four Indians were hanged together in Bastion Square or Lower Bastion Street as it was then called. Public executions were one of Victoria's more lugubrious forms of entertainment until they were abolished in 1870. They generally took place outside the courthouse which was until 1860 in the old Colonial Police Barracks.

Sometimes justice miscarried as when an Indian, so old he had to be carried to the gallows, was executed and his son, a year afterwards, confessed to the murder.

The crime of the four Indians hanged on May 3, 1863, though gruesome, testified to the resentment felt by Indians at the white man's intrusion. They had murdered three white men and a 15-year-old girl. One white, Bill Brady, had landed on a small island south of Salt Spring Island with a companion John Henlee. They were in their tent after dinner when shots rang out. Brady was mortally wounded, but Henlee, though shot in three places, fought off the inrushing Indians and even managed to row his dying partner to Oak Bay.

The murdered girl was Caroline Harvey, married daughter of a German settler Frederick Marks, murdered with her father on Saturna Island.

According to Indian witnesses Marks was shot as he sat on a rock and Caroline was chased, caught, stabbed to death and her stripped body thrown into the sea with a piece of stove tied to her hair.

During the search for the suspects Charles Bryden, a seaman on H.M.S. *Forward*, was killed by a shot fired from Kuper Island which was being bombarded by the warship. Ah-Chee-Wun and two other Indians hanged for the death of Bryden. Another Lamalchi Indian Um-Whangh hanged for the murder of Caroline Harvey. Ah-Chee-Wun was considered guilty also of the murder of Frederick Marks and Caroline Harvey. He had boasted of having murdered 10 whites ... presumably gold-seekers canoeing over to the Mainland. But as he was already convicted for the murder of Bryden the other charges were not proceeded with.

Caroline Harvey is buried in Pioneer Square adjacent to Christ Church Cathedral. The City cemetery was originally at the southwest corner of Douglas and Johnson (the block with Dorman's Men's Wear on the corner), but the bodies were transferred in 1860 to the Quadra Street site.

It was Begbie's duty to confirm all death sentences, but apart from his legal activities he was prominent in the arts. He was first president of the Victoria Philharmonic Society formed in 1859. He bought the old Hudson's Bay Company fur warehouses on Government Street and converted them into the Victoria Theatre. The theatre was demolished after hosting many famous stage personalities, including Mr. and Mrs. Charles Keen in 1864. Today's Churchill Hotel stands at the approximate entrance to the theatre. The Victoria Theatre could seat 500, but it was in the sixties not the only entertainment hall. A room under Goodacre's butcher shop, corner Government and Johnson Streets, named the "New Idea" was used for minstrel shows and light comedy.

The "New Idea" later become the "Omineca." There was also Moore's Hall at the northwest corner of the present Post Office (Yates and Langley Streets).

Theatres seemed to spring up and disappear almost overnight in the early days. A touring group in 1859 played in the Royal Hotel on Wharf Street and called it the Royal Theatre. The next year a group played in a music hall on Government Street (the "New Idea"?) and called it the Colonial Theatre.

Begbie's Victoria Theatre was renamed the Royal Theatre in 1867.

Some of the internal complications of the theatre world were revealed by bankrupt touring company promoter John Potter in 1863. He complained that he had enjoyed full houses but very little money. His high-living partner, he alleged, had lived high on the town and tendered theatre tickets in payment. Potter also suspected his doorkeeper who was at all times "very flush." To top all when Potter went to renew the lease on the theatre he found it had been leased to the doorkeeper. The doorkeeper then had a fight with the cashier and the latter absconded with the cash, leaving Potter holding the bag of unpaid bills.

But touring companies were few and far between. In general, Victorians had to generate their own entertainment. The Victoria Amateur Club had some clever comedians and actors. Their repertoire included Shakespeare's plays and other popular features such as *Coleen Bawn*, *Boots of the Swan*, *Who Stole My Pocket Book* and *Henry Dunbar*. Performances with a political slant were very much appreciated in a town so politically conscious as Victoria and the readings by visiting authors were well attended.

Among the original members of the Victoria Amateur Club who

performed in the Royal Theatre were Charles Clarke, W. M. Anderson, C. B. Tenniel, Arthur Keast, Lumley Franklin, S. Farwell, H. C. Courtney, H. Ruston, Joseph Barnett, Ben Griffin (of the Boomerang Inn), Godfrey Brown, W. J. Collingham and Alex Phillips.

Admission prices varied between 50 cents and $1.50. These prices were high in relation to the wages of the day, but as entertainment was scarce and the proceeds went to charity, to attend was a citizen's duty.

The Orphans of St. Ann, the hospital and the fire brigades were regular beneficiaries from performances.

Other cultural activities which came as a result of the gold rush and the influx of businessmen and officials included the Philharmonic Society, which provided the Victoria Theatre's first orchestra since John Tod's fiddle. Members were Digby Palmer, F. S. Bushell and Messrs. Gunter, Roberts and Hayes, all performances being directed by R. G. Marsh.

The Oddfellows had their first meeting at Fort and Langley Streets in 1864, sponsored by California visitors. Later the Oddfellows moved to the site of the B.C. Cement Building, Fort and Wharf (now used for a dance club), and in 1880 to their present building at 1323 Douglas. The Germania Sing Verein (beer and song, sometimes more beer than song) was popular in the early 60's and in 1862, H. Heisterman (the name of a real estate firm today) started a library with 160 members at 111 Government Street (between Johnson and Yates).

Also in being were the St. Andrew's Society founded in 1859 ... it had 100 members in 1863 and their names appear in the City directory of that year, also those of the Masonic Lodge. The Lodge stood at the southwest corner of Langley and Yates. A new building went up in 1878 costing $12,000 at the northwest corner of Fisgard and Douglas and, with additions made in 1903, still stands.

The Mechanics' Literary Institute, started in 1864 with F. Swanwick as chairman, catered to the growing number of literary citizens. It had two spacious rooms in Fardon's Building, the entrance being on Langley Street next to Hibben and Carswell's corner

(Yates and Langley south side). Hibben and Carswell were the pioneer stationers and booksellers of Victoria.

An unusual society was the Chebra Bekus Cholim Ukedis Ha. In the 1863 directory, the Society states that it was organized in the month of Seva. First assumption that this was a mystic cult is dispelled by the names of the directors . . . Keyser, Davis and Levy.

In the religious field Victoria then as now has always been most church-conscious. The Rt. Rev. George Hills, first bishop of British Columbia, who was, with Sir James Douglas and Sir Matthew Baillie Begbie, one of the three most influential of early citizens, wrote to a friend on his arrival in Victoria in 1860: "The congregation here contains a larger proportion of shrewd, thrifty, intelligent educated gentlemen than any in England outside London. The Church (Christ Church) holds 400 and five-sixths of them are men."

In 1861 with 600 permanent residents the city had five churches. As is the case today, those seeking religious truth had a wide choice from the orthodox churches to the less-traditional efforts of Harmony Hall and "New Messiahs." Many San Francisco evangelists came here and they fought for each other's sheep with no holds barred.

One reverend gentleman in 1861 won a house and lot in a beer saloon crap game.

Another influx of San Francisco evangelists followed the great earthquake of 1906. They plagued inmates of saloons and hotels urging them to "beware of the wrath to come" and to mend their sinful ways, acting on the assumption that if San Francisco had had no saloons there would have been no earthquake.

One of Victoria's early proselytizers was the Reverend A. G. Garrett of Cedar Plains Church (he later became a bishop in the Episcopal Church of America). Aided by the choir of Christ Church he used to preach from a barrel to departing and not too sober gold-seekers on Wharf Street.

But true to their crusading traditions the Roman Catholics were first in the field here. The first R.C. church in the province was St. Charles, established in Esquimalt in 1847.

34

It was followed in 1853 by another building — a mere shanty full of cracks on Courtney Street between Douglas and Government Streets. Oblate Father Lamfritt built and plastered the building with clay with his own hands.

Bishop Demers, who crossed over Puget's Sound in an Indian canoe in 1852, built St. Andrew's Church on Humboldt Street in 1858. The *British Colonist* of those days reported that "it is built without much regard to the niceties of architectural design," but sweetened its criticism with praise of the paintings and carvings, the work of Father Michaud. This building is now the chapel of St. Ann's Academy. The present St. Andrew's on Blanshard Street was built at a cost of around $60,000 in 1892. Originally it had two spires but one blew off in a most untimely storm on Christmas Day 1905.

At Broad and Pandora was Victoria's original Methodist church, opened in 1860.

The site was later that of the Brackman-Ker (millers) Building and now carries a furniture showroom. The 1891 land boom brought a $30,000 windfall to the Methodists and they replaced their church with the present steepled Metropolitan United Church at Pandora and Quadra dedicated in 1891. Demolished to make room for the church was the house built by C. Sharp in 1858 which was then the only house on Pandora.

A similar windfall befell the First Presbyterian Church originally at the corner of Blanshard and Pandora. Their church, opened in 1863, sold for a fancy price in 1912 and was replaced with the present First United Church at Quadra and Balmoral.

The Baptists were early on the scene with the Church of Calvary (Reverend Wm. Carnes) on Herald Street near the present site of Hudson's Bay Company store. This church went up in flames in 1876 and was replaced with the new Emmanuel Baptist Church in 1886. This church still stands at Fernwood and Gladstone Streets. Other early churches include St. Stephen's in Saanich (1862), St. Paul's, Esquimalt (1866), St. James in James Bay (now demolished) built in 1884 and St. Luke's, Cedar Plains, opened in 1862.

Unfortunately the history of Victoria churches is not altogether peaceful. George Hills, for example, first Anglican bishop of British

Columbia, had a very difficult time, although he came with all the authority of a consecrated Bishop of the Diocese of British Columbia, created by the issue of Royal Letters Patent by Queen Victoria on January 12, 1859. This tall, white-haired and aristocratic-looking son of an English admiral arrived here in 1860 and was met by the Reverend E. Cridge, former Hudson's Bay Company chaplain and leader of the Anglican community. Together the two men trudged the three-mile trail, knee-deep in mud from Esquimalt to Victoria, where a group of ladies had procured a small house and prepared a meal for the first ordained bishop.

Cridge was a little apprehensive and, one may assume in the light of events, rather jealous at the arrival of a supervisory ecclesiastic.

He was inclined to evangelical rather than conservative church practice, but if he was jealous he dissimulated well because Bishop Hills was soon writing to a friend that "Cridge is a truly good man . . . he enters into all my plans and is a great support to me." The Bishop was soon to be disillusioned.

Bishop Hills was a dedicated and indefatigable worker. He organized the Victoria diocese and appointed Reverend Robert J. Dundas to conduct services in the Victoria courthouse on Sunday mornings and at St. Paul's in the afternoons. The Reverend R. Dawson was made incumbent at Craigflower and the Reverend E. Cridge, Dean of Christ Church.

The Bishop also consecrated the Victoria District Church (Christ Church) as the first Cathedral in the province.

For 32 years Bishop Hills was head, but not the undisputed head of the Anglican Church in British Columbia.

His antagonist was the short, bearded, kindly but rather obstinate Dean Cridge, who, one is inclined to suspect, thought that he and not George Hills should have been the first Bishop. As years went by, the Dean became a thorn in the flesh of Bishop Hills, causing him great distress.

The Dean's jealousy and resentment can be understood. He was an old-timer compared with the Bishop, having been appointed Colonial Chaplain in 1854. He had many friends and the Hudson's Bay Company built the Victoria District Church for him in 1856. The Church was only a small, wooden, box-like building where the new Court House now stands, but in it the Dean performed all church services including weddings, baptisms and funerals, a funeral costing only $1 which included grave digging and tolling of the bell.

The Victoria District Church was supplemented in 1860 with the so-called Iron Church, or St. John's. This was a corrugated-iron building sent out from England by the well-known benefactress Miss (afterwards Baroness) Burdett-Coutts of the famous London banking family. This lady also endowed generously the B.C. bishopric as she had already endowed the bishoprics of Adelaide and Capetown. The Iron Church was erected on Douglas Street where the Hudson's Bay Company store now stands and served until 1913 when it was demolished. Old-timers remember it chiefly because of its capacity to amplify outside noises. A passing tramcar or dray could make the service temporarily inaudible. First rector of St. John's was the Reverend R. Dundas, who later became canon of Winchester.

Christ Church, oldest of Anglican churches, has been rebuilt three times. The first wooden building burned down in 1869. The alarm was given (somewhat suspiciously many Anglicans thought) by a cassocked R.C. padre hurrying home to supper. A new Christ Church went up on the same site in 1872. The present Cathedral adjacent to Pioneer Square was constructed by Parfitt Bros. and consecrated in 1929.

Christ Church has, incidentally, the oldest vital statistics on the coast which were begun in 1837 by the Reverend Herbert Beaver, chaplain in Fort Vancouver, Washington, before the Hudson's Bay Company transferred its Pacific Northwest headquarters to Victoria.

Dean Cridge's antipathy towards Bishop Hills intensified with the years, many of which were spent by the Bishop organizing his vast diocese under conditions of great hardship and sometimes physical danger. The differences between the two men finally came into the open at the consecration of the new Christ Church Cathedral in 1873. The brawling, locking of church doors and verbal and written accusations which accompanied and followed this event seemed more appropriate to the times of Oliver Cromwell.

For the consecration Dean Cridge had invited Wm. Reece, Archdeacon of Vancouver Island, to preach. In his sermon Mr. Reece suggested encouragement of a moderate ritual, maintaining that ritual springs from a revived religious life. When he had finished his sermon Dean Cridge jumped to his feet and shouted:

"This is the first time Ritualism has been preached here. So far as I am concerned it shall be the last." Cridge's supporters in the Church showed their approval of his outburst by clapping and stamping of feet.

There is no evidence that Bishop Hills had pre-knowledge of Mr. Reece's views, but he took Dean Cridge to task for his unseemly behaviour and other offences. The Bishop's representations still further incensed the Dean who went on to publicly repudiate the Bishop and his authority. When the Bishop forbade the Dean to preach, the Dean's supporters locked the Cathedral and prevented the Dean's removal.

Finally as Dean Cridge denied the authority of the Ecclesiastical Court the Bishop took the case to the Supreme Court of British Columbia, which gave judgment against Dean Cridge. The irascible Dean then took his supporters to worship at the First Presbyterian Church on Pandora and later built a new church, the Reformed Episcopal Church (Church of Our Lord) on Humboldt Street. It stands there today, Victoria's oldest church building, flanked by the recently constructed Cridge Memorial Hall.

Some people maintain that Sir James Douglas, the Chief Justice and many other leading citizens were secretly in sympathy with the stormy Dean. Judge Begbie in fact remitted to Cridge the court costs which he had incurred defending himself against Bishop Hills.

The Anglican Church went from strength to strength in spite of the dispute. In 1879 the huge British Columbia diocese was subdivided by the formation of the dioceses of New Westminster and Caledonia.

A great building boom accompanied the expanding suburbs in the years 1940-1960.

Archbishop H. E. Sexton, recently retired, is the only bishop of the Diocese to become an Archbishop and holds the record for continuous service (32 years) as Bishop of the Diocese.

The dissension within the Anglican Church community followed closely on that which rent the Presbyterian Church.

The dispute contributed to Royal Governor Seymour's view that "Victorians were tempest torn and excited." Long term result of the dispute was to give Victoria two churches catering to Presbyterians ... St. Andrew's Presbyterian Church on Douglas Street and the First United Church at Quadra and Balmoral which combines Methodist and Presbyterian beliefs.

Trouble in the Presbyterian community followed the arrival of the Reverend Thomas Somerville in the early sixties. Somerville wanted a clearly defined system of Church government under the Church of Scotland. But many local Presbyterians wanted to carry on as before, catering to all Presbyterians under a very loose system of administration. Many felt a debt of gratitude to the Irish Church which had supported them financially.

The Rev. T. Somerville's irritation with church elders was sharpened by the fact that his modest salary was constantly in arrears. He called a meeting of his supporters in the Mechanics' Institute and announced his resignation. When he went to preach a farewell sermon the following Sunday, the *Colonist* of September 10, 1866 relates, he found the Pandora Street church locked up and his opponents refused to give him the key. Tempers got short and were shaping up for a free-for-all outside the Church doors when Somerville was admitted, mounted the pulpit and managed to calm his supporters. He maintained that rebels had usurped his functions. He arranged for his supporters, the bulk of the congregation, to hold services in the old Gymnasium Hall on Broughton Street. Then he set about organizing a new church, as a result of which St. Andrew's Presbyterian Church came into being, originally at the corner of Courtney and Gordon Streets (in 1869) and now at 680 Courtney.

The hard-core "Old Believers" who disputed Somerville's authority found themselves, as a result, unable to hold services for nine years. He in fact put the First Presbyterian Church temporarily out of business.

First Presbyterian minister in Victoria was the Reverend John Hall who made a lone trek from Esquimalt to Victoria in 1861. He was sent out by the Irish Presbyterian Church and as his earlier letters show had his moments of despondency. Victoria was teeming with gold-seekers and their shacks and he had great difficulty in finding any Presbyterians or anybody who knew what Presbyterianism was. His luck changed when he walked into the Bank of British North America and asked a man whether he was a Presbyterian. The man was Alexander Wilson who answered "yes" and helped him trace others of the faith.

The first Presbyterian service was held in Moore's Music Hall. A site was then bought at the northwest corner of Blanshard and Pandora and services started in 1863.

To bring the Church story up to date, Victoria in 1970 had 70 church and religious organizations, Anglican churches being predominant, for a population of 180,000, but the number of church buildings was far greater than these figures indicate because many churches had added annexes to cope with growth of congregations. The abundance of churches which are exempted from taxes was a matter of concern to some city and municipal officials.

Against this concern must be set the undoubted benefits to the taxpayer through the services given by religious organizations and especially the older churches like the Anglican and the Roman Catholic.

Human beings have since they were cave men always needed a power beyond themselves to which to turn for consolation, hope and inspiration in those times of great stress from which few are immune in their journey through life. In the troubled post-World War II years when all values are questioned and civilization itself is in a state of flux the need for belief in an omnipotent and wise Creator has been greater than ever. There can be little doubt that organized religion has played and is playing a significant role in reducing the number of people who might otherwise have needed costly taxpayer-subsidized care to enable them to overcome their problems.

Chapter 4

THE ROYAL GOVERNORS

A COLOURFUL BACKDROP to the social stage in Victoria's formative years was provided by the royal governors. Royal governors had far more influence than the lieutenant-governors who succeeded them when British Columbia became part of Canada in 1871. They were representatives of the British Empire to which the Island belonged, men of good breeding, absolutely incorruptible and skilled in administration.

Of the five royal governors between 1850 and 1871 all except Richard Blanshard were men of private means to supplement their not ungenerous salaries. Their social gatherings and other semi-regal functions offset the isolation of life in a small and distant colony and gave stimulous to the modest catering, dressmaking, liquor vending and carriage businesses, besides contributing to general conviviality.

Blanshard, the pecuniary exception, had a "raw deal." He was the first Royal Governor of the Colony and arrived in Victoria on March 9, 1850 in H.M.S. *Driver*. Our tribute to him is Blanshard Street. This 32-year-old tall, aristocratic, but by no means robust gentleman presented his credentials at a solemn ceremony in the Fort thereby instituting British government in the Pacific Northwest.

This proved to be the highlight of his governorship for Blanshard could not get his salary, a staff or even a place to live. He had to stay at first on board H.M.S. *Driver*. His only subjects if one excluded the servants of the Hudson's Bay Company were Captain Grant and his eight grumbling men.

Naturally melancholic on account of the malaria from which he suffered, Blanshard found nothing at Victoria to lighten his spirits. After a time he was lodged in the Fort while a residence for him was being built on Government Street. The Hudson's Bay Company which at that time controlled all trade used to mark up 300% on cost price for groceries and other imported necessities. Blanshard found the cost of living financially embarrassing. The Colonial Office whose servant he was did not help his pecuniary position. They charged him personally with the legal expenses involved in settling a mining dispute and for his out-of-pocket expenditure in a military expedition he organized to protect an isolated settlement.

Blanshard did manage to get a council set up to deal with the grievances of Grant, Langford, Staines and others. He also kept tabs on Hudson's Bay Company spending for which they were to be reimbursed on relinquishing their lease of the settlement. He left in September 1851 after 18 months here. His health had given way and his private fortune was, he wrote, "utterly insufficient for the mere cost of living here so high have prices been run up by the Hudson's Bay Company." A crowning insult ... he was asked by the Colonial Office to pay his fare home.

Douglas, who had fully expected to become first Royal Governor, succeeded Blanshard and with access to the right people in London and knowledge of local conditions, made a much better job of it. When Douglas's term of office terminated in 1864, Arthur Edward Kennedy, a generous spender succeeded him. His spending was the more welcome because of the economic gloom which followed the gold rushes. A boom city became a city of despair overnight when in 1865 the usual spring rush to the gold diggings failed to materialize.

Miners had left behind large unpaid debts, overstocked retailers and warehouses bulging with unsaleable merchandise. The extent of the decline is shown by exports. They were $809,000 (including gold) for one month in 1858 and only $29,448 for the whole year of 1867. The government was heavily in debt to the Bank of British Columbia which refused further credit and many badly needed public works had to be cancelled.

Kennedy arrived in 1864 when economic storm clouds were already low on the horizon. But without hesitation the Assembly voted a $2,000 welcoming fiesta. Kennedy brought with him his wife and two charming daughters Georgina and Elizabeth Henrietta. These daughters had good voices which were in succeeding months to bring nostalgic tears to many eyes with their rendering of "God Save the Queen." Gun salutes, musical fanfares, naval bands, fireworks and much drinking at wayside saloons accompanied the vice-regal procession from Esquimalt to Victoria, where it was discovered that by an oversight on the part of the organizers no living accommodation had been provided.

The Kennedys' had to put up in the St. George Hotel on View Street. There the Germania Sing Verein, entering in the spirit of the occasion, continued to serenade the Royal Governor long after he had gone to bed. In the end, the host of the St. George yielded to this choral blackmail and invited them in to quench their not inconsiderable thirst which automatically terminated the singing.

Kennedy's first concern was to get somewhere to lay his head and entertain . . . the latter being a social activity into which he was continually prodded by his active daughters. He rented temporarily "Fairfield" (now 601 Trutch Street) the home of Joseph Trutch, the Cariboo Road builder, mining promoter and astute politician. The house still stands and gives a fair idea of what was in those days considered a higher class residence, but "Fairfield" was a temporary expedient. On Rockland Hill was a dwelling known as Cary Castle. It was built by George Hunter Cary, a former Attorney-General of Vancouver Island, who sold it to Mrs. Elizabeth Miles, widow of a Hudson's Bay Company official.

She resold it to the Royal Governor for $19,000. The Government then on Kennedy's urgings spent $21,000 to complete the building. Its uncompleted state was due to the fact that George Cary, who was always in a rush, quick-witted, rheumatic and excitable, decided to build the residence before counting the cost. He nearly lost his last penny and was glad to sell it to Mrs. Miles when only one wing was completed.

Both Dr. Helmcken and De Cosmos who were very anti-Establishment opposed the spending, but Kennedy, the handsome Irishman, pleased the crowds. They liked him to spend . . . it meant jobs for them, and so they gave his opponents a rough time at the hustings.

Although Victoria had only 6,000 people, so many crowded into Cary Castle when Kennedy entertained that anybody who fell down ran the danger of becoming a pattern on the floorboards! Women complained bitterly of the dilapidated state of their wear after Kennedy balls. A Victoria newspaper made the understatement of the year when it referred to the first ball ever given in the Colony as being "inconveniently crowded."

Frederick Seymour, 1864-66, Royal Governor of the Mainland colony of British Columbia and later of the combined colonies of Vancouver Island and British Columbia, was equally popular in his capital, thirsty New Westminster. His unregal appearance (he was slight, frail and bald) and equally unregal voice (squeaky and sometimes inaudible) was offset by great personal generosity. He spent freely of the taxpayers' money as well. When, much against his personal inclinations, he had to take up residence in Victoria, he spent a lot of money on Cary Castle and its cricket pitch. He was criticized by some for his free spending, but in fact the Colony was 11 months in arrear with his salary and he was paying the Bank of British Columbia 18% interest on the overdraft. Seymour felt it was a gentleman's duty to look after his servants and nothing distressed him more than having to dismiss some of them after he had taken a cut in salary to help out the Colony.

In Victoria the duties of royal governors brought them into contact with what one must blushingly admit were a unique assortment of semi-educated political opportunists, many of them newcomers to the Colony. Headline-conscious, they criticized the royal governors frequently. The latter, in turn, did not pull their punches. To Royal Governor Kennedy is attributed the remark that "Victoria has two classes . . . those who are convicts and those who ought to be convicts." But this remark has also been attributed to an Australian lieutenant-governor in regard to the citizens of Australia at that time. Kennedy thought legislators manipulated laws to suit their own pockets. They could not give themselves raises, they got no pay. But they were land speculators. A case in point was when the legislators voted to abolish taxes on real estate. It transpired that many of them were in arrears with taxes on land they had bought during the boom. When the slump came they could not meet the assessments on their property.

George Tomline Gordon, Treasurer of the Vancouver Island Colony, entered into the spirit of the times by defalcating with $3,000 of the taxpayers' money. Tall, red-headed, bearded and be-whiskered, Gordon used to boast that people were polite to him because he owed them money. The judge was less polite and awarded him three years in jail, but money talks even behind bars and Gordon disappeared from jail. At the same time by contrast a transient, Thomas Rice, got six months for stealing a fellow roomer's coat.

Frederick Seymour was very involved in the controversy as to whether the capital of the combined colonies should be in Victoria or New Westminster. Victoria politicians mostly favoured Victoria, but some who had real estate holdings in New Westminster were for the Mainland site. New Westminster land speculators and officials who had their homes in "Imperial Stumpfield" wanted the com-bined Parliament to be there of course.

Seymour left no doubt as to his preferences. He thought Victoria only suited to be "a fishing place." He liked his New Westminster subjects and did his best to divert trade from Victoria to New Westminster.

He told London that Victoria had a half-alien restless population — ill at ease with itself. He also voiced the view when certain tran-sient merchants pressed for Confederation with Canada that "it was the expression of a disheartened community looking for change of any kind."

The decision to locate Parliament here delighted most Victorians, but dismayed Seymour and New Westminster.

The life cycle of royal governors in Victoria soon became fairly predictable. Fanfares and cheers on arrival . . . growing criticism . . . praise and sentimental tears on departure or death. Two royal governors are buried in Victoria, namely Frederick Seymour in the Esquimalt naval cemetery and James Douglas in Ross Bay cemetery. Seymour died of dysentery off Bella Coola on January 10, 1869 while settling an Indian dispute. Kennedy — "Old Deportment" as

45

he was called behind his back, departed amidst copious weeping for a post in Hong Kong, later to die at sea off Aden.

Anthony Musgrave, last of the royal governors to brighten Victoria life with Imperial tradition, held office from 1869 to 1871. His personal fortune was considerably increased by marriage with a connection of the wealthy American Cyrus Field. He had been Seymour's private secretary in Antigua, was talkative, intelligent and reported to have Creole blood. One of his two sisters married John Trutch, brother of the Commissioner of Lands and Works. Musgrave became a cripple after setting a precedent in having a broken leg set by a local Canadian doctor. He thereby increased his popularity with the anti-British element at the cost of his gait. During his term of office, a few score German, Jewish and other residents signed a petition urging the United States to annex the Colony. This aroused great local furore, but Musgrave did not attach much importance to it. He said most of the petitioners were not even naturalized citizens.

The petitioners didn't really wish the U.S. to annex the Colony. They were using a form of blackmail to get the British government to bail out the nearly-bankrupt community.

Musgrave had to contend with the grievances of officials displaced by Confederation, and he obtained pensions for them. He also contended with the grievances of those who thought severance of close ties with Britain prejudiced their future and betrayed their loyalty. Musgrave, like the other royal governors (including Douglas) had no high opinion of agitators for Confederation. He thought they were chiefly concerned with promoting their own interests. To Musgrave fell the unpleasant task of telling the Legislative Council that whether they liked it or not, the British government wanted the combined Vancouver Island and Mainland colonies to join up with the rest of Canada.

The royal governors in their time had formidable powers.

Legislative assembly members might propose (they sat proposing in session over 310 days one year), but the royal governors disposed. They could withhold civil list salaries and funds from Crown land grants. The opposition they encountered rose from two differing ideas of the purpose of government. The royal governors, echoing

46

the Mother Country's views, wanted the Colonies to pay their way. To this end in the recession times which ruled during most of the years they were in office (Douglas's periods of office excepted) they imposed stringent economies, cutting down on public works.

The local politicians regarded government primarily as a cow to be milked. They endeavoured to make use of the broadened franchise to blackmail the royal governors and the British Government, finding support among those suffering from poverty and those envious of the status and emoluments of British officials imported to run the Colony.

The amalgamation of the two colonies of Vancouver Island and British Columbia in 1866, the centennial of which was recently celebrated was viewed with gloom by many Victorians. A salute was fired by the Royal Navy in harbour here to mark the occasion. Douglas thought a funeral procession would have been more appropriate. Confederation with Canada in 1871 was equally a cause for regret by many of Victoria's staunchest citizens. They foresaw an unwelcome change from incorruptible British administration to the pork-barrel politics of Eastern Canada.

But Victoria was given no choice. Britain in the 1860's did not want the colonies and they had to do as she wished or risk abandonment by London and eventual absorption by the United States.

The social precedents set by the royal governors have fortunately been continued by the lieutenant-governors and add greatly to Victoria's social scene. Opening of Parliament remains the most important official function. Lieutenant-governors also receive visiting royalty, heads of state and ambassadors.

The annual dinner to legislators, the State Ball (recently revived after being dropped for some years), the New Year reception open to all male residents and the July garden party are the main social events. Invitations to the garden party are sent to those who have signed the Government House register. Many Vancouver and other out-of-town British Columbians attend all events.

A list of lieutenant-governors and royal governors will be found in the appendix.

Chapter 5

A STORMY DECADE

THE LAST EIGHT YEARS OF THE 1870 to 1880 decade were with the exception of the 1930 depression years the most dismal in Victoria's economic history.

The population declined from 7,900 when the last royal governor left office in 1871 to under 6,000 ten years later. Hundreds became destitute. Hundreds more emigrated to the States where conditions were not much better. Many went back to Eastern Canada or worked their way by ship to England.

Yet this was the Confederation decade. It started off with the brightest prospects. By 1870, Victoria had partially recovered from the letdowns which followed the Fraser River and Cariboo gold rushes. With the departure of the transient gold-seekers and merchants and the establishment of the Legislature for the whole of British Columbia in Victoria, the city's economy seemed to be on a reduced but firmer base. In fact during Anthony Musgrave's two years as royal governor (1869-71) the city's population had doubled.

Joseph Trutch, the first Lieutenant-Governor who succeded Musgrave, had brought back from Ottawa most generous terms in return for the province joining the Confederation. They included construction of a trans-Canada railroad terminating in Victoria, work to begin within two years. The province was to receive $100,000 per annum for its graciousness in allowing Ottawa to build it. Small wonder that on Confederation Day, July 19, 1871, Victoria celebrated with a glorious binge. People crowded the taverns and streets drinking and singing, watching the Roman candles lit for the occasion, and listening to congratulatory speeches, the firing of naval guns in the harbour and the ringing of church bells. Victoria seemed to "have it made."

The shrewder citizens saw government jobs, political appointments, contracts for supplying the railroad builders, endless opportunities in real estate speculation and all the benefits obtainable through distant federal supervision of expenditures incurred locally.

Had anybody told the roistering crowds that within a decade the premier of a poverty-stricken and despairing province would be suggesting that Vancouver Island become a separate kingdom with its own queen, H.R.H. Princess Louise, he would have been considered a super-Jeremiah.

By 1871 dwellings had stretched beyond the Douglas-Johnson-Courtenay-Wharf street boundaries of 1862 to Pembroke Street in the north, easterly to Quadra, to a good part of James Bay in the south with Wharf Street, as before in the west. But within this area were many vacant lots.

Before the 1858 Fraser River stampede there were very few dwellings which could be called residences.

There was James Douglas's home where the Provincial Museum now is (a tablet marks its site). Orchard House was built in the early 1860's at 600 Michigan, almost opposite the home of Macdonald, the unfortunate banker.

Out of town, a couple of hundred feet north of Fort Rodd was Belmont House, built by Chief Justice David Cameron about 1855. Belmont House overlooked Esquimalt Lagoon. Not a trace of it remains today. It was the scene of many gay parties in its time and its grounds later became part of Hatley Park (Royal Roads). David Cameron owed his affluence to Royal Governor Douglas, his brother-in-law. The appointment created great friction because Cameron did not have many qualifications except his kinship with Douglas. He had been an unsuccessful cloth dealer in Scotland and a coal mines clerk before being promoted to the Bench.

Also erected in this period (in 1863) was the home on Carr Street (now incorporated in Government Street) where the talented Victorian artist Emily Carr was to be born eight years later. The Carr

49

residence on the northeast corner of Simcoe and Government Streets is now being restored by the Emily Carr Foundation.

Emily was known as "Klee Wyck" (the smiling one) by the Indians in whose villages she painted. She did not do much smiling at home, being thought a wilful child by her family. She was happier with the Carr's cows than with her sisters, and was frequently banished to the barn to keep the cows company where she could indulge unimpeded in her enjoyment of cigarettes. Her new bold style of painting earned her nothing but hostility in Victoria and Emily frequently stuffed her work in the garbage can. When after her father's death the family fell on hard times Emily lived on Simcoe Street and took in boarders. Not one to be trifled with, she turned the hose on one of them.

Not until she was 58 did Emily become famous, Ottawa having recognized her talent. She was careless of her appearance . . . many living residents recall her pushing a battered pram downtown for groceries, her petticoat showing beneath her skirt; but she was meticulous in her work.

No Canadian artist has excelled her in ability to portray British Columbian mountain, forest and sea. No artist has managed to emulate the stark, almost savage majesty she brought to her studies of nature. Her work today is highly prized and very valuable. She died in 1945.

The Carr home was originally on a 10-acre lot which provided the family with vegetables and milk as was the custom of the times. The lot was subdivided to allow room for a hotel, the Park Hotel, the site now occupied by the Emily Carr apartments on Douglas Street. Buyer of the site in 1863 was Bill Lush who promised he wouldn't run a tavern, but soon broke his promise and the Carr family had to put up a fence to shield them from the noise and drunks.

Bill Lush came to a bad end. He assaulted a Royal Navy marine for which the magistrate fined him $150. He went back to his tavern, swallowed strychnine and died.

Vernon Villa, later renamed Ivy Hill, was the home of Donald Fraser, M.L.A. It was built in the early 1860's. Although it no longer exists, the wall round its grounds between Rupert and Vancouver streets can still be seen and encloses a raised parking lot. Some years after it was built it became the home of Mr. and Mrs. Charles Vernon, Charles being a pottery manufacturer and gold commissioner and related to Donald Fraser. Mrs. Vernon was the daughter of Mrs. Duncan McTavish, and Mrs. McTavish bought the home from her daughter and renamed it Ivy Hill. A path led up Ivy Hill to the R. P. Rithet family next door.

A wedding (famous in its time) took place from Ivy Hill ... that of Margaret Elizabeth McTavish to a wealthy New Yorker, Dr. E. Fuller.

The McTavish's, of course, were one of the great landowning families of Victoria.

Although Victoria in the early 1870's was, architecturally, nothing to call attention to, the pioneers could congratulate themselves that they had at least made a dent in what was till they came, an Indian preserve.

A start had been made on hospitals (St. Joseph's and what was to become the Royal Jubilee), education was looked after in the Colonial and Craigflower schools, a police court and judiciary were functioning.

The three hospital buildings erected in Esquimalt in 1855 to accommodate possible casualities from the Crimean War were still in existence. They have since been demolished ... the last of them in 1939. Public buildings included the new Court House (1860) and the Colonial Police Barracks (1861) in the Birdcage assembly of buildings, the firehall on Yates Street (1861), the drill room and the jail on Langley Street (built 1862).

The Wootton home of California redwood went up in 1859 at Courtney and Quadra. The house was demolished in 1952 and the site is now that of the fine new Y.M.C.A. building. The Woottons are a well-known Victoria family. Henry Wootton, a former ship's officer, arrived here in 1858 and got the position of Harbourmaster to which was later added that of Postmaster, the previous postmaster having disappeared with a large sum of money.

He brought out his wife from England and their daughter Anne married Elliott Hammond King. The latter was not so fortunate in his attempts to get a livelihood. He started a newsaper, calling it the

51

Victoria Gazette. But the former *Victoria Gazette* had stopped publishing only a few months before and the publishers sued him for using the name of their paper. The *Victoria Gazette* had earlier printed all official bulletins and it seems that Elliott Hammond King's secondary object in starting a new *Gazette* was to get the job of Queen's Printer. But his newspaper folded and nothing came of the job.

The Wootton-King alliance yielded a daughter, Annie and two sons, Henry and Ted. The sons founded the still functioning King Bros. shipbrokers. Henry also helped to fit out Victoria's famous dug-out *Tillicum*. The 30-foot *Tillicum* sailed with Captain John Voss and a newspaperman named Luxton from Oak Bay and across the Pacific in 1904. Luxton deserted the vessel at first opportunity, Voss took on another crewman, who was washed overboard, and eventually arrived in Margate, England, after an epic 40,000-mile voyage.

The story of the *Tillicum* thrilled readers all over the world. In London Captain Voss was made a Fellow of the Royal Geographical Society, but he was a man of uncertain temper and departed England leaving the *Tillicum* to rot. It was brought back to Victoria thanks largely to the efforts of Geo. I. Warren who helped to locate her and induced two Greenwich Yacht Club members to part with her. He raised the funds for her return by freighter and she is now lodged in the city's Maritime Museum.*

Citizens evinced mercurial optimism during the first few years of the Confederation decade. There was much private and public building. Erin Hall, home of the Nesbitts (a grandson is well known as a Victoria historian and for his laudable efforts to preserve what is worth preserving in our environment) went up in 1874.

A novelty of Erin Hall was a 20,000-gallon water tank which supplied every room. The house cost around $10,000 ($75,000 today). The site with its several acres now houses many smaller dwellings.

The original Samuel Nesbitt had a biscuit factory at 59 Yates

* George I. Warren was for over 30 years commissioner of the Victoria and Island Publicity Bureau when the famous slogan was coined: "Follow the Birds to Victoria."

Street (Yates at Broad, south side) and the tin boxes in which the biscuits were packed were much prized by the Indians as coffins. Later, Nesbitt's cracker factory moved to Fort Street, between Langley and Wharf Streets.

Wentworth Villa went up on Fort Street hill, a mile from town. It was the home of Mrs. Blinkhorn who arrived with her husband and niece Martha Cheney in 1851 after a seven-month voyage round the Cape in the 300-ton barque *Tory*. The building with its "sugar cake" eaves still stands at 1156 Fort and houses antiques (The Connoisseur Shop). The Blinkhorns managed the Bilston Farm at Metchosin.

When her husband died Mrs. Blinkhorn moved into Wentworth Villa with her niece who had meanwhile married Captain Henry Ella, a handsome officer of the Hudson's Bay Company. The dearly-loved old lady died at the ripe age of 80 leaving many good works behind her.

Captain Henry Ella's tragic death in 1873 while crossing Burrard Inlet in a canoe (the taxi of those days) ended 18 years of happy married life for Martha. Before and after marriage Martha kept a detailed diary of life among the few who made up Victoria's early society. People walked, canoed and rode tremendous distances. Company was sought for its own sake. John Muir of Muir's sawmill in Sooke (he bought it from Captain Grant) and his sons John and Archibald used to ride to the Metchosin farm. Captain Grant, the erratic surveyor, travelled to Sooke by canoe, calling in at Metchosin on the way. Martha travelled by canoe to the Governor's ball at Fort Victoria and attended a party on the warship *Trincomalee*, riding horseback back to Bilston farm next day.

The Langfords (including daughters) and Mrs. Skinner and baby used to visit Metchosin on foot. Dr. Helmcken frequently walked from Victoria or his View Royal farm to Metchosin. Prominent people Martha mentions in her diary include the Rev. Robert Staines (the ecclesiastical pig fancier) and wife, Governor James Douglas, Captain and Mrs. Cooper, Mr. and Mrs. Barr, the two Miss Reids, Mr. Newton, Mr. Pearse, Mr. McKay and Mr. Martin.

Captain Cooper and James Douglas never agreed. The captain was a stout, irascible former Hudson's Bay skipper and a thorn in the governor's side from the moment he arrived. He met Blinkhorn on the voyage out and with him built a schooner to ship lumber to San Francisco. Then he tried to ship cranberries from the Mainland. Douglas regarded both moves as an infringement of the Company's trading rights and banned the cranberry shipments.

But Douglas needed cash to run the Colony. Liquor then, as now, seemed a promising source of revenue.

The moral issue — debauching of Indians and Company employees could also be invoked. Douglas proposed to license liquor vendors and also that members of the Executive Council be barred from the trade. Cooper being in partnership with notorious liquor vendor James Yates (Yates Tavern on Yates Street) at first angrily opposed Douglas, but Douglas knew his man. After being generously plied with H.B. liquor, Cooper agreed to his proposals.

An hour or two later, as the effects of the hospitality wore off, Cooper's earlier objections returned. He visited his partner in Yates Tavern and stimulated by more alcohol and the bawling out he received from Yates he staggered into the street yelling "Down with the Hudson's Bay Company! Down with monopoly!" Finally he went down himself for more than the count — most enjoyable for the onlookers.

Cooper sold out in 1856, went to England and protested against the high-handedness of the Company.

He came back to Victoria and when Britain took over the Colony from the Hudson's Bay Company was, to the disgust of Douglas, appointed harbourmaster in 1859. Insult to injury, he hadn't paid the Company for his land and owed a large debt to their store. Cooper was a surety for the *British Colonist* which under editor De Cosmos constantly abused Douglas. He later sold out his Esquimalt land at a profit and went to New Westminster, heading a campaign for a subsidized steamer service to San Francisco which would put the Mainland in a more competitive position with Victoria . . . again to Douglas's annoyance.

Martha Cheney frequently mentions hurricane-like winds and rains and bad trails. She churned butter, did the ironing and all things deemed proper for a well brought up young lady. She led a

OLD PARLIAMENT BUILDINGS
(the Birdcages) viewed from the
waterfront.

OUTSIDE VIEW OF VICTORIA.

Page 29.

VICTORIA IN THE LATE 1850's
Artist's sketch of waterfront showing
newly-built James Bay Bridge,
Victoria District Church (later
Christ Church) in background, the
Hudson's Bay Company warehouse
(tall building on left) on what is
now Wharf Street and the old Fort
Victoria dwellings, centre. Ship
in forefront is S.S. *Beaver*.

WINDSOR HOTEL
still standing, reputed to be the
oldest in Victoria.

THOMAS HARRIS
Victoria's first mayor.

THE QUEEN'S MARKET
Harris' butcher shop, the first
in Victoria.

A STREET IN VICTORIA.

VIEW OF YATES STREET IN 1852 from Government to Wharf Streets. Commercial establishments include: Adelphi Saloon, Kady Gambitz Drygoods Store, the first established in Victoria; Bank of British North America, first bank in Victoria; Moore & Co., druggists, corner Yates and Langley Streets; auction house on Wharf. In this artist's sketch most of the figures shown are intended to represent Chinese and Indians.

THIS MODEST PIONEER FARMHOUSE
is representative of better dwellings of
the time. It was the home of the
Blinkhorns who farmed in Metchosin.

SIR ANTHONY MUSGRAVE
the last Royal Governor of
British Columbia.

very busy life and left numerous children and grandchildren when she died well on in years in Wentworth Villa.

Another home in Martha Cheney's time was that of Henry Pering Pellew Crease (the legal firm of Crease & Co. perpetuates his name) who built "Pentrelew" in 1874. The name is Cornish for "sloping two ways" and the home, now the Victoria Truth Centre, sloped towards Linden and Rockland.

Henry Crease was born in Cornwall, the son of Captain Harry Crease, R.N. He became the first barrister in Victoria when he arrived in 1858 and later a member of the Legislative Council and Justice of the Supreme Court.

Crease was known as the "Father of the Bar" and in view of the times in which he lived it is important to state that this was a legal and not bibulous qualification. His wife must have been very devoted to him. She made the journey via the Panama with three daughters. After surviving the blows of this voyage and six years in New Westminster, she suffered a blow on land when the Crease home burned down just as they were about to move in. The burned home was replaced with "Pentrelew" and it was a very gay place. Lady Crease as she became after her husband was knighted reckoned that every admiral in the Royal Navy had climbed as a midshipman the cherry trees in the five-acre Pentrelew grounds.

A few hundred yards from "Pentrelew" was the home of banker A. A. Green which is now the Victoria Art Gallery. Banker Green must have taken great business risks for the Land Registry records show that his land was consigned to creditors. The home was acquired by David Spencer who moved there in 1910.

Henry Crease and David Spencer jointly purchased a 10-acre estate (see map). David Spencer, in addition to looking after his extensive retailing interests, found time to raise 13 children. The children grew up in a 10-room home built in 1874 at the south end of James Bay Bridge. One son, Chris, built a home next door to his father in James Bay and lived there until 1910. After David Spencer moved with his remaining children into what is now the Art Gallery, his original James Bay home became the Poplars boarding house . . . a somewhat unsavoury place according to then current reports. Next door to Chris Spencer lived Cameron, a clothing merchant.

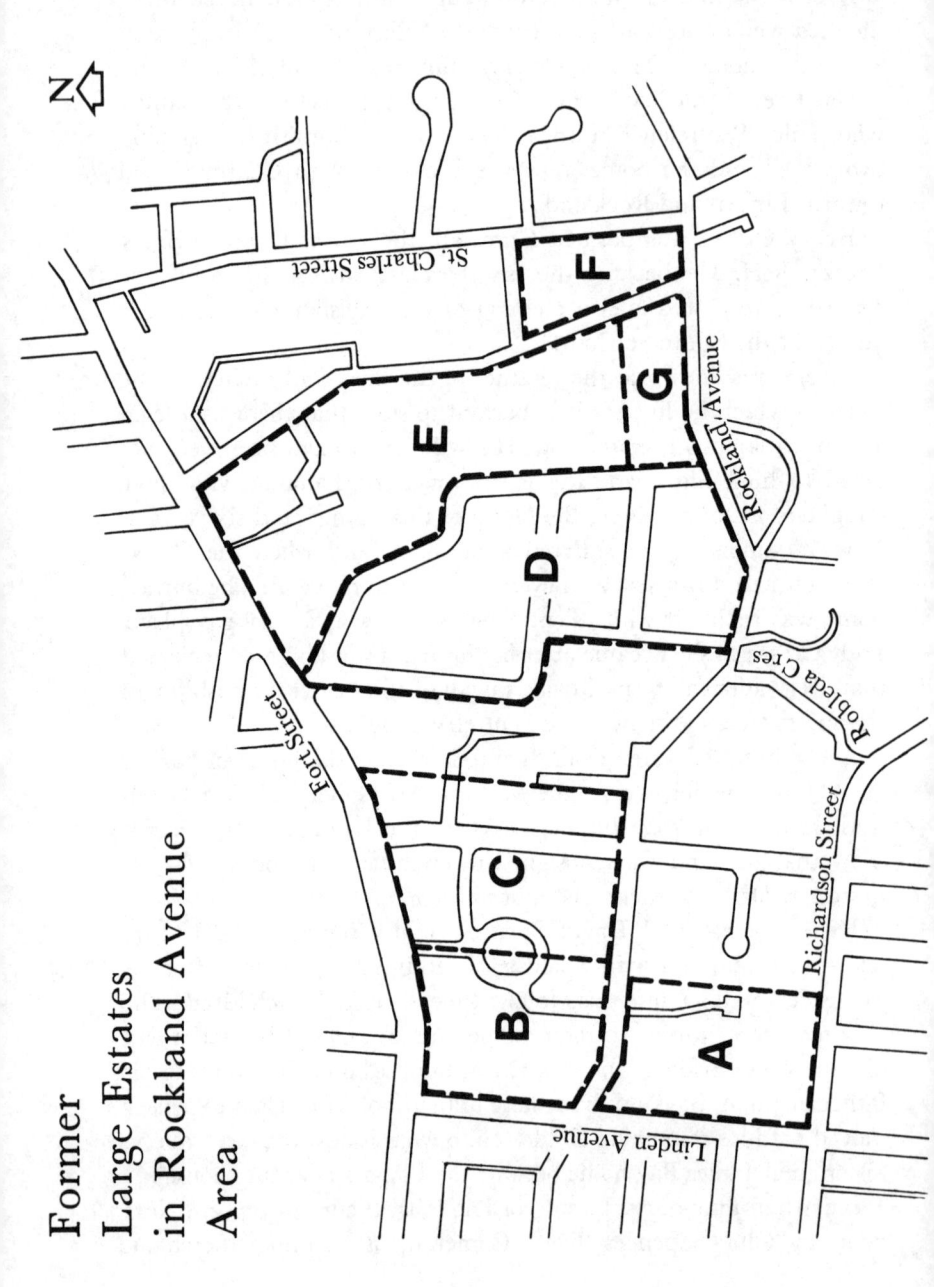

Former
Large Estates
in Rockland Avenue
Area

Cameron's home was pulled down in 1905 to allow the extension of Birdcage Walk which ran from the James Bay side of the bridge to Michigan Street.

Enlivening the somewhat sombre decade was the marriage in 1878 of Martha, youngest daughter of Sir James Douglas to C.P.R. survey official Dennis R. Harris at the Reformed Episcopal Church. This was one of the unforeseen by-products of Confederation.

Bridesmaids were the Misses Helmcken, McTavish, Gridge, Mac-Donald, Langley, Wallace, Tolmie and Bushby. Some of them seem to have been a bit overworked. Their names appear at numerous weddings. The groomsmen were Messrs. R. Gridge, A. W. Jones and A. Mackenzie. Martha and her husband did not travel far for their honeymoon. Destination was Steven's Hotel, Saanich.

Two years before, another well-known Victoria resident tied the marital knot for the second time. B. W. Pearse of Fernwood married Miss Jennie Palmer. The Misses McTavish and MacDonald were again among the bridesmaids.

Pearse who, it will be recalled, laid out the townsite with Pemberton, built Fernwood, a small stone house, at Vining and Begbie Streets in 1860. To judge by the frequency with which his name appears on title deeds, he must have speculated a lot and done very well out of land during the gold rushes. Fernwood, with additions made in 1883, became a two-storey mansion of 15 rooms. The estate was bounded by Fort, Haultain, Victoria High School and Richmond (Jubilee Hospital).

Pearse died in 1902. The estate was valued at $290,000 and the

---

A   THE LAURELS

B   SPENCER (ART GALLERY)

C   PENTRELEW (CREASE)

D   CRAIGDARROCH (DUNSMUIR)

E   NESBITT

F   PRIOR

G   BARNARD (DUVALS)

house demolished in 1969. Pearse became resident engineer of the Public Works Department of Canada after Confederation. It is remarkable as one follows the careers of eminent Victorians how politics and public appointments were intertwined. Take the case of Senator William John MacDonald. His home, "Armadale," was the showplace of Victoria for many years. The stone-towered two-storey mansion stood in 28 acres of park at Ogden Point. It was built in 1876 by the Senator, who, incidentally is responsible for Victoria Day becoming a national holiday.

"Armadale" had a dining room 18 x 20 feet, a library 14 x 18 feet and a 12-foot-wide entrance hall. MacDonald Park in James Bay is part of the estate and Niagara Street cuts through the driveway out of which used to emerge the senator's handsome equipage.

"Armadale" was a centre of political and social life and a home away from home for Royal Navy officers. John MacDonald was by all worldly portents a successful man. A pioneer resident, he lived after marriage in 1857 in "Glendale," a cottage on Gordon Street which later became the Badminton Club and then the site of the first Union Club building.

Of his six children, Mary married a Royal Navy commander in 1896 and Flora the manager of the Bank of British North America, Gavin Hamilton Burns, in 1890. In its shabby later years "Armadale" became a night spot, fell into ruin and was demolished in this century.

Other notable homes built in the early 1870's were the Charles home at 1038 Fort Street (north side, west of Cook). It was on an acre of land. Wm. Charles was a senior Hudson's Bay Company official. Avalon Villa fronting on Beacon Hill Park was built in 1870 by Peter John Leech, who discovered the Leechtown gold. Peter Leech could have operated a travel agency without ever consulting a map. Before coming here with the Royal Engineers in 1858 he had served in the Crimean War and with General Charles Gordon in Khartoum. He then surveyed northern British Columbia, and on one trip was reduced to making soup out of a dogskin coat, being saved from starvation only by the arrival of some Kispiox Indians.

He laid out the Bella Coola townsite, managed a Hudson's Bay store and became city engineer of Victoria. About $100,000 in gold was taken from the Leech River which is named after him. Leech was one of the lucky few to get a bride from the brideship *Tynemouth*. Mary MacDonald was one of four sisters in the ship and Mrs. Leech became well known as the organist in the Reverend Cridge's Reformed Episcopal Church.

"Avalon" was an ugly two-storeyed house. When it was built Beacon Hill Park opposite was deep forest with a frog pond. There was no Douglas Street. The Goodacre Towers apartment (north corner of Avalon Street) is now on the site.

As a result of Confederation several Federal buildings went up, providing welcome employment. A new wooden drill hall near the Birdcage buildings was built in 1874. Formerly volunteers had drilled in premises on Broughton Street.

H.M.C.S. Malahat on Wharf Street, believed to be the oldest Federal building in Victoria, was started in 1871 and completed three years later. It was originally the Custom House and became the Armed Services recruiting centre in 1959.

The City Council was also infected by the initial enthusiasm engendered by Confederation. The Council approved a water by-law to borrow $100,000 and in 1873 the foundation stone was laid of the Victoria Waterworks Co. Previously water had been brought from Spring Ridge (at Fernwood and Vining Streets) by the Spring Ridge Waterworks Co., the price having fallen from 25 cents a bucket in 1858 to 20 buckets for $1 in the early seventies.

The roof fell in on all this optimism and prosperity in 1873. A financial panic hit the continent. Ottawa, on whose promises Victoria's future was predicted, was as badly hit as any. Factories and shops closed down. Unemployment became rife. Revenues declined.

For Ottawa it was fiscally and politically impossible to honour the generous offers made to Lieutenant-Governor Trutch in return for British Columbia joining Confederation. It hit Victoria like a thunderbolt to learn that construction of the trans-Canada railroad would not only be postponed, but the terminus when it was built would not be in Victoria. To soften the blow Lord Carnarvon, Governor-General, proposed immediate construction of the Esquimalt & Nanaimo Railway, but the Ottawa government would have none of it.

Despair gripped every heart in Victoria. Her whole future seemed blighted. With one decision Ottawa had knocked away the main prop of her economy. Despairing of an economic recovery, residents became politically instead of business activated. What could be extracted from Ottawa became the burning topic in the Legislature, in clubs, in business houses, saloons and homes.

Chapter 6

POLITICS AND PERSONALITIES

As a result of the political turmoil many new colourful personalities emerged during the 1870-80 decade to add excitement to the social and legislative scene.

There were no political parties — they came in first with Premier McBride in 1903—but M.L.A.'s and their supporters switched from one or other combination according to where the "mostest" was promised. The rallying cry for patriots was the never-failing vote-getter today, namely: "unfair treatment by outside interests."

In the earliest years of the Colony the Hudson's Bay Company was the whipping boy, accused of benefitting its shareholders at the expense of settlers. When Vancouver Island became a Crown Colony the British government aroused the ire of many because of its alleged neglect and parsimony. When British Columbia became part of Canada, Ottawa became the culprit, allegedly depriving the province of its rightful share of Canada's revenue, an attitude — whether well based or not — still common today.

The lengths to which British Columbians were prepared to go to extract money from Ottawa is shown by their pressing Ottawa to accept the province's population in 1870 as 60,000 when in fact it was only 36,247 as far as could be ascertained from the dubious records kept. Nor were the politicians in the East sprouting angels' wings. Urging support for this or other measure from their local political friends they were careful to assure them that their interests (real estate, trade, or otherwise) would not be affected.

British Columbia's first premier made no great contribution to political or social life. The chief claim to fame of John Foster McCreight, premier 1871-72, was his honesty. He had the reputation of being crochety and ill-tempered, but he was really intolerant of politicians although elected for Victoria. Lieutenant-Governor Joseph Trutch persuaded him to accept the premiership of the first united parliament of Vancouver Island and the Mainland.

As a lawyer, McCreight was an educated man, in contrast to the other politicians whom the lieutenant-governor described as "a queer kittle cattle ... a wild team to handle." They were too wild for McCreight who quit the premiership over a very small matter after a year and was glad to do so. Politics were definitely not his line. He was a fiery tempered Irishman who arrived here from Australia in 1860 and upset Chief Justice Begbie by daring him to use outside the court the words he had used inside. Begbie twice exiled him to "Siberia" — the legal term for the Cariboo, the drawback being that with the gold rushes over, there was nobody to judge. It was only one stage removed from solitary confinement. McCreight did not shine socially. He lived on Michigan Street near Birdcage Walk.

He was apparently married for the name of Mrs. McCreight appears with his as guest at a social function, but little was seen of her and the marriage certificate was not among his papers.

He achieved temporary notoriety by publicly punching a Dr. Rumsey on the nose and was fined for so doing. Neither assailant nor assaulted ever revealed the reason for the set-to. Perhaps there wasn't one.

McCreight was an ardent supporter of Christ Church, but shocked the Church and friends by suddenly turning Roman Catholic. He left Victoria in 1897 never to return.

British Columbia's first cabinet ministers were paid $3,500 a year, the equivalent being about $35,000 today. Their spending was a substantial contribution to the city's economy. M.L.A.'s got no pay, but were suspected of helping themselves to generous "pickings." In one session of the Legislature a motion was put that a return be made of all amounts paid to members. It was turned down. The *Colonist* commented: "The public thought the M.L.A.'s services were free, but there is more than a suspicion that some have been paid and well paid for their services."

Royal Governor Seymour charged outright in 1869 that many M.L.A.'s "made pickings on the quiet."

After McCreight came De Cosmos (1872-74). Amor De Cosmos, the West's first radical, was born plain Bill Smith, legitimate off-spring of James and Charlotte Esther Smith of Windsor, Nova Scotia. He changed his name to the Latin equivalent of "Lover of the Universe" because when he was an itinerant photographer in the California goldfields he found himself submerged beneath hundreds of Bill Smiths. He arrived in Victoria with the gold-seekers, but swiftly decided that there was more pay dirt in politics. Socially De Cosmos was an alcoholic beacon in a toper's maze. Nearly all men drank heavily, but De Cosmos seldom seemed to eat. Wine and whiskey drinking on the Pacific coast parallelled the gin-drinking in industrial England with one important exception. Britain's gin palaces catered to the working classes, whereas wine and whiskey drinking was indulged in heavily by all classes throughout the west. Successful men were proud of their wine cellars.

Some blame the shortage of women and absence of domestic life for the heavy drinking. Naval officers endeavouring to round up partners for a ball in 1860 could find only 30 young ladies — some of them half-breeds — in the whole of Vancouver Island. It was estimated that males at that time outnumbered females by 100 to 1.

The situation was relieved, by the arrival of 62 imported females among 270 passengers in the S.S. *Tynemouth* in September 1862. The women were sent out under the auspices of the London Female Emigration Society. There would have been 96 of them, but San Francisco, where the *Tynemouth* called, was just as short of women as Victoria. Thirty-four went ashore there and didn't return to the ship.

For Victoria, arrival of the *Tynemouth* was a gala event. All shops and other businesses closed for the day and crowds of sex-starved settlers and miners tried to board the ship in Esquimalt where she tied up. But they had to wait until the passengers were brought to Victoria in the gunboat *Forward* and quartered in the Colonial Police Barracks in James Bay. Most of the women found partners within a few days and many of their descendants live here today.

But even in Victoria, according to local legend, some of them "went missing" as far as husbands were concerned, but they were not missing from the local scene.

In the same year the *Seaman's Bride* was due here from Australia with 23 females. They were permitted ashore in San Francisco and stayed ashore. As to the type of lady, Australia was as short of women as Canada and it is hard to believe that Australia was parting with her best.

The arrival of the *Thames City* with a detachment of Royal Engineers in April 1859 brought 118 men, but only 31 women to the Colony. In 1862 a ship from Britain arrived with 250 passengers, among them only 25 women and, worse still, 20 of them were married. There were not enough women to go round for the few hundred local residents, let alone the tens of thousands of transient miners. It was not to be wondered at. The long voyage round the Cape from Britain was perilous and inflicted great hardships. When to this is added the roughness and monotony of a pioneer's living it is understandable why many of the early fur traders partnered Indian women.

James Douglas's wife Amelia was the offspring of Hudson's Bay chief factor William Connolly and an Indian wife. Factor John Tod, who owned a large part of Oak Bay, partnered three Indians. One of them he called his "singing Lola" but her vindictive and stern look in a photograph seems to indicate that she "went off song" after a few years of John. Mary Tod Island off the Oak Bay Marina is named after one of his daughters.

De Cosmos didn't marry at all. His interests were in other directions. He was launched into political life by the *British Colonist* (now *Victoria Daily Colonist*) which he founded. It was not, however, the first newspaper. The pioneer newspaper was the *Victoria Gazette* edited in 1858 by American immigrants Williston and Bartlett. Their literary efforts were preceded by those of Robert Melrose who is sometimes hailed as Victoria's first journalist. Robert Melrose, a Scot, arrived in Victoria in 1853 to work on Craigflower Farm where he lodged with his wife in a rough shack. Mrs. Melrose

64

did all the work and raised daughter Ellen (born in 1854): Robert raised his glass and kept a meticulous diary of the alcoholic content of his fellow immigrants.

He kept a daily record telling with the precision of a breathalyzer whether they were one-quarter, half-, three-quarters, or dead drunk. A red letter day in Mrs. Melrose's hard life was when H.R.H. Princess Louise, a daughter of Queen Victoria, visited her, accepted a jug of home-made cream and gave her $5 to show her appreciation. A truthful line in Melrose's diary reads: "It would almost take a line of packet ships running regularly between here and San Francisco to supply this isle with grog, so great a thirst prevails amongst its inhabitants." Melrose was probably among the horde of "Egyptian locusts" as they were termed who descended on a newly-built ship in 1869 and consumed all the liquor and food before the christening party arrived. The builder was indignant. The invited guests indignant. The *Colonist* wrote: "The young socialite who was to have christened the ship left in a great huff."

Meanwhile the shipwrights dealt Bacchanalian blows at the blocks and the ship slid unchristened into the water.

"What shall we call her?" shouted the head carpenter on the receding vessel. "Call her?" echoed the desperate owner with a vengeful glance at the departing "locusts": "Call her the Bums" and *B.U.M.S.* she was christened.

Ship christenings (as indeed any free entertainment) can be counted on to draw Victorians in crowds. Harold Husband, president of V.M.D. shipyards, in 1962 publicly invited "friends" to attend the launching of the ferry *Queen of Victoria*. He found he had so many "friends" he had to abandon the custom.

The *Victoria Gazette* changed hands in the year it started after going daily at 12½¢ (about $1 per copy by today's values) and expired a few months later.

An employee in the leaky Wharf Street shed where the *British Colonist* was printed was David W. Higgins.

Higgins was an able but quarrelsome journalist. His career was punctuated with libel cases. Halifax-born, he arrived in Victoria in 1858 and soon quarrelled with De Cosmos. He set up the rival *Victoria Daily Chronicle* in a press he brought from the defunct

Victoria Gazette. Meanwhile De Cosmos had sold the *British Colonist* to the staff. Both Higgins' *Chronicle* and the *British Colonist* found the going tough. Higgins merged the two papers into the *British Colonist and Victoria Chronicle*, then, after six years, renamed the paper *Victoria Colonist*.

Higgins, like De Cosmos, had his eye on politics and the financial rewards attached thereto. He sold out in 1886, became an M.L.A., Speaker of the House and president of the National Electric Tramway & Light Co. He wrote two books *Mystic Spring* and *Passing of a Race* and married in the year of his arrival a local girl, Mary Jane, third daughter of J. T. Pidwell, a Cornish Methodist, whose home was at the corner of Douglas and Humboldt Streets, now a parking lot.

In 1885 he built one of Victoria's finest homes "Regents Park" at the west corner of Fort and St. Charles Streets, the scene of many gay social events.

The *Victoria Colonist* was printed in the Hibben-Bone building on the site of what is now the Churchill Hotel on Government Street in 1882: the old Victoria (Royal) Theatre was demolished to make room for it. The newspaper moved to View and Broad Street near the present Canada Trust Building about 1900 and in 1951 to its present location on Douglas Street where it combined printing facilities with those of its former rival, the *Victoria Daily Times*. The latter, a Liberal paper, was started as a weekly, price $2 per year, by Senator Wm. Templeman in 1884 and was published until 1951 in the "Times Building" on Fort at Broad, a building now sublet into offices. But this was not the first attempt at a Liberal paper in Victoria. De Cosmos, dissatisfied with the treatment he was getting from the *Colonist* got his brother to start the Liberal *Standard* in 1874.

Victoria has been a publisher's graveyard. Through the years it has had the *Telegraph, Express, News, Weekly Sentinel, Globe, Evening Post* (publisher W. J. McDowell), *Home Journal* and *Observer*. In the 1860's, it had a French newspaper *Le Courier de la Nouvelle Caledonia*, the editor of which was reputed to be a count, but finished up as a waiter. In 1869 John Robson, the New Westminster publisher and politician, moved his expiring *Columbian* here and it was absorbed by the *Colonist*, of which he later became editor.

Douglas, who was constantly attacked by De Cosmos in the *British Colonist*, ignored the criticisms and seems to have regarded the "Lover of the Universe" as a species of cockroach. But others were less patient. Hudson's Bay Company official Rod Finlayson beat him up in 1862. Robert Dunsmuir, the coal-mining magnate, wore out an umbrella on De Cosmos' shoulders when the latter accosted him aggressively on the street. A few minutes afterwards De Cosmos emerged from his editorial den to make some unpleasant remarks to Mayor Rithet. The mayor punched him around and chased him back to his sanctum. Residents also retold gleefully in 1866 the story of a legislator who crooked De Cosmos' head under his head and treated the face to what was described as "severe but merited chastisement."

The fiery-tempered legislator had intended to throw De Cosmos from the James Bay Bridge into "the drink," but Dr. Helmcken intervened and prevented this. Sir James Douglas afterwards told Helmcken pointedly that his jurisdiction as Speaker of the House was inside not outside parliament. Helmcken's intervention had apparently deprived the governor of a great pleasure.

The Colony was in a bad way financially when De Cosmos took on the premiership. It was still worse off when he left. But Victorians got plenty of entertainment. De Cosmos' electioneering was a roisterer's delight, very often accompanied by free drinks, band music, torch parades from the home of one prominent supporter to another, terminating sometimes with a grand drink-in at the old Colonial Inn. De Cosmos could speak longer than any man of the time. He spoke once for 24 hours continuously in Parliament.

Refreshing his falsetto voice with frequent sips of spiked eggnog he captivated audiences with his mixture of half-truths, oversimplifications, innuendos and downright untruths. He told the malcontents what they wanted to hear and could reinforce his oratory with copious tears. He was somewhat of a political chameleon, changing colour with his changing interests. De Cosmos was at various times for and against

(1) Victoria being a free port;

67

(2) Confederation;

(3) Parliament being located here;

(4) A transcontinental railroad.

He indulged freely in political blackmail. By threatening secession he hoped to get more money out of Ottawa. The location of the terminus of the projected Trans-Canada railroad was a football for conflicting real estate interests.

Eventually De Cosmos left provincial for Federal politics. His departure was hailed with uneasy relief. Many wondered what he would get up to in Ottawa.

Victoria rejected him altogether at the polls in 1892 and he became a lonely old man, indulging in interminable walks and embarrassing men and women with his fixed stare. He seemed to be trying to remember faces. In his last year he was insane and under constant surveillance. Few people troubled to attend his funeral in Ross Bay cemetery, but many years after his death the *Victoria Daily Colonist* erected an imposing monument over his grave. He is also commemorated with a plaque in the rotunda of Parliament Buildings. He found many more admirers in the twentieth than the nineteenth century. Ottawa even discovered that "he was a leader in the struggle for responsible government" . . . although anybody more irresponsible it would be hard to find.

After De Cosmos came Premier George Anthony Walkem. Out of the wreckage of Confederation promises Victoria had managed to salvage the promise of a drydock.

Construction of the drydock became a financial burden and political scandal. The first pile was driven in 1876. Eleven years elapsed before it was finished. It was to be 481 feet long and the Dominion Government guaranteed 5% interest on the cost for 10 years. The project went wrong from the start. There was some shockingly bad figure work. Item: cement estimated at $3,000 cost $250,000. Item: total cost of dock estimated at $500,000; actual cost $1,175,000.

The cement was ordered from England by Premier Walkem and stored in Selleck's warehouse at a rental of $80 a month. First stored in 1871 it was still being stored 20 years later. In 1882 a fire broke out in Selleck's Hotel adjoining the "fireproof warehouse," leading to a loss of $30,000 in cement. Many contractors were ruined. So great was the administrative tangle that the Dominion Government, despairing of sorting it out, took over the whole project.

The drydock finally completed in 1887 (H.M.S. *Cormorant* was the first ship to use it) was replaced in 1927 by the new $5,000,000 dock, 1,150 feet long, which is used today. Its replacement was partly a result of the anti-unemployment campaign following World War I. It has been useful for many merchant and war vessels, but it has proved an even more useful source of revenue for dockyard employees and consequently Victoria as a whole in the years since World War II.

The drydock scandal drove Premier Walkem from office. He was premier on two occasions, from 1874-76 and 1878-82. A short, bespectacled man, he was pleased with his resemblance to Rudyard Kipling. An Irishman of English descent, his father arrived with the Royal Engineers: he became prominent in Victoria's social life when he married Sophie Edith Rhodes, whose father was a partner in Rhodes & Janion, well known auctioneers and merchants; their warehouse was on the waterfront at Store and Johnson and the derelict Janion Hotel still stands.

Walkem could paint animals very well and some went so far as to call him a second Landseer. He lived after marriage in "Maplehurst," the large Henry Rhodes property, boundaries of which were Galt, Blanshard, Princess and Quadra Streets. The residence was just north of where the Victoria Memorial Arena now is. He died there in 1908 at the age of 81.

"Maplehurst" was the scene of many garden parties, notably one in 1874 featuring an "Aunt Sally" and a "post office" from which young postmistresses issued most gushing epistles.

Walkem and his great friend De Cosmos went to London at the taxpayers' expense to put their view that Ottawa was falling down on its railroad promise. The *Victoria Colonist* said the mission was a failure. The *Victoria Standard*, run by Charles, brother of De Cosmos, said it was a success. Walkem gained popularity, but contributed to depression by buying votes with a reckless public works programme. Unable to borrow more locally, he borrowed from Ottawa threatening secession to gain his ends.

69

When he resigned the premiership in 1882 the *Colonist* said his only success in public life was advancing his private fortune. "He has led his country into debt, difficulty and dishonour and now abandons it to its fate."

It relented on his death and said he "was a man of more than ordinary talents."

A. C. Elliott, another Irishman, who took over in the year 1876-78 between Walkem's two terms of office, was welcomed in Victoria society partly because his only daughter Mary Rachel married the only son of Sir James Douglas, but also because as Victoria police magistrate he was in the public eye. There was some resentment at the fact that he began to draw two salaries at the same time . . . as legislator and city police magistrate. He got over this hurdle by continuing the police magistrate's job without pay.

Elliott was of a retiring disposition, unsuited to the hurly-burly of politics. He had great personal courage and once entered a hostile Skeena village alone to apprehend a murderer.

He is buried in Ross Bay cemetery.

Before condemning too harshly the apparent unscrupulousness of our early politicians it must be remembered that opportunities for advancement outside politics were few. The population was small and engaged chiefly in what are now termed the service industries . . . that is supplying local needs. The export and import trade was largely dominated by the Hudson's Bay Company. The Royal Navy had their steady suppliers among farmers and merchants. San Francisco provided a good market for lumber. The much-coveted salaried official positions were in the early years filled almost entirely by qualified men from the United Kingdom. For lawyers and the unskilled two avenues were open . . . real estate and politics.

Land was cheap. Buying it on time payments was not beyond the means of those with modest capital, but paying the taxes until it could be resold at a profit called for reserve capital or a good job, especially in a declining market.

The value of land could be multiplied if a road or railroad were built near it. This desirable end was the aim of much political manipulation. Many government expenditures could be shaped to benefit landowners and many politicians directed their efforts to increasing the value of their holdings. These efforts resulted in much public works expenditure being incurred on projects of no benefit to the people whatever, plunging the province into debt.

When Victoria in 1878 decided that more was to be gained by fighting than co-operating with Ottawa John A. MacDonald, who had lost his seat in Kingston, Ontario, was offered a Victoria seat. He went to Ottawa as Victoria's champion, later becoming prime minister.

The same decade saw two of the few new buildings in the city for many years, namely the first Dominion Hotel and Rickman's Brick Works on the site of the old Globe Hotel.

The Globe Hotel was the first building erected in the former Hudson's Bay Company enclosure when the Company sold its lots on Government Street between Fort and Bastion Streets in 1861. The Dominion Hotel replaced the "What Cheer House," a tavern operated since the early sixties by Thomas Mitchell from Swansea, Wales. Mitchell had some success with his gold diggings in the Cariboo and built the "What Cheer House" with the proceeds. After selling out he turned to farming in Saanich.

Chapter 7

THE PARLIAMENT BUILDINGS

THE MOST DIGNIFIED and aesthetically-pleasing structure in Victoria and indeed in all of British Columbia is the Central Legislative Building on the Inner Harbour waterfront. It was opened in 1898, at a time which saw industrial, political, technical and social changes as bewildering to our forefathers as those of recent years have been to us.

In 1880 Victoria's population was only 6,000. By 1900 it was 20,219, representing a threefold increase in 20 years. In spite of periodical short-term setbacks, the city in general hummed with industry, diversified to an extent the city has never since achieved. Sealing, salmon-canning, shipbuilding and ship chandlering, the carriage trade, and brewing were among industries which provided employment for 12,000 workers, one half of them in fish canneries: one third of invested capital was in sash and door factories.

The Portland newspaper *The West Shore* described Victoria in in 1889 as "a city pre-eminently to delight the heart of the tourist with more than a dozen good hotels, one or two of them world-renowned." It went on to portray the city as the largest and wealthiest in the province with the largest iron works on the Pacific coast outside San Francisco (the Albion Iron Works), five boot and shoe factories, a sawmill, planing mill, box factory, wire works, corset factory, vinegar and pickling establishments, meat packing house, cooperage works, a dozen cigar factories, two soap works, book binderies, several breweries, and so on.

The *Victoria Times* in 1890 claimed that the city had three times the combined wealth of Nanaimo, Vancouver and New Westminster. It estimated the personal property of citizens to be worth $6,386,830. It was a remarkable transformation when one recalls that only seven years before, the City's three electric streetlights were turned off when the moon was shining in order to save electricity.

In 1889, 32 sealers left Victoria and brought back pelts valued at $247,170. In the same year salmon valued at $1,890,200 was exported in 335,458 cases. The Dunsmuirs who spent generously in Victoria as for instance in the building of Craigdarroch Castle, earned their money mainly from coal and in one year exported 5,798,307 tons from Nanaimo.

Although there were temporary economic setbacks, notably the United States financial panic in the years 1893 to 1897, the optimism engendered by the prosperous years was carried over in the decision to erect a Parliament Building worthy of the province. There was a political motive too.

The establishment of the Parliament Buildings in Victoria was and is still a sore point with many on the Mainland. Originally, it will be recalled, the province consisted of two Crown colonies, both with their own legislature. Vancouver Island with Victoria as capital was one. New Caledonia, capital in New Westminster, was the other. The colonies were united in 1866 when both were hopelessly in debt. Vancouver Island owed $293,689 and the Mainland colony $1,002,953. The service of Vancouver Island's debt consumed one-third of the revenue. Location of parliament would bring immense advantages to whichever capital was chosen. It would increase real estate values owing to the transfer of civil servants to the new capital (with consequent declines in real estate values in the old capital); it meant more employment, more influencing of government expenditure, political appointments and legislation which would probably favour the chosen capital at the expense of its rival.

Victoria must acknowledge its debt to King Alcohol for being chosen as the site of the combined parliament. Both Victoria and New Westminster had their spokesmen. New Westminster entrusted to Captain William Hales Franklyn presentation of its case to the Legislative Council. Franklyn, a Nanaimo magistrate, was a former P.&O. captain who lost his job for misconduct. Franklyn was "half-seas over" when he began to read his carefully-prepared speech. He found his script rather blurred. The Council recessed to allow him time to recover, but according to one version, while he was recovering, a Victoria champion removed the lenses from his eyeglass frames. After the recess he could not read at all. When the vote was put, New Westminster lost the day.

The replacement of the old "Birdcages" by the fine stone Central Building would, many Victorians thought, silence once and for all those Mainlanders who kept up a constant agitation about Parliament being located here. But even as late as 1914 when the east and west wings were added to the Main Building, many on the Mainland were still pressing for the Legislative Buildings to be transferred brick by brick if necessary to the Mainland.

The Mainland can, of course, point to its population and industry far exceeding that of Vancouver Island as a reason for locating Parliament across the water. But, on the other hand, Victoria is the oldest British colony on the Pacific coast. Without Victoria and its shrewd pioneer administrator James Douglas, there might never have been a Canadian New Westminster or Vancouver. The establishment of the Vancouver Island settlement in 1848 played a significant role in the negotiation of the Oregon Boundary Treaty which left all land north of the 49th parallel to Canada (an exception being made for the southern part of Vancouver Island on which Victoria is situated).

The scope and cost of the Parliament Building evoked much criticism. When it was started in 1893 by order of Premier Theodore Davie the total provincial population was only 175,000 and that of Victoria only 17,000.

The cost of the building was to be $600,000 — an enormous sum when the annual revenue of the province was only $1,500,000. In fact it actually cost $923,000, half as much again as the estimate. It was opened by Premier J. H. Turner in 1898. Turner arrived here at the time of the gold rush, developed a successful business as carpet merchant and after the premiership was appointed B.C. Agent

General in London. He had a beautiful home at the corner of Bay and Pleasant Streets (Point Ellice), was a keen horticulturalist and achieved a life ambition when he retired in London on a property near the famous Kew Gardens.

As premier, Turner headed a power party which consisted chiefly of businessmen who had made their stake in mining, salmon canning, railroad construction and wholesale merchandising. Among them were many of his former business associates.

With minor exceptions only local materials and local labour were used in construction. The foundations and steps are of granite from Nelson Inlet in the Malaspina Strait. The masonry is faced with andesite from the Haddington Quarries, 200 miles north of Victoria, while the slate for the roof, enduring because of its high silica and alumina content, came from Jervis Inlet.

The minor exceptions are the hand-wrought iron gates at the main entrance which came from London, England, and the marble lining the rotunda which is from Tennessee. Labour in the 1890's had not acquired the militancy of later years and only two strikes marred construction, neither of them over wages.

A stonecutters' strike was caused by a workman being accused of spoiling a stone. The masons' strike which followed was due to accusations that they were holding up the work. This strike was settled when the masonry contractor fortuitously drowned while on his way to the quarries. Although pleased to have the job of building the Legislature, many Victoria workmen could not rid themselves of the idea that others (foreigners) might be getting undue benefits. To counter malicious rumours, Fred Adams, contractor for the masons' work, found it necessary to publish a list of names and nationalities of those employed, proving that out of several score workmen only seven were United States citizens. Contracts were awarded inter alia to Bishop & Sherborne, carpenters, Richard Drake, plasterers, Albion Iron Works Co., H. T. Flett, plumbing, W. H. Perry, coppersmith and E. Spillman, painters. Superintendent of Works was E. C. Howell with Victor Moretti as fresco artist and decorator.

Following the drowning of Adams, McGregor & Jones took over as general contractors and it is interesting to note that Fred Mc-

Gregor, a son of the contractor, is Canada's champion and Victoria's senior life insurance salesman.

Designs for the building were invited from all over the continent. Winner was a 26-year-old English architect who had arrived in Victoria only a month earlier. He was Frank Mawson Rattenbury who already had a number of public buildings in England to his credit.

The front of the main Parliament Building is imposing with the statues of Sir Matthew Baillie Begbie and Sir James Douglas flanking the entrance. But many people consider the rear even more attractive than the front. The east and west wings which were added in 1912 at a cost of $1,000,000 are seen to better advantage from the rear because of the greater depth of frontage.

The east and west wings doubled the floor area of the Main Building. The inset figures at the rear portray Sir Anthony Musgrave, Chief Maquinna of Nootka, and John Bunyan substituting for David Thomson who located the source of the Columbia River. The sculptor could find no likeness of Thomson from which to portray him in stone, but the daughter of the famous explorer said he was John Bunyan's double, so the author of *Pilgrim's Progress* impersonating Thomson is the result. On the library wing are more sculptures. C. Maroza, the artist, had a sculptor's gala with them. Chief Maquinna and Chief Justice Begbie are both double features. Statues to them already existed elsewhere in the buildings. Others are of John McLoughlin, Hudson's Bay factor, Dr. J. S. Helmcken, first speaker of the House, Captain Cook, Sir James Douglas, Sir Francis Drake, Lord Lytton (to whom our first officials owed their appointments), Sir Anthony Musgrave and General Moody.

Many well-known politicians of the time would have liked to have been immortalized in stone on the buildings. One may assume that the decision to sculpt two men who had little to do with Vancouver Island, namely Captain Cook and Sir Francis Drake, saved a lot of heartburn among rival claimants.

The visitor cannot miss the murals in the rotunda, the work of Victoria's George Southwell, and should also see the photographs of Victoria Cross heroes.

A curious oversight by architect Rattenbury was the omission of washrooms in the Main Building. R. Rigan, the caretaker, noted "the entire absence of anything in the shape of lavatory accommodation for either ladies or gents which has been found very awkward at times when entertainment is in progress. We are compelled to furnish the crudest accommodation for the ladies and gents who have a long distance to travel before reaching a lavatory and then find it crowded."

Unwittingly the reader of Mr. Rigan's notes conjures up the picture of a tremendous run on fire buckets as the caretaker answers the frantic appeals of panic-stricken guests.

Outlining of the buildings at night with over 3,000 light bulbs, which were first switched on for Queen Victoria's Diamond Jubilee in 1897, was a happy thought. It continues today and as a result the Parliament Buildings are beyond doubt the most photographed buildings in the province. Many of the original bulbs have never been replaced. The Buildings were illuminated even before completed, so proud was Victoria of them. H.M. ships *Imperieuse* and *Amphion* and the American battleships *Columbine* and *Alert* arrived here for the first illumination. Official opening of the Main Legislative Building was in 1899.

Rattenbury, who designed the Parliament Buildings, was also responsible for the Empress Hotel, C.P.S. Pavilion, Crystal Gardens, renovation of the Courthouse (on Bastion Square) and Bank of Montreal buildings, the latter on Government Street.

His home in Victoria was on Beach Drive and is now the Glenlyon Preparatory School for boys. His fame as an architect was overshadowed by the drama of his death. In Victoria he met a Mrs. Caledon Dolly (maiden name Alma Victoria Clark) and the result of the liaison was the citing of the latter as co-respondent by Rattenbury's first wife. Mrs. Caledon Dolly was 31 when she met Rattenbury, many years younger than the architect, pretty, highly strung and married twice before. Her first husband was killed in World War I. She left her second husband and returned to Victoria to strike up a friendship with Rattenbury. He married her after his divorce and took her to England in 1928. They resided in Bournemouth, but there the architect became melancholic and obsessed with financial forebodings. Both he and the new Mrs. Rattenbury were heavy drinkers. Mrs. Rattenbury used to accuse him of being parsimonious, but they tolerated each other, leading separate lives under the same roof.

Before long Mrs. Rattenbury became enamoured of a 19-year-old chauffeur-handyman by the name of George Percy Stoner, whom she had engaged. In 1935, seven years after their return to England, the architect, reclining in a chair, was attacked from behind and murdered with a blow from a carpenter's mallet. Both Stoner and Mrs. Rattenbury were charged with murder, but the case against Mrs. Rattenbury could not be proved. Stoner stoutly maintained that he alone was responsible. He was sentenced to penal servitude for life and soon after the sentence Mrs. Rattenbury stabbed herself to death.

Rattenbury's free classic style design of the Parliament Buildings with their copper-sheathed cupolas are a great tourist attraction. The canning and sealing, shipbuilding and manufacturing which prompted the optimism of the times are now mostly history. But tourism has remained: the Main Building was responsible for drawing 70,000 tourists here in 1899, and Parliament has continued to be a main tourist attraction ever since.

The location of the province's main body of civil servants in Victoria (about 5,000 are located here) has proved an immense boon to the economy, constitutes the city's biggest single payroll and insures it to an appreciable extent against economic ups and downs. To the salaries of civil servants must be added the spending by members of the Legislature, by visiting businessmen and dignitaries and the considerable outlays on the grounds and on maintenance and office supplies. The civil service has also been largely responsible for Victoria's conservative character. Method and unhurried routine which are the hallmarks of government administrators is reflected in the more settled manner of life of many residents. They live here and wish to stay here. Their interests are in the beautiful gardens for which Victoria is renowned, in the multitude of cultural societies and in municipal government in which many play a prominent role.

But this also led until recent years to a passiveness and non-aggressive approach to living which led many outside critics to describe Victoria as "the only cemetery with a shopping centre."

All business was in tried and trusted hands, which joined to form a circle into which newcomers found it very difficult to break. It was possibly responsible for an overemphasis on safety as evidenced by the multiplicity of traffic lights and "stop" signs and restrictions which visitors from the Mainland find galling.

A visit to the Legislative Assembly chamber which was modelled on that of the Mother of Parliaments is, of course, imperative for the visitor. Equally impressive is the Provincial Library. The grounds of the Legislative Buildings are also of great interest to the historically-minded. The fine Victoria Centennial Fountain at the rear of the Buildings, was activated in 1962. Native fauna from which British Columbia Indians derived their totems are modelled around the fountain. Flanking Parliament Buildings on the west is the Confederation Garden opened in 1967 with its fountain and eternal flame, shields of the provinces, and other symbols of Canadian identity.

Facing the waterfront is a plinth paying tribute to Sir James Douglas, Royal Governor and Commander-in-Chief of the Colony for many years.

The profusion of flags in front and behind the Parliament Buildings can be somewhat confusing to the foreign visitor. The Maple Leaf on the main flagstaff was first flown as the new flag of Canada in 1965. It superseded the Canadian Ensign with its four quarterings depicting the national emblems of England, Scotland, Ireland and France. The Maple Leaf flag has met with a less enthusiastic reception in Victoria than in other parts of Canada and indeed, in 1970, the substitution of the Maple Leaf for the Union Jack was challenged for its legality in the courts by a Victoria citizen. Victoria's affection for the Union Jack derives partly from the fact that the city was until recently predominantly British, but also because the Royal Canadian Navy warships stationed here were modelled predominantly on British naval tradition.

Many Canadian soldiers who fought under the Union Jack and mothers who lost their sons in the two World Wars in which Canadian contingents made Canada's reputation as a fighting nation have an emotional attachment to it.

The Maple Leaf flag, on the other hand, appealed to the pride of many Canadian-born citizens who felt the Dominion had now grown up and was entitled in its own right to be an independent nation.

The British tradition is remembered in the Union Jack flying from a separate flagstaff and in the flag held by Captain Vancouver whose statue adorns the main cupola. Another acknowledgment of the link with Britain is made in the separate British Columbia flag. This flag was authorized for use in the province in 1960 and has "three silver and blue wavy bars from the bottom of which a shining half sun in natural colours under the Union Jack bearing in the centre a golden antique crown."

Occupying a central position of honour on the Parliament lawns is the statue of Queen Victoria from which our city derives its name. Mounted on a base of Swedish granite, it is the work of Allan Bruce Joy, a well-known London architect of his period, who was not at all pleased with its siting. He intended the statue to be nearer the main entrance to the Legislative Buildings where the fountain, built by a New York firm at a cost of $1400 in 1905, is situated. He complained that the Queen's statue in its present location can be viewed only "at the risk of being run over by a car or falling in the water."

In the northeast corner of the grounds is the War Memorial.

Chapter 8

THE WAR MEMORIAL AND TWO WORLD WARS

VICTORIA'S WAR MEMORIAL on the lawn fronting Parliament Buildings was unveiled by Lieutenant-Governor Walter C. Nichol in 1925, funds for the Memorial having been raised by public subscription. At the time the Memorial paid tribute to those who lost their lives in World War I, but, like the Cenotaph in London's Whitehall, it now also acknowledges our debt to those who made the supreme sacrifice in World War II.

The inauguration of the Remembrance Day services at the Memorial was due to C. A. Gill of the Royal Canadian Legion who worked many years to get the participation of the Services in the annual tribute. The colourful standards of the Legionaries, the uniforms of those in the Armed Services, the cadets' bands, singing of traditional hymns, two minutes silence, sounding of the "Last Post" and "Reveille," followed by the laying of wreaths, make Remembrance Day at the Memorial Victoria's most poignant and impressive ceremony.

The sculpture itself is the work of two brothers, Sidney and Vernon Marech of Farnborough, Kent.

How many Victorians lost their lives in the two world wars will probably never be known. Many born in Victoria did not enlist in their native town, but reported to the recruiting depot nearest to where they happened to be when war broke out. Many who enlisted in Victoria and did their training at the Central School, Willows and Gordon Head camps were from other towns and provinces.

There is no record of their names and origin except in regimental registers which are dispersed in various cities of Canada. A further complication is caused by the military system whereby men were transferred from one unit to another as exigencies demanded and evidence of original unit identity is very hard to trace.

What is known is that about 8,000 men enlisted in Victoria in World War I and in World War II. The Canadian Scottish with headquarters in Victoria, lost 402 killed in battles which included the Normandy landing, Caen, Falaise, Calais, the Scheldt and Northwest Europe.

Then, of course, there were the many scores of men from Victoria who served in the Air Force (some in the R.A.F.), the Imperial forces, in the Royal Canadian and Royal Navies and in the merchant service.

In both world wars Victoria was a very patriotic town, but like Britain, which is not a military-minded country, it tended to neglect the armed forces in peace time. Through the peaceful decades which preceded World War I, the spirit of service was kept alive by men like James Douglas, Colonels J. H. Turner, Charles Houghton, E. G. Prior, R. Wolfenden and others who encouraged and sometimes themselves organized militia units. But in spite of their efforts the neglect was sometimes appalling. For instance at one time the coastal guns defending Victoria were found stuffed with sticks and stones and everything moveable around the batteries had been stolen. Macaulay, the tall, lean sheepfarmer after whom Macaulay's Point is named, drowned in a powder barge which was so badly maintained that it sank at night in Esquimalt Harbour.

Secure in the protection of the Royal Navy, most citizens were not greatly interested in military life, but Victoria nevertheless was seldom without some troops. First here were the Royal Engineers who arrived in 1858. Some of them were housed in three wooden huts built by James Douglas at the head of Skinner's Cove. The huts have since been destroyed.

The scarlet-coated Royal Marines arrived the next year, most of them being sent to San Juan occupied at that time by Hudson's Bay Company men and American settlers. That was the year of the "Pig War" when Lyman Cutler, an American settler, shot a Hudson's Bay Company pig and British and Americans faced each other belligerently. Eventually San Juan was ceded to America, the Marines leaving it in 1871. In 1860 the Victoria Rifle Volunteers, a local militia unit was formed. J. H. Turner, who later became premier of the province, is credited with its organization. About the same time an unofficial military unit came into being, the "African Rifles." Among the 300 negroes who came here with the gold rush were some who resented not being allowed to join and wear the gorgeous uniforms of the mostly American-manned fire brigades. They salved their racial pride by forming a militia unit with even more resplendent attire including plumed shakos as headgear until Douglas told them they were not wanted.

By 1861 the Birdcages had been erected and the Victoria Rifles became the Vancouver Island Volunteer Rifles, drilling in a wooden shed in James Bay. In course of time this shed was replaced by a drill hall which is now used to house the Motor Vehicle Branch of the Provincial Government. In 1864 the V.I. Volunteer Rifles again changed their name, this time to the Victoria Volunteer Rifles.

The next step was the organization in 1878 of the Victoria Battery of Garrison Artillery under the command of Captain C. J. Dupont, whose home was in Stadacona Park, a large part of which he owned. But the whole set-up was somewhat confused.

So many changes of name and switchings of loyalties occurred among the volunteer units that it was decided to stabilize the situation. Artillery and Rifles amalgamated in 1883 to form what has now become the Fifth B.C. Field Battery Canadian Garrison Artillery, with headquarters at Bay Street Armouries. The Battery is one of Canada's few militia units with a continuous history. Twenty-six men of the Battery went to the Boer War, some losing their lives at Paardeburg Drift. A plaque to those killed is at the entrance to the Bay Street Armouries. Their records show that 777 men went overseas in World War I, 55 were killed, 148 wounded and 56 awards were won. But in World War I infantrymen were in greater demand than gunners and the casualties of the Fifth Battery were incurred mainly in line regiments for which they volunteered. Chief of these were the 50th Gordon Highlanders and 88th Victoria Fusiliers, both of which were very active in Victoria prior to the outbreak of World War I. The 50th Gordon Highlanders and the 88th Victoria Fusiliers were in the 1st Canadian Division assembled at Valcartier. They furnished reinforcements for such well-known battalions as the 30th, 48th, 60th and 88th, many men of the 30th reinforcing again the 7th Btn., C.E.F.

The 16th Btn. C.E.F., was made up of Gordon Highlanders in Victoria and the Seaforths from Vancouver. Victoria men also fought in the 47th and 67th Battalions. Plaques to the 50th Gordons, the 88th Fusiliers and the 2nd Canadian Pioneers (previously 48th Btn.) have a deserved place of honour in the Parliament Buildings.

The 2nd Canadian Mounted Rifles was recruited chiefly in the Okanagan, and one who joined them as a trooper was a young Englishman, George Pearkes, later to earn a V.C. and many other decorations and to become, with ex-servicemen at least, the most popular lieutenant-governor the province has ever had.

Following Confederation it seemed wrong to many people that Victoria should depend for her defence entirely on the Royal Navy, British troops and local patriots in the militia. Moves were made in Ottawa and in 1887 Victoria got the first regular unit of an all Canadian force when 100 officers and men of "C" Battery arrived from Quebec City and Kingston, Ontario, and were housed in the old Fair Building on Beacon Hill. It was bad accommodation and combined with other disadvantages led to many desertions. Among the disadvantages was the fact that the men of "C" Battery were outclassed socially both by the Royal Navy and by the dockyard employees. Victorians were enthusiastic dancers and the dockyard employees staged dances in far more appealing surroundings than those of "C" Battery in the old Fair Building.

Towards the end of the nineteenth century both the Canadian and British governments began to show greater interest in Pacific coastal defences. The outcome was that in 1897 the British government was paid £112,000 to build the Esquimalt fortifications plus £147,500 per annum for Royal Marine Artillery and Royal Engineer detachments.

As a consequence 78 officers and men arrived in Victoria, dismantled the old earthworks at Finlayson and Macaulay Points and

Brothers Island built at the time of the Russian war scare in 1878, and installed the then ultramodern six-inch disappearing guns at Fort Rodd Hill and Macaulay Point, and 12-pound quick-firing guns at Duntze Head, Belmont and Black Rock. The Fort Rodd Hill installations (Fort Rodd is named after Lieutenant John Rodd of H.M.S. survey vessel *Fisgard*) are well worth a visit, as also the nearby Fisgard lighthouse, built with bricks brought round the Horn.

In World War II Victoria was ringed with modern batteries from Ogden Point to Mary Hill, but with the advent of more sophisticated methods of defence all were declared obsolete in 1956. The guns were never in action against an enemy as Victoria fortunately was spared the bombardments, bombings and rockets which made life hazardous in many belligerent countries.

But the loss of many of its finest citizens overseas brought grief to numerous households. The declaration of war on Germany in August 1914 transformed Victoria overnight. Hundreds rushed to the colours. The militia were called up. By the fall of 1914, the city was almost without able-bodied male civilians. Nearly all the physically fit were in uniform. The knickerbockered remittance men and ramrod-back ex-Imperial Army officers who had succeeded the ranchers and bearded Naval officers of the 1890's disappeared from the Union and Pacific clubs. Victoria's young men, like those of all belligerent countries, were eager to get into the war "before it was all over." Most people thought that it would last six months at the outside.

Women were equally enthusiastic. Nurses volunteered for overseas duty. Women applied to follow their husbands to England. Miss Kathleen Dunsmuir ran a soup kitchen at Boulogne. Concerts and theatre performances were staged exclusively to enable the purchase of comforts for the troops. The English, French and Belgian national anthems featured at many charity concerts.

The departure in August 1914 of the city's first detachments for overseas service gave rise to scenes of unprecedented fervour. Nearly 100 officers and men of the 5th regiment headed by captains P. T. Stern, R. P. Clark, lieutenants K. H. Bomill, W. B. Shaw and Captain the Rev. Wm. Barton, together with detachments of the

Corps of Guides and the Canadian Signal Corps embarked on the Canadian Pacific steamer *Princess Mary*. Crowds swung along with the troops on the march to the wharf, school children serenaded them on the Empress Hotel lawn with "The Maple Leaf Forever," "Rule Britannia" and "God Save the King"; three military bands played simultaneously on the wharf and contingents from the High-landers, the Fusiliers and every militia unit in the city were present to see them off.

The Gordon Highlanders (eight officers and 226 men) of the 50th regiment headed by Majors Lorne Ross and Garnet B. Hughes and the 88th Victoria Fusiliers under Major Byng Hall, left about the same time commanded by Lieutenant-Colonel A. W. Currie.

Immediately on the outbreak of war every officer of the Fusiliers volunteered unconditionally for overseas service. A first contingent of 250 went to the front with captains Cooper and Harvey. Two young lieutenants, Ford-Young and Hay, resigned their commissions rather than be left behind.

The many unemployed and panhandlers disappeared from Douglas, Government and Johnson Streets. The drill hall on Menzies Street (the Bay Street Armouries were only begun in 1913), the Willows Fair Grounds, Work Point Barracks (built in 1890) and the Central School resounded to the shouts of drill sergeants, military music and the tramp of heavy boots. Then the first letters began to arrive from the front. The unexpected nature of the warfare they revealed was as appalling to civilians at home as to the soldiers themselves. Describing his first Christmas in Flanders an officer wrote: "It is pretty beastly in the firing line, very wet and in places over one's knees in mud where some of the trenches have been flooded and it is quite hopeless to try to keep warm.

"We take a waterproof sheet and blanket each to the trenches and there are dugouts where we try to sleep. But the cold is damn-able. We have lost so many pairs of shoes in the mud that we are being fitted out with boots and puttees."

The enemy's use of poison gas shocked everybody. A soldier wrote to the *Colonist*: "The gas the enemy uses is terrible. One's eyes are simply running with water and one can hardly breathe. It hangs around for hours, choking and blinding the men."

ARTHUR EDWARD KENNEDY
Royal Governor, 1864-66.

CHIEF JUSTICE
MATTHEW BAILLIE BEGBIE

BISHOP GEORGE HILLS

THE OLD IRON CHURCH
(St. John's)

BLANSHARD STREET ABOUT 1890
This view was taken looking north
from where the Dominion Hotel
is situated. In left foreground
a brewery, now the site of the Public
Library. The tall building almost
next door was demolished to make
room for the Kaiserhof (now Kent
Apartment) Hotel. In right foreground vacant plot is now site of
B.C. Telephone building and beyond
it the Jewish Synagogue and centre
the First Presbyterian Church (built
in 1862) on the site of the present
B.C. Hydro building. The spire
of St. John's (Iron) Church, now
Hudson's Bay Company department
store site, on extreme left in
background. Two blocks beyond the
Church, buildings gave way to
fields and bush.

EMILY CARR

surrounded by the many pets
she loved so well.

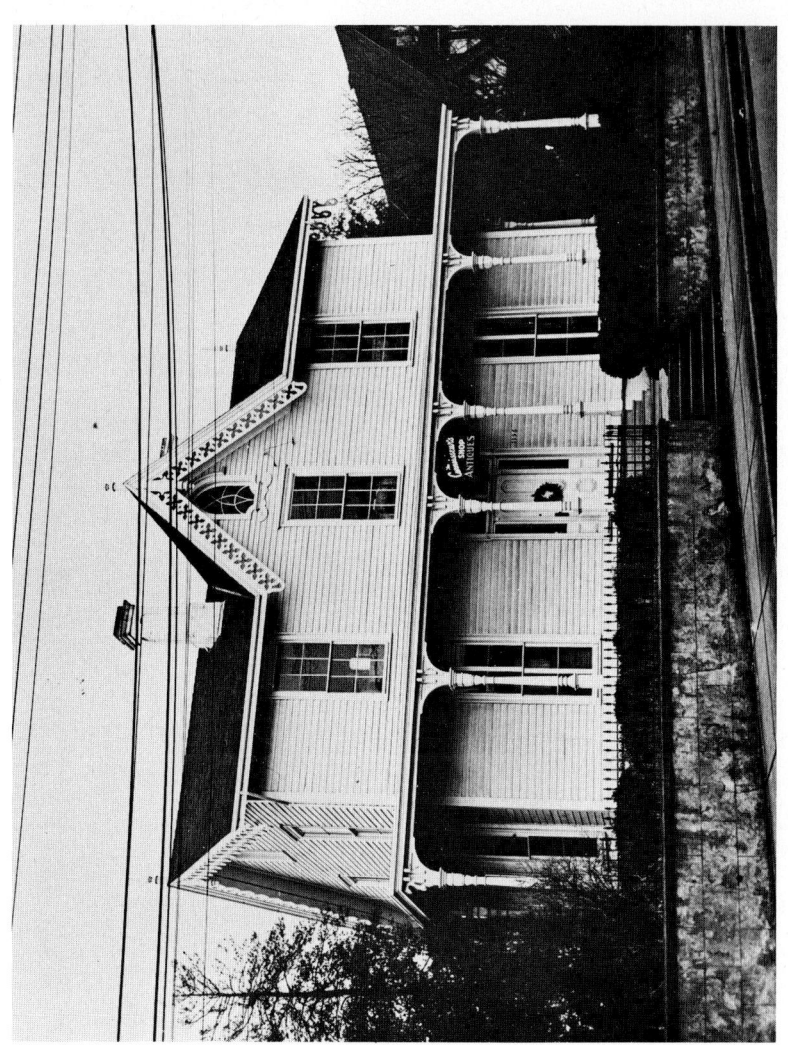

THE FORMER ELLA HOME
still standing on upper Fort Street.

MARTHA CHENEY
(Mrs. Henry B. Ella)

MRS. THOMAS BLINKHORN
who worked hard for good causes,
including the first women's infirmary.

The loss of life was frightening both to the men and civilians: a soldier in the famous Seventh Battalion wrote home: "We had our whack. For ten minutes we slaughtered Germans line after line until we had lost two-thirds of our men and they got round our right flank. We had no artillery support while they were pounding hell out of us all the time and many men were laid low by poison gas. Our regiment fought splendidly and I am proud of them but am sorry to say there are very few left. It is awful to think that so many of my comrades are dead."

Other men described the devastating effect of the big German guns, the terrible sufferings of wounded French women and children and the efforts they made to succour them, but there was never a note of despondency in published letters: "Nobody was the least bit frightened at the coming attack," wrote one man. "In fact we rather enjoyed it at first. But people kept getting killed in so many ways it became a nightmare. A man falls beside you and you just heave him out of the way like a sack of flour."

Another wrote: "It's wonderful how soon you get accustomed to things. The German attack was beaten off and here we are in our billets with gramophone blaring away while the Germans are blowing up houses only 200 yards away."

Ypres, the Somme, Amiens, Arras, Vimy Ridge, Paschendaele ... there was hardly a major battle in which Victorians did not fight. Many wounded were brought here to convalesce, notably at the Esquimalt Hospital and Stadacona Park, and many liked Victoria so much they made it their future home.

The wounded were invited into private homes, and given privileged seats at theatres and concerts: even cricket matches were staged between local ladies and convalescing soldiers. Mrs. R. H. Pooley and a number of her friends played an eleven from the Esquimalt Hospital. The soldiers won although some of them had to bat with one hand and bowl left-handed! The Victoria Patriotic Fund staged performances in the Royal and other theatres throughout the war for the benefit of the troops.

But as names and photographs of those "Who Died for Empire" continued to appear with painful frequency under banner headlines in the local papers war weariness set in. There was hardly a family including the most prominent which was not bereaved. The 10th Battalion which included many Victorians had 180 men left, the 16th Battalion 300 out of 600 men. Losses were felt the more keenly in Victoria because it was a small intimate city with many families inter-married and where everyone knew everyone.

It is noteworthy that the Victoria area furnished an outstanding military figure. Lieutenant-Colonel A. W. Currie, a former Sidney school teacher and realtor reached the apex of his career when he was appointed commander of the Canadian Corps in succession to Sir Julian Byng. Currie enlisted in Victoria's 5th Regiment as far back as in 1894, reached the rank of lieutenant-colonel, retired as commanding officer in 1913 and in 1914 assumed command of the 50th Regiment (Gordon Highlanders). His appreciation of the role of artillery in saving the lives of infantrymen was of immense benefit to Field Marshal Haig and, it is said, saved Haig's reputation.

This was the major factor in his promotion to commander of the Canadian Corps although some people allege, wrongly that his friendship with Sir Richard McBride, former British Columbia premier who had become Agent-General in London, played a role. The appointment was not popular with some Victorians because as a civilian Currie ran a real estate firm which like others in that business was prominent in the pre-1914 land speculation boom and many of his clients lost their life savings. But he was as much a victim of the mass hysteria as other people.

The First World War was followed by influenza just as devastating in Victoria as in the rest of the world.

World War II was a very different affair and Canada's soldiers had more national identity than in World War I. In 1914-18 Canada's fighting men were largely British-born or of British descent, whereas their sons of World War II were mostly Dominion-born and bred.

World War II was hailed with no martial music, no patriotic songs and concerts, no enthusiasm. Everybody anticipated a repetition of the slaughter which marked World War I. There was great fear of submarines and for this reason troops left Victoria behind a curtain of secrecy.

Between the two wars military units had been reorganized. The

88th Regiment Victoria Fusiliers and 50th Regiment Gordon High-landers ceased to exist, and in 1921 the Canadian Scottish Regiment was created inheriting the traditions and honours of the 16th Battalion to which the 50th Gordons contributed so heavily in World War I. Those interested in the fine record of this regiment should read *Ready for the Fray* by Professor R. H. Roy of the University of Victoria. The Canadian Scottish are proud of the fact that they are the only regiment to have been given freedom of the City of Victoria, but still prouder of the Oak Leaf awarded to the 16th Battalion for the attack on Kitchener's Wood in April 1915.

As was the case in World War I, local women in the years 1939-45 did their best to supply comforts to the troops. One of the more notable efforts was by the Women's Auxiliary to the Canadian Scottish who purchased a lot on Despard Avenue from the city for a nominal payment and built a five-room bungalow with largely donated labour and materials. They raffled the bungalow and made a profit of nearly $5,000. The astonishing thing (some said it could only happen in Victoria) was that the raffle was won by an American, who later came and lived in the house for a few years.

During both world wars the Victoria home front had its anxious moments.

There were some in retrospect amusing episodes. For example, in 1914 Victoria was apprehensive of the German battle squadron under Graf Von Spee which was operating around the tip of the South American continent, 8,000 miles away. It may be noted that the British Admiralty did not consider it even a remote possibility that the German squadron would head north, and the eventual interception and destruction of the German warships by Sir Frederick Sturdee's battle squadron off the Falkland Islands in December 1914 amply justified their strategic appraisal.

But Premier McBride hastily purchased in Seattle for the sum of $1,150,000 two submarines to defend Vancouver and Victoria. They had no torpedoes, were without trained crews and were paid for cloak-and-dagger fashion with a cheque handed over by the chief janitor of the Parliament Buildings and a civil servant.

On their way to Esquimalt the submarines narrowly escaped being sunk by the gunners of Black Rock Battery.

Being manned by dockyard crews ignorant of submarines, they did not know how to submerge and the only recognition signal they could give was feeble waving with a handkerchief, according to W. Berkeley Monteith, a member of No. 29 gun crew at Black Rock which sighted them.

Again in 1914 when the German cruiser *Leipzig* was reported off the Mexican coast the only Victoria-based and completely obsolete warship *Rainbow* was dispatched to escort back to Esquimalt the *Shearwater* which was off San Francisco and carried no wireless.

Floating wreckage was reported the next day and Victorians assumed with logical pessimism that it was the *Rainbow*. Fortunately for the Canadian crew the *Rainbow* never contacted the *Leipzig*.

As regards World War II, a *Victoria Times* reporter reminisced in 1958: "The scorching breath of war swished the face of B.C. several times during the last 100 years. People lived like moles after Pearl Harbour and the invasion of the Aleutians. There were air raid shelters, gas masks, emergency food supplies. There was a total black out. Slits took the place of headlights. Sirens were installed, air raid wardens were on duty. Ships to Vancouver ran without lights after a U.S. freighter was torpedoed 30 miles away."

When a Japanese submarine dropped a shell or two on Estevan lighthouse on the other side of Vancouver Island many residents contemplated evacuation. A curfew was declared, troops were confined to barracks and preparations made for a full scale enemy invasion.

Even the presence of the troop transport *Queen Elizabeth* in Esquimalt for a few days gave many the jitters because they thought it might lead to a Japanese bombing attack.

Victorians thought the drydock would be a prime target for Japanese bombers, but the Japanese apparently did not share this view. The thousands of tons of cement embodied in a drydock make it a most unrewarding target for bombers. Nor were Victoria's anxieties shared by Ottawa. It considered that any risk from the Japanese was more than counterbalanced by the United States' entry into the war as an Ally. It held to its 1914 view that the Atlantic was the main theatre for Canadian naval operations and never returned any of the four destroyers stationed on this coast which were ordered to Halifax in 1939.

And although the Royal Navy last maintained a station here in 1905, the year in which Canada took over responsibility for her own defence, visits by British warships were frequent.

H.M.S. *Kent* and at least two other Royal Navy cruisers were here on August 4, 1914, the day war was declared. They were part of the squadron badly mauled later by the German battle-squadron comprising the *Scharnhorst, Gneisenau* and *Leipzig* in the Battle of Coronel off the South American coast. This battle was followed by the Falkland Islands engagement when all the German ships were sunk by H.M. battle-cruisers *Invincible, Inflexible* and *Indefatigable*.

H.M.S. *Kent* returned to Victoria in 1915 after the battle and officers and men were given a tremendous welcome in Victoria. The Pacific Club went so far as to put on a special banquet and entertainment for the officers.

On the home front, the most enduring effect of the wars was the emancipation of women. As in other belligerent countries women donned overalls, put their hair beneath caps and worked alongside men in factories and shipyards. The shipbuilding facilities of Victoria were a great asset to the Allied cause and the influx of workers quickened the pace of life. Yarrows shipyards alone for the two peak years of World War II had 2,500 on its payroll including 480 women, and built five corvettes, two 10,000-ton cargo ships, 17 frigates and five LST's (landing ship tanks). The great Esquimalt shipyard, successor to the B.C. Marine Railway Company and bought in 1914 by Alfred Yarrow,* also overhauled the machinery of the *Queen Elizabeth* and of many other ships. V.M.D. launched 20 10,000-ton "Victory" ships and two 8,000-ton steel ships.

The wartime housing built for the shipyard workers has now largely disappeared.

* Yarrows has been operated by the Wallace family as an affiliate of Vancouver's Burrard Drydock Co., since 1946. The Burrard Drydock Company was successor to Wallace Shipyards, Vancouver, founded by former Brixham (Devon) shipbuilder Alfred Wallace. Of his two sons, Clarence, who was lieutenant-governor 1950-55, served as private in the 5th Battalion in World War I, while his brother Hubert is vice-president and managing director of Yarrows. John Wallace, son of Hubert, is general manager.

What will disappear only with death is the spirit of comradeship which unites ex-servicemen in every country . . . a comradeship born of hardships and dangers unselfishly shared.

The very lively branches of the Canadian Legion, Army, Navy and Air Force Vets, the Air Force Association and the mess of the Canadian Scottish testify to the enduring nature of this comradeship.

The Air Force Association, incidentally, includes many former members of the R.A.F. training squadron stationed at Patricia Bay airport in World War II. They fell in love with Victoria and decided to make their homes here.

It has become the custom in recent years to question the wisdom of the sacrifices made during the two World Wars and to criticize the generals in command, but men act and react according to the circumstances of their times.

Serving men did their duty as they saw it. Those ex-servicemen who gather round the War Memorial on Remembrance Day are conscious of the fact that the Allied victories, for which so many of their comrades gave their lives, spared Canada the crushing burden of reparations and catastrophic inflation after World War I. It is thanks to these men that following Hitler's defeat we have a lieutenant-governor instead of a Nazi Gauleiter in Government House.

The majestic Parliament Buildings, symbolizing as they do the democratic system of government for which the Armed Services fought are a truly fitting background for the War Memorial.

> They shall not grow old
>   as we that are left grow old;
> Age shall not weary them,
>   nor the years condemn:
> At the going down of the sun
>   and in the morning
> We will remember them.

Chapter 9

SOCIAL CHANGES
THE BIG BUSINESSMAN BECOMES FASHIONABLE

UNCHALLENGED LEADERS OF society and industry at the turn of the eighteenth century — the period which saw the construction of the Main Legislative Building — were the Dunsmuirs. Robert Dunsmuir, founder of the family fortunes, came to Vancouver Island from the coal mines of Ayrshire in 1851. He was a skilled miner anxious to improve his lot and on the voyage out promised his wife he would build her a castle. He fulfilled his promise in later years by building Craigdarroch Castle in Victoria, one of the city's outstanding buildings. But for many years before he achieved success he lived in what was little better than a shack, surrounded by Indians, in the then coal-mining village of Nanaimo. He spent all his spare time searching for coal and was rewarded with the discovery of the seams at Departure Bay, which to us today is better known as a terminal of the B.C. Ferry system, and went on to become the largest and wealthiest employer in British Columbia. Reminders of the Dunsmuir activities abound in the Nanaimo area in the form of slag heaps, shafts, loading chutes and miners' cottages . . . now mostly abandoned.

Robert Dunsmuir's prestige rivalled that of the lieutenant-governors. He spent immense sums in Victoria, buying houses for his kinfolk, investing in various enterprises and providing much employment here. Robert Dunsmuir was that rarity in his era, a straight business man. No suspicion of political jobbery ever touched him. The *Victoria Times* was on one occasion rash enough to accuse him of using government to suit his own ends. He sued the newspaper, represented by his lawyer Theo Davie (later a premier of the province) and it cost the defendants $500 and very considerable legal fees.

In contrast to our own days, large fortunes in Robert Dunsmuir's time did not excite envy. Politicians had not yet begun to exploit artificially-stimulated jealousy of the wealthy as a step to political power, camouflaging this jealousy under slogans such as "social reform," "social justice," the "new society" or other catch phrase. Wealthy men were admired . . . to the extent that when Robert Dunsmuir returned here from one of his business trips to San Francisco he was serenaded by employees of the Albion Iron Works which he reorganized. Although Robert Dunsmuir made his money chiefly around Nanaimo he spent it largely in Victoria.

His first Victoria home was "Fairview," opposite the Legislative Building at the junction of Quebec and Menzies Streets. From the description of a fancy dress ball given there in 1885 we get an idea of leading people. Guests included E. G. Prior who was later premier. His firm, Prior's Hardware, became part of Mac & Mac (McLennan, McFeely & Prior) the great hardware merchants; Mrs. Bullen, Miss Helmcken, Mr. Irving, Sir Anthony Musgrave and, in full naval uniform, Sir Michael Culmie Seymour and Captain Ross.

In 1886 Emily, a Dunsmuir daughter, married Mr. Snowden from the Fairview residence.

From the same home daughter Mary Heab married Henry Croft and lived afterwards at Mount Adelaide. This splendid home in Esquimalt was later purchased by Sam Matson, publisher of the *Daily Colonist*. The surviving Mrs. Matson willed the property to the Salvation Army and it was demolished in 1959 to make room for the Army's "Matson Lodge" on Dunsmuir Road.

Another Dunsmuir marriage took place in 1891. The uniting of Jessie Sophia, Robert's sixth daughter, to Sir Richard John Musgrave of Waterford, Ireland, was the social highlight of the season. Prominent citizens at the Christ Church Cathedral ceremony included Robert Patterson, who later played a prominent role in promoting the railroad to Sidney, and R. P. Rithet, a most enterprising Victoria businessman. From the *Victoria Times* description: "The wedding was the most fashionable and brilliant in Victoria's history ... the body of Christ Church Cathedral was filled with invited guests, while hundreds of ladies and dozens of gentlemen not so fortunate crowded the side streets, the aisles and the church-yard.

"The bride's dress was of white and silver brocade, with full court train, brocaded in silver in the pattern of the Prince of Wales crest; veil and trimmings of Honiton lace." The six bridesmaids were Miss Effie Dunsmuir, Miss Musgrave, Miss Maude Dunsmuir, Miss Lizzie Harvey, Miss Birdie Dunsmuir and Miss F. Ward (the latter the daughter of a prominent merchant).

Afterwards "between 200 and 300 guests spent several hours merrily at Craigdarroch Castle, the home of the bride, the band of H.M.S. *Warspite* being present to enliven proceedings."

To give an idea of Dunsmuir's wealth — in 1883 he bought out his partner in the Departure Bay mines for $600,000 in cash (about $4,250,000 today). One of his sons, Alexander, who became an alcoholic, thought nothing of paying $20,000 for a necklace as a gift and left $645,000 to his brother James. He also built Oakland House in Berkeley, California, and 75 acres of wooded and formal gardens, which is now the property of the City of Berkeley.

Craigdarroch Castle itself was built on 20 acres which stretched from Fort Street to Rockland Avenue (see map). It went up in 1889 and cost $650,000. The world was scoured for the finest of hardwoods. Leaded glass was imported from Italy and the impos-ing staircase built in Chicago. The mansion had 35 fireplaces, a billiard and ballroom and a 63-foot-long living room. The double driveway curved to Fort Street where what is now the junction of Joan Crescent and Craigdarroch Road was the entrance.

Robert Dunsmuir died before the Castle was finished and his widow moved in and lived there until she died in 1908. The grounds were then subdivided and sold. Everyone owning a lot was given one chance on a draw for the Castle itself. The winner was Mr. Cameron of the Westholme Lumber Co., who mortgaged it to the Bank of Montreal. The B. of M. foreclosed on the mortgage and sold the Castle to the city for $35,000. During World War I, Craig-

95

darroch was a convalescent home for servicemen; it then became headquarters of the Victoria and then the Greater Victoria School Board.

The Victoria Conservatory of Music is now established in the mansion and hopes to have found there permanent headquarters. Since the Victoria School of Music was instituted in 1897 it has had three homes . . . first was in the Institute Hall next to St. Andrew's Cathedral facing View Street where the Bishop's house stood in 1950 and then on Pandora between Broad and Government Streets.

Robert Dunsmuir, a kindly man, was treated with almost royal deference by Victoria's citizens. When he entered the city council chambers, which he did very rarely, mayor and aldermen rose to their feet and remained standing until he was seated. In addition to reorganizing the Albion Iron Works, he brought in American associates (Crocker, Stanford, Huntingdon and Hopkins — California's "Big Four") to launch the Esquimalt and Nanaimo Railroad and bring the terminus to Store Street, in Victoria.

He was as generous in private as he was careful in business, an instance of his generosity being when he chartered a steamer to bring daughter Marion and her bridegroom to Victoria after the Nanaimo wedding. Robert Dunsmuir owned not only mines. He had a fleet of steamers, was a large shareholder in the Canadian Pacific Navigation Co. and chief shareholder in the Victoria Theatre of which he was an ardent patron. The *Colonist* editorialized on his death that he hadn't an enemy in the world.

His second son James took over his father's business interests, became premier of British Columbia in 1901 and lieutenant-governor 1906-09. He offset the excessive drinking of his brother Alex by becoming a total abstainer. Victoria remembers James today chiefly because of Hatley Park.

Another Dunsmuir residence was Burleith, the gates and stone fence of which are still to be seen on Craigflower Road.

James and his American wife lived in "Burleith" after Mrs. Robert Dunsmuir (the widow) went to Craigdarroch. Many gay parties were held there, but it was ruined by fire around 1932 after they moved to Hatley Park. James had eight daughters and two sons, the eldest daughter married Major Guy Audain, whose son

James is well known in Victoria as an author and racehorse owner.

Hatley Park (Royal Roads) which was built in 1911 had in its 700 acres Italian and Japanese gardens, fish pools, a conservatory, sunken gardens and dozens of other beautiful features which make it still today one of Victoria's greatest assets. The estate was bought by the Canadian government after Mrs. James Dunsmuir passed on in 1937 and is used as a training centre for future officers of the Armed Services. The mansion, Hatley Castle, was designed by Samuel McClure, who became Victoria's leading architect.*

McClure, studious by nature, was the son of a Royal Engineer and like his father was an expert telegraphist. He turned to architecture and his homes characterized by stone or stained shingle lower exterior and half-timbered plaster on the upper storeys were noted for their spacious entrance halls and staircases and their leaded glass windows.

Notable examples are the Olde England Inn, "Kingsmount" at 305 Denison, the Harry Gladwell home 1770 Rockland, "Illahie"† built in 1907 for Biggerstaff Wilson, the Gibson house on 1590 York Place (now owned by lawyer Howard Harman) and the Glen Rosa rest home at 644 Linden.

McClure died in 1929.

The pre-eminence of the Dunsmuirs marked a decided change in Victoria's social values. It would have been impossible for the Dunsmuirs to have attained such eminence 25 years earlier. Acceptability in the higher social circles was, until the 1890's, judged by different standards — those engaged in "trade" were considered to rank lower than those of good birth and holding official positions.

In Victoria's earliest years the question of birth did not arise because the only "society" existing was that of senior Hudson's Bay Company officials and officers of the Royal Navy stationed here. James Douglas was the undisputed head of all and, in a small settlement where every face was familiar, social distinctions could not be rigid. Even as Royal Governor of Vancouver Island (1851-64)

---

* The Canadian Government bought Hatley Park with all buildings and 700 acres of land for $75,000!

† Corner of Charles and Maud streets.

97

Douglas made a point of inviting "all but the riff-raff" to his parties at the Fort.

Friendship with Douglas put the hallmark on social acceptance. To be invited to take a bumpy ride in his springless carriage . . . an invitation he frequently extended to the wife of Bishop Cridge and other ladies . . . was an honour not lightly to be declined. For men it was a privilege to be asked to accompany him on a Saturday afternoon country ride or in the S.S. *Beaver* to visit San Juan and the Company's farm managed by Mr. Griffiths.

If Douglas was on the top rung of the social ladder, on the bottom (assuming that he eventually made it) were characters of uncertain origin like Blanket Bill. Blanket Bill when a very old man in Bellingham claimed to have instituted Victoria's first mail service by canoe to Seattle. He got his name because when captured by Indians they swapped him, he claimed, for a blanket (presumably a new one) offered by James Douglas. Advancing years brought celebrity to Blanket Bill, but his memory had unfortunately gone and his disjointed and sometimes incoherent reminiscences (not all due to age), interrupted by long, unexplained silences were of little benefit to historians. But he claimed to be well known in Victoria.

The mostly English gentlemen-farmers who arrived with their servants soon after Victoria was founded introduced a lighter-hearted and, the Scots old-timers thought, a light-headed note into society. Most of them had their expenses paid by the Puget's Sound Agricultural Company for whom they acted as bailiffs and then, as now, expense accounts were subject to abuse. They and their daughters enjoyed dancing, singing, horseback-riding, picnics, visits to H.M. warships and all-night parties. Many parties had to be all night ones for, as Martha Cheney describes in her diary, distances between the farmhouses and the H.M. ships were too great to permit return the same day and heavy drinking seems to have been customary among the men. The wives and daughters of the immigrant farmers wore bustles when entertaining . . . a form of dress regarded by the Scots in the same light as many elderly regard the miniskirt of today.

Officers of the Royal Navy stationed here shared the same ideas of entertainment as the gentlemen farmers. To them Royal Governor Douglas was "Old Square Toes" (not in his hearing of course). He and his cronies could join in the fun if they liked. Fortunately Douglas, no doubt egged on by his daughters, chose to like, insisting at the same time on due respect for the dignity of his office. As senior official in the Colony he could condone the new attitudes without losing prestige, although he disapproved of the extravagant expenditure. He may even at times have welcomed the change.

As the population of Victoria slowly grew, Hudson's Bay officials looked for financial opportunities outside the strictly regulated sphere of their salaried employment. The Company could make money by trade and by selling land. What was more natural than the purchase of land by Company officials?

Prominent employees like Tod, Yale, Finlayson, McNeill and Pemberton were among those who purchased land around Victoria at the then current price of $1 an acre and by so doing they enhanced their financial and social standing. A new land-owning class was in course of formation. Land ownership received further encouragement when the Company and the Crown permitted purchase by instalments. Those who purchased downtown lots prior to the gold rush made a handsome profit provided they sold out in time, but much of the land purchased in outlying areas remained uncultivated for years and the purchasers had to wait a long time for the return on their investment.

New elements entered society with the 1858 and subsequent gold rushes. Mostly they were fly-by-nighters. Downtown Victoria was for them a sort of fair ground where they pitched their booths and made their sales of camp equipment, shovels, barrows, picks, lamps, drink, clothing, provisions and boots to transient gold-seekers.

W. & J. Wilson, clothiers, on Government Street, were an exception. William Wilson, who arrived here in 1862, bought out the Henry Gillard store on Government Street and was later joined by his brother Joseph to form W. & J. Wilson. William became an M.L.A. and died here at the age of 84 in 1922. The Wilsons have been connected directly and indirectly with numerous enterprises in the city . . . carriage trade, groceries, finance . . . and one Wilson, Richard, was a recent mayor of Victoria.

People who made money by "trade" were, however, never regarded as in the upper echelons of society: landownership and official position ... with the government, the Hudson's Bay Company or the Royal Navy remained the hallmarks of the "upper crust."

Honoured guests at a ball given by the Royal Governor in New Westminster were Matthew Baillie-Begbie, W. A. Young, Colonial Secretary, whose wife was a niece of James Douglas; A. G. Henry Pering Pellew Crease, the leading Victoria lawyer; Joseph Wm. Trutch, Commissioner of Lands and Works; W. D. Hamley, Collector of Customs; Chartres Brew, Superintendent of Police; Arthur T. Bushby, Captain James Cooper, Harbourmaster; Robert Ker, Auditor-General; Registrar of Court Charles E. Pooley and Colonel R. Wolfenden, Queen's Printer.

Wolfenden was a former sergeant with the Royal Engineers, but had a knowledge of printing.

The titles given these officials when the whole white population of British Columbia was about 6,000 seem rather grandiose to us today, but perhaps they were no more out of place than our 11 parliaments, 10 premiers and one prime minister for a population of about 21 million.

It is interesting to note that drunkenness was not a prerogative of civilians. The band of the British flagship which was to play at the New Westminster ball arrived so drunk that the Royal Engineers' band was hastily rounded up to substitute.

More evidence of the "togetherness" of the official classes is seen in honoured guests at a concert given in St. John's Church in 1873. They included Joseph Trutch, Admiral Hillyar, the ubiquitous Begbie, Judge Gray and Sir James Douglas.

Tradesmen, on the other hand, were expected to remain tradesmen and while this may have been irritating to many from over the border, there was no way of breaking the barrier. Birth and breeding (provided the breeding was supplemented with a private income) also played a large part in social acceptance. When Lady Jane Franklin, wife of the famous Arctic explorer Captain Sir John Franklin, R.N., paid a visit to Mayor and Mrs. Harris, her A.D.C. referred, somewhat snobbishly it seems to us today, to the reception they could expect: "Will your ladyship wash 'er 'ands?" and narrated with great gusto how the reception went exactly according to expectations. Harris was the wealthiest man in town, but still a "tradesman." Another indication of the prerogative of birth is the remark made by Lord Dufferin, the governor-general, about Anthony Walkem, premier from 1874-76. He wrote: "He (Walkem) is not, I imagine, a person of any great consideration. He is a lawyer in a small village (Victoria) and the son of a clerk in the Dominion Militia Department, so that in one's intercourse with him one has to be on guard against the intellectual frailties engendered by his professional antecedents."

In other words, the aristocrats of those days didn't think race horses could be bred from draught-horses. People accepted this maxim and their place in life. Those were the days when the hymn was sung, unamended:

> The rich man in his castle, the poor man at his gate,
> God made them high or lowly, he ordered their estate.

In all societies birds of a feather have tended to flock together. Before the advent of an established mercantile class, officials and their kin flocked very much together. We read that at a society gathering in 1870 the Hon. Arthur T. Bushby, son-in-law of Sir James Douglas, sang in a rich tenor "Soft Sleep Be Thine," "Banks of Allan Water," "Gently Sighs the Breeze." Mr. Haverick, an official from Yale, gave impersonations in "The Stagestruck Hero"; Mrs. Needham, wife of Chief Justice Needham, played the piano for her daughter singing "The Forsaken," "When the Swallows Fly Home." Her singing reduced strong men to tears, said the newspaper comment.

The tradesmen classes similarly had their social occasions in the philharmonic, dramatic, fire brigade and other societies. None of them clashed and the Church in those days as in these was a point of contact for all stratas of society.

Without a doubt the most popular of all institutions in Victoria ... a popularity which continued until it left Victoria in 1905 ... was the Royal Navy. The Navy joined in every activity. As early as 1858 it staged Victoria's first cricket match when a team from H.M.S. *Satellite* played the Pioneer Cricket Club. The Navy was important economically. A battleship like the *Sutlej* would have a complement of 600, all of them spenders. In 1873 the Royal Navy had five ships here with 1800 men. The Navy Yard had many permanent employees, all of whom were fed with mostly local produce. Victoria felt great pride in the security provided by the Royal Navy. This was given expression to by the *Daily Colonist* in 1890 in a comment on the ball tendered to Rear Admiral Hotham and officers of the Pacific Squadron. It wrote: "The event is looked upon not only as a recognition of the many courtesies received at the hands of the officers, but as an attempt at making the representatives of Britain's maritime power feel that though they sojourned among colonists, their lot had fallen among British subjects whose ambition for Britain's welfare is the same as theirs, whose hope is that they may ever continue to be one of England's most substantial bulwarks as well as her chief colony."

The first and the second dry dock in Esquimalt were a direct result of Royal Navy interest. The latest and largest dock was built after an inspection tour by Lord Jellicoe. It was as a result of his visit that the *Queen Elizabeth* could dock here in World War II. Some older residents still remember the Royal Navy ratings, many of them fine bearded men. They were seldom quarrelsome, full of fun and spent freely of their modest pay.

Socially the bands of the warships provided first class music for weddings, Victoria day celebrations, funerals, sporting events and many other occasions. Jack Tar was always willing to give a hand in fighting fires or floods. Citizens thought so highly of the naval ratings that they protested to the Admiral about them being put on chain gangs with other common malefactors for breaches of discipline (mostly desertion) and the Admiralty felt compelled to stop the practice. As to the officers they were gentlemen, often with private means and among them were some very eligible bachelors.

Captain Langford's oldest daughter married Captain Joslin, R.N. The third married a Lieutenant Bill. The second oldest married outside the Navy, to Captain Lewis of the Hudson's Bay Company. Thomas Skinner's daughter (the first white girl born in Victoria) also married a naval officer. The marrying habit was not confined to officers. Many tars became engaged locally but there was a regrettable tendency by many to forget their obligations when they left.

All Victorians grieved for the four midshipmen from H.M.S. *Warspite* who drowned off Race Rocks in 1891 after leaving Pedder Bay in a canoe to get salmon; the monument erected by their sorrowing parents is still maintained carefully in the Canadian Forces Base in Esquimalt (formerly H.M.C.S. Naden).

Until recent years the Navy, whether R.N. or R.C.N., always enjoyed marked preference in Victoria. The Canadian admirals who succeeded the British were on a par socially with the lieutenant-governors and their presence or absence could make or mar a social occasion. One of the best remembered of recent admirals is Rear-Admiral W. M. Landymore, a short, energetic officer with a distinguished war career, who fell a victim to unification of the Armed Services. Victoria's affection for and identification with the Navy is now exercised through Rear Admiral H. A. Porter, whose title is Commander, Maritime Forces, Pacific Coast, but H.M.C.S. Naden is commemorated in the Naden band, first founded in 1932, whose performances in the Victoria Day parade always draw enthusiastic applause.

It is sad to record that in Post World War II years relations between civilians and navy men deteriorated in Victoria. Young navy men stationed here resented what they called the "smugness" of Victorians devoted to their homes, gardens and families and apparently quite ignorant of the fact that Victoria, as a seaport, offered sailors very little indeed in the way of entertainment . . . entertainment which they considered they had a right to expect.

Victoria merchants, on the other hand, watched with growing concern the vast quantities of merchandise bought overseas by the crews of warships stationed here. They noted also that the so-called "goodwill" cruises which enabled crews to buy so much more cheaply in San Francisco, Hong Kong or Japan, seemed to coincide with Christmas or other buying seasons. The retailers also noted the enlargement of retail purchasing facilities within the "Naden" area for members of the Service in direct competition with them; as private enterprise is the backbone of all taxation, they felt they should not have to compete with tax-subsidized services.

After the navy officers and Hudson's Bay Company officials in early years the senior officials enjoyed precedence. The first civil list in 1859 totalled £5,300. Principal officials were Matthew Baillie Begbie, Chartres Brew, Captain James Cooper, Wymouth O. Hamley, Captain W. Driscoll Gossett, R.E., treasurer, whose iron house from England has previously been mentioned, W. A. G. Young, and George H. Cary, Attorney-General.

With the advent of more representative government the ranks of officialdom became diluted with political appointees. Some of the jobs were entirely superfluous, but they provided jobs for supporters of the politicians. Begbie commented on the appointment of a second chief justice that "it was as necessary as a 13th wheel to a railroad truck." This dilution led to a downgrading in social status of government officials generally. The original appointees were much higher on the list of socially acceptables.

A corollary of this was the upgrading of the mercantile section of the community. The last 20 years of the nineteenth century saw the emergence of leading merchants as a separate class, although they were often at the same time landowners, politicians and industrialists. Good family became of less account. A good bank account of paramount importance.

It is to these merchants that Victoria owes many of its finest homes of the period. Some of these homes do not seem so magnificent to us today as they are often dwarfed by high-rise apartments erected near them, or their surroundings are diminished by the building of smaller, modern dwellings, but in their time they were palaces compared with the homes of the working people. The fine woodwork, minstrel balconies and imposing staircases were something the ordinary man saw only as a servant. Even as late as the 1930's, a reporter invited to describe a reception at one of these fine homes would think he was really entering high society.

Who were these people, where were their homes, how did they make their money?

Chapter 10

FAMOUS MEN AND FAMOUS HOMES

ONE OF THEM WAS R. P. Rithet, a great friend of the Dunsmuirs, whose home "Hollybank" was among the most gracious of Victoria mansions. "Hollybank" was built by Rithet in 1875. Rithet later became a mayor of Victoria and his firm Rithet Agencies Ltd. on Fort Street is one of the oldest real estate and insurance houses in Victoria.

Rithet, like many of the merchants who became important socially had to wait a long time for prominence. He came here in 1862 and married Elizabeth Jane Munro, one of the three daughters of Hudson's Bay factor Alexander Munro.

Rithet got his start here with Sproat & Company. Gilbert H. Sproat managed the lumber mills at Alberni in 1863 and built up a very large business with San Francisco and Victoria. In the last of the early gold rush years he shipped one million board feet of lumber to Victoria, so great was the demand for hotel, saloon and dwelling construction. To handle this business he established a commission house in Victoria under the name of Sproat & Company. This firm also handled commissions and insurance and Rithet was his right hand man.

After the gold rushes Gilbert Sproat became discouraged with Alberni and maintained that the district was too rugged for profitable lumber operations. Present day Alberni proves him to have been an unreliable forecaster. Sproat Lake is named after him.

Rithet left Victoria in 1869 to take charge of the San Francisco end of Sproat & Company's business and the *Colonist* bade him fulsome goodbyes. But they were rather premature. Rithet was back three years later and became partner in the firm of Welch, Rithet & Co. After being elected mayor in 1885 he entered politics and became M.L.A. in 1889. He then went on to found his own wholesale house which prospered exceedingly in the Klondike gold rush of 1898. Rithet and other enterprising Victoria merchants were able to persuade tens of thousands of gold-fever-racked stampeders in Seattle and San Francisco that Victoria was the best point in which to buy supplies for the Klondike and the best port of embarkation to the north.

The Vancouver and Victoria boards of trade even advocated through brochures that gold-seekers go all the way to the Klondike via the Ashcroft trail and thence overland north. Very few, if any, who took this trail ever reached journey's end. During the Klondike gold rush the streets of Victoria were like a madhouse. To quote Pierre Berton's *Klondike*, the city was "invaded by Scots, Irish, Germans, Australians, Americans, garbed in outlandish costumes and dragging oxen and horses along roadways piled high with sacks of provisions, knockdown boats, fur robes, etc." Our merchants did a roaring trade and the Klondike laid the foundation of many fortunes. Horses fit only for the glue factory were sold at outlandish prices. One ship the S.S. *Bristol* left here with 600 horses housed in 2-foot-wide stalls. It had to return it was so top heavy. But the accommodation for the gold-seekers was not much better and near riots broke out on many ships.

Rithet built Rithet's wharves at Dallas and Simcoe Streets, later part of the site of V.M.D. shipyards, had a steamship named after him, developed a large farm and was a well-known horse fancier.

"Hollybank" which sat in several acres facing Beacon Hill Park, had all the then accepted signs of success; stables, barns, tennis and croquet courts, a rose garden. Gertrude, a Rithet girl, married Laurence A. Genge, whose family lived next door at the corner of Humboldt and Vancouver. The former Genge home still stands and is now known as "Grant Manor."

R. P. Rithet died at "Hollybank" in 1919 and Mrs. Rithet lived there until her 100th year, dying in 1950. An iron fence from "Hollybank" is in the Legislative Square.

Before the Genge's moved next door to "Hollybank," the Roman Catholic Bishop Lootens had a cottage there. The cottage was removed to make room for the Genge home and was located until recently at 1012 Pendergast Street. In the past few months it has been demolished to make room for the Barcelona Apartments. Bishop Lootens' cottage was transported on rollers, a process which took several days. Moving in this way over even a comparatively short distance often made a resident very difficult to find. He would be neither at his old or his new address. His home was somewhere between the two. If the weather was very bad a house could get stuck in a road and block it for weeks at a time. How recent is Victoria's history is illustrated by the fact that the late Premier Byron "Boss" Johnson as a boy helped his father remove the Lootens' cottage.

Shotbolt, the druggist, whose store was on the south side of Johnson Street, between Government Street and Oriental Alley, built a fine home called "Hollywood" on what is now known as Shotbolt Place. His store with its enormous glass flagons of presumably coloured water is now gone and a saw sharpening service and other businesses are on the site. Also gone are his home and 10-acre estate at Shotbolt Place. Many smaller houses are now on the site. Thomas Shotbolt like his contemporary Rithet waited a long time to achieve social recognition. He came to Victoria from England in 1863, was a leading merchant by 1880 and died aged 79 in 1922.

In addition to his pharmacy business Thomas Shotbolt was one of the promoters of the street lighting and railway system and the turnabout for the Fairfield Road streetcar was outside his driveway near the Margaret Jenkins school.

Shotbolt Place on Gonzales Hill was in one of Victoria's most fashionable areas, namely the Fairfield, Rockland, Fort Street and St. Charles Street district. In the area were Craigdarroch Castle, Government House and homes like those of Dr. Thos. Jones, pioneer dentist; J. A. Sayward, lumber magnate; Robert Ward, merchant and broker; James Angus, brother of the C.P.R. president; Rout Harvey, merchant; senator Harry Barnard; physician J. C. Davie,

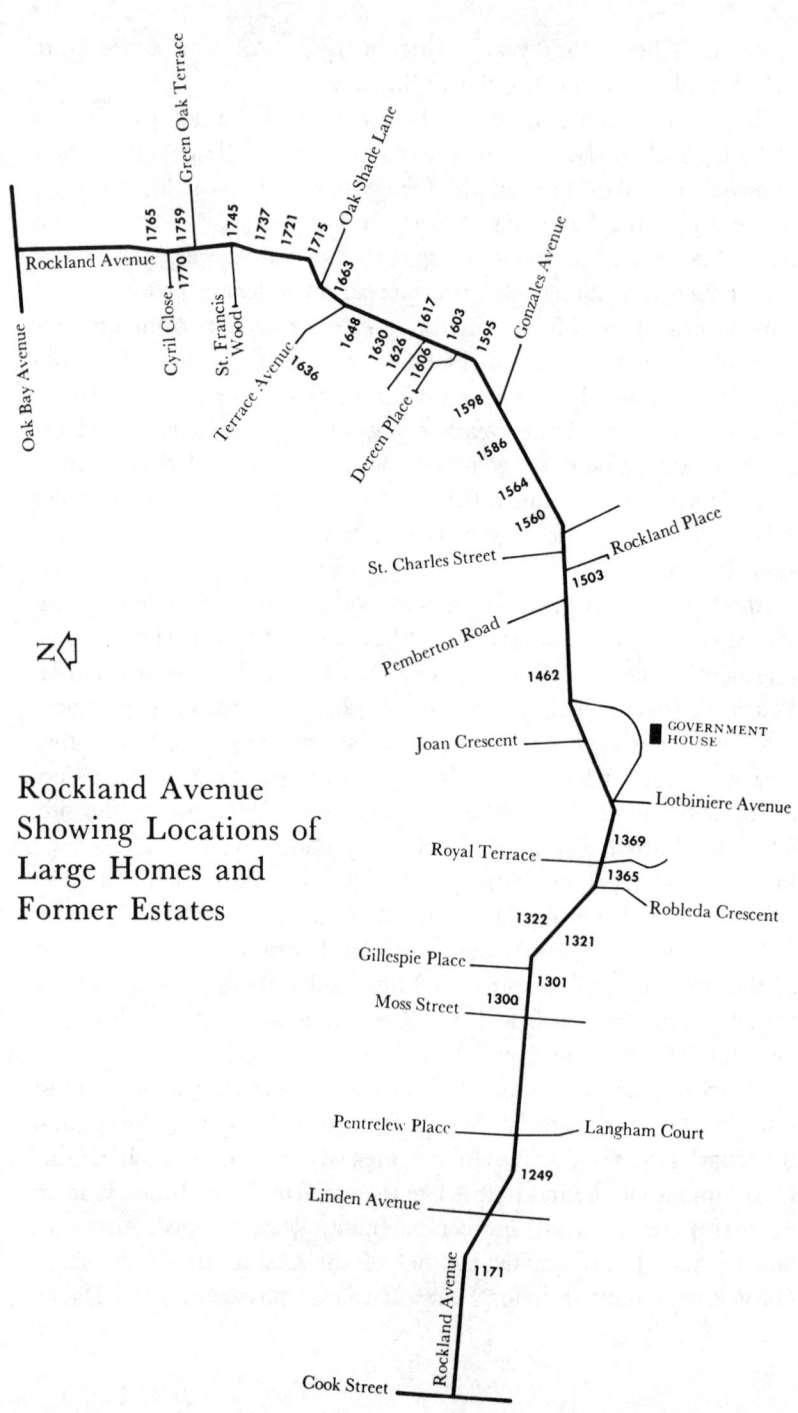

Rockland Avenue
Showing Locations of
Large Homes and
Former Estates

KEY TO MAP OF ROCKLAND AVENUE
COOK STREET TO OAK BAY AVENUE

EVEN NUMBERS

1300 Former site of "Gisburn," built in 1880's and owned successively by Robert Irving, J. B. Hobson, retired financier, and Jack Rithet.

1322 Caroline Macklem home. Built in 1894 for Hewitt Bostock who started the *Province* newspaper in downtown Victoria. This later became the *Vancouver Daily Province*. Bostock became a senator and the home was afterwards occupied by J. D. Prentice, rancher.

1462 "Duvals," now Mary Manor apartment house, see page 113.

1560 Built by Duncan Ross, prominent Liberal.

1564 Built 1870's.

1586 Built 1907 for S. J. Pitts, wholesale merchant. The condition of this house has been much criticized since it was acquired by a junk dealer.

1606 "Dereen," built for noted realtor R. S. Day.

1626 Formerly the home of E. V. Bodwell, K.C. Now owned and occupied by B. Russell Ker.

1630 Builder was lumberman W. J. Macaulay who owned the Chemainus Mill.

1636 This house stands well back on Terrace Avenue almost next to the water tower. Built in 1892 by W. J. Macaulay (see No. 1630).

1648 "Newholm," built in 1897 for A. S. Dumbleton. Dumbleton had to leave Victoria after litigation involving his handling of trust funds. Many prominent families were concerned.

1770 Built around 1906. Was home of Biggerstaff Wilson, one of the sons of pioneer clothier William Wilson and father of ex-mayor Richard Biggerstaff Wilson.

ODD NUMBERS

1171 "Dundalk," Rockland at Linden, a turreted house built in the early 1900's by Arthur Jones, who came here as a Scots gentleman from Inverness, but went into real estate. It was built for his brother Dr. Thomas J. Jones, pioneer dentist.

1249 "The Laurels," built in 1885 for Robert Ward, a prominent merchant, who at the height of his career left Victoria for England without any explanation and never returned. The grounds extended to Linden Avenue in the west and south to Richardson. "The Laurels" later became the home of the Collegiate School and St. George's School for Girls. The auditorium of the Langham Court Theatre is a former schoolroom in the grounds of the residence.

1301 Several smaller houses and two sequoia trees mark the site of the former "Oakmeade," a show-house of its time, built in the early 1890's for J. A. Sayward, well-known lumberman who also built the Sayward Building on Douglas Street. An old Sayward barn still stands below "Ellesmere" (see No. 1321).

1321 "Ellesmere," built in 1899 for James Angus, brother of the C.P.R. president.

1365 Believed to have been built in 1912.

1369 "Stoneyhurst," built in the 1870's for Rout Harvey. He arrived here with his family in 1861 and later joined Turner, Beeton & Co., prominent merchants. Harvey built "Stoneyhurst" in seven acres and members of his family lived there until 1906.

1503 Built in 1885 for J. C. Davie, noted physician. The home is in Rockland Place and is now called Rockland Apartments. Dr. Davie was one of five sons brought out from Merton, Surrey, by their father, a member of the Royal College of Surgeons. One son, Alexander Edmund Batson Davie, became a lawyer, went into partnership with C. E. Pooley, married Constance Langford Skinner and was premier 1887-89, dying while in office. Dr. J. C. Davie created a sensation by eloping with a daughter of J. H. Todd, the industrialist.

1595 Former site of "Gonzales," see page 108.

1603 Built in 1899 for A. E. McPhillips, lawyer and judge. The old coach house can be seen from Rockland Avenue, but the house lies well back.

1617 Rockland Avenue Hospital built in 1906 by D. J. Angus of Montreal. The site is believed formerly to have been that of Cuyler Holland's house. Cuyler Holland was a prominent realtor and connected with B.C. Land & Investment Co. (see page 200 sequ.).

1663 Now an apartment house. A member of Molson's banking family lived there.

1715 "Hochelaga," built in 1892 for A. J. C. Galletly, manager,

Bank of Montreal. "Hochelaga" is the Indian name for Montreal. Galletly's wife and daughter were drowned with many others in the S.S. *Clallum* off Trial Island in 1904. His sister came out to keep house for him and he built a smaller house for her at No. 1737.

1721 Built in 1890 by Henry Dumbleton for his son A. S. Dumbleton who had to leave Victoria (see No. 1648).

1745 House with granite pillars: built in 1890 for Lyman Duff, prominent lawyer who went to Ottawa.

1759 "Barclay Manor," built in the 1920's by Hon. Walter C. Nichol who was lieutenant-governor from 1920-26. Nichol came to Victoria from the east as a reporter in 1894, bought the *Province* (see No. 1322) and published it as a weekly in Victoria in the old Presbyterian Church at the northeast corner of Gordon and Courtney Streets. He moved the newspaper to Vancouver in 1898 where it became the *Vancouver Daily Province*.

1765 Malvern House College.

Joseph Despard Pemberton, Culyer Holland, the Galpins, David Higgins, *Colonist* publisher and many others.

The Pembertons from Dublin were one of Victoria's best-known families. Joseph Despard Pemberton became the province's first surveyor-general and the extent of his landholdings can be seen from attached map. His $10,000 ($150,000 today) home "Gonzales" built in 1885 at the southeast corner of St. Charles and Rockland Avenue had 20 rooms, five bathrooms, a billiard room, library, conservatory and, of course, a tower as was then the fashion.

"Gonzales" became a girl's school in 1945 and was demolished in 1952. The large estate is subdivided to make room for many smaller dwellings. The Pemberton name is commemorated in Pemberton Park on Richardson Street, Pemberton Road and in many other "Pemberton's" throughout the province. Joseph Despard had six children, three sons, Fred, Will and J. D. Junior, and three daughters.

One daughter, Sophie, who married Canon Beanlands of Christ Church, became a noted artist after studying in Paris and London. Another daughter, Susan, founded the Alexandra Club for Women with headquarters in the ivy-covered building on Courtney Street which later became the R.C.M.P. headquarters.

Daughter Aida married Robert Beavan, the realtor, insurance agent and clothier, who was for a short time premier of British Columbia. Their home was where the White House apartments are on Beach Drive, opposite Oak Bay Beach Hotel and the adjacent Native Plant Park was a gift by the late Mrs. Beavan to the Oak Bay municipality.

Of Joseph Despard's three sons, Fred was a noted horticulturalist and is credited with introducing holly to Vancouver Island. His two daughters, Mrs. H. C. Holmes and Mrs. L. Harvey, are here today.

Two grandsons, Captain F. Despard Pemberton and Warren Pemberton (sons of Fred Pemberton) were killed in World War I. Capt. F. D. Pemberton was an R.F.C. pilot and was killed when attacked by German fighters.

Augustus F. Pemberton arrived here in 1855, four years after his brother Joseph. He farmed for three years and then like most sensible men got an official post and became Police Commissioner for Victoria. He was a staunch supporter of the Anglican Church and once narrowly escaped death. He was helping to put out a fire in the loft of Christ Church when he fell through the plaster ceiling and would have continued to the floor if he had not been caught by the roof beams.

He married a sister of Chartres Brew, Inspector of Police, and it is not unreasonable to assume that the marriage played a role in his selection for the post of police commissioner. Quite naturally, inter-related families in Victoria helped each other, the posts given to his kin by Sir James Douglas being an outstanding example. Augustus Pemberton met his future bride when at her brother's request he waited on her when she arrived by ship from England. It was a case of love at first sight and the couple walked hand in hand from Esquimalt to the city. They were married in 1861 and had three children — Chartres, Cecil and Evaline Mary; Evaline being the first registered nurse in Canada; she died in 1965.

Rockland Avenue on which "Gonzales" was built in 1895 began at St. Charles Street and continued northeast to what is now Oak Bay Avenue. From St. Charles Street west what is now Rockland Avenue was called Belcher Street.

The oldest still standing home on what was then Belcher Street is "Duvals" (now 1462 Rockland) opposite Government House. It was built by Mrs. Elizabeth Miles in 1860. She was a very capable woman. Her husband, a government official, died two days after their marriage. Later she bought Government House (Cary Castle as it was then known) and sold it to Royal Governor Kennedy. Still later "Duvals" belonged to Chief Justice Joseph Needham and was bought in 1870 by Francis J. Barnard who had made a lot of money with his Cariboo Express Services during the gold rushes. He deserved to make money. He started his express service the hard way by personally carrying mail on his back and walking from one end of the Cariboo to the other. It was many months before he got the government mail contract. His son Harry became an M.L.A. and senator and died in "Duvals" in 1954.

In spite of the fact that a minimum suburban lot had to be five acres in extent, the property was not large and the grounds extended only 200 feet back from Rockland (Belcher) between Joan Crescent and Pemberton Road. Craigdarroch Castle grounds seem to have jutted into the "Duvals" property because the railings round the old Craigdarroch lodge can still be seen between the "Duvals" driveway entrance and Joan Crescent.

A few hundred feet northeast of "Duvals" is "The Priory." This house is at 729 Pemberton Avenue and the five-acre grounds were once bounded by Angus Road in the north, Rockland, Pemberton and St. Charles. It was built in 1885 by the Hon. E. G. Prior, coal mine inspector, businessman (Prior's Hardware Store), militia colonel, premier and lieutenant-governor. Prior's first wife was Suzette, youngest of John Work's daughters.

The land between "Duvals" and Fort Street belonged to biscuit-manufacturer Samuel Nesbitt, the site of whose residence has been a vacant lot since it burned down in 1960. Carberry Gardens off Fort Street formed the driveway to Nesbitt's home, "Erin Hall," (see index).

Nearby in Regent's Place is the former home of David W. Higgins, the journalist-politician-businessman whose career is outlined elsewhere (see index). The house at Fort and St. Charles Street is now being renovated and is evidence of the considerable progress Higgins made since pitching his tent on Douglas Street in 1858 and sending his contributions to the *British Colonist* for which he worked on a free-lance basis.

But fine homes were not confined to the Rockland Avenue area. Oak Bay obtained and still has a really fine home at 1587 York Place, built in 1898 by Charles Tupper, who is sometimes called the "Father of Confederation." Confederation is the offspring of so many so-called "fathers" that it must find its parentage rather confusing if not promiscuous.

Charles Tupper was a Victoria lawyer who lived at the York Place home for nine years and then left for Vancouver.

Charles Hayward, a pioneer carpenter who constructed the scaffolding for hangings on Bastion Street built his home on Vancouver Street. The site of this now demolished house is the parking lot on Meares Street opposite the Montreal Trust Building. The Hayward grandchildren were brought up in the still-standing green house at No. 1005 Cook Street (Rockland at Cook). The house was noted for its spiral staircase . . . very rare at the time it was built. The home is now used by the Roman Catholic Church as a recreation centre, or was until recently.

From scaffolding and its victims to the undertaker business was a logical step and Hayward's Funeral Chapel, of which his grandson is a director, was founded by him.

C. E. Pooley, one-time Court Registrar and then Speaker of the House, lawyer, and confidant of Robert Dunsmuir, built "Fernhill" at Lampson and Esquimalt. A short distance away was "Ferniehirst" built in the 1860's by Robert Ker from Dalkeith, Scotland, father of David Russell who was partner in the great Brackman-Ker milling complex and founded the family fortunes. "Ferniehirst" stood in 150 acres of land bounded by the Colquitz River in the north, the Gorge (then known as The Arm) in the south, Portage Inlet in the west and Tillicum Road. Tillicum was the boundary between the Ker and the James Yates properties. "Clahowa Tillicum" means in Indian talk "How do you do, friend?" Yates and Ker used to greet each other over the boundary fence with "Clahowa Tillicum?" and as a result when the road replaced the fence it was called Tillicum.

Ker Avenue was the approximate site of "Ferniehirst" and nearby roads Davida Street, Inez Drive, Arnot Drive and Walter Avenue perpetuate Ker family names. Pioneer Robert Ker, several of whose descendants live here today, met his death in an unusual manner. There was a terrific snowstorm on New Year's Day 1879. Robert Ker left on horseback late in the evening for the Gorge Hotel. He never came back and was found dead in the snow the next morning. There is a brass plaque in his memory in St. John's Church of which he was a pioneer member. He was successively auditor-general and paymaster general, being retired on pension after Confederation together with many other officials. He had been 14 years in government service.

Douglas Street near what is now called the Fountain or Humber Green was another favoured residential area. Henry Heisterman, who started Victoria's first library after he failed to find gold in the Cariboo, built a fine home where the Scott Block now is. He built up a big business in real estate and insurance. Nearby was the fine rococco home of the Erb (brewing) family and the homes of Noel Shakespeare (2663 Blanshard), mayor and postmaster, Theo Davie and Roderick Finlayson and round the corner at Hillside Farm, Mrs. John Work. Ludwig Emil Erb owned the Victoria-Phoenix Brewery and his wife was a great entertainer considering 200 guests a modest gathering. Today's Labatt's Brewery on Government Street is successor to Victoria-Phoenix Brewery.

Captain Victor Jacobsen, the sealing captain, an industry which poured money into Victoria, built his home at 507 Head Street, Esquimalt. It was extensively restored by its owner in 1969.

James Bay was also very popular as a residential area. There were 26 homes on Menzies Street between Bellevue and Dallas Road, most of them with large grounds. Usually there were only two houses to a block.

Among residents were John A. Kerr, Wm. McDowell, Captain J. J. Irving, H. A. Rudge, Frederick Elworthy, Thomas Trounce who was responsible for Trounce Alley, Timothy Tobin, Captain D. Urquhart and Theodore Davie whose first wife was Blanche Baker of Saanich; she was only 14 when he married her.

In 1970, Premier Robson's house, built in 1885 at the northwest corner of Michigan and Government Streets and next to it the house of his son-in-law and daughter Mr. and Mrs. Joseph Hunter, were being used as government offices. Robson, a compulsive talker, was the powerful boss "axeman" of politics in his time. At first he decried and hated Victoria, but grew to love the city so much that he later lived here.

Robson was one of 16 children and came to British Columbia to look for gold, found none and gained a living splitting shingles. He then turned to newspaper work. As editor of the *British Columbian* he was very anti-Douglas, blew hot and cold on Confederation and was knocked down and severely hurt by a political opponent. As later editor of the *Colonist* he got $250 a month, but doubled his emoluments when he obtained the post of paymaster and purveyor to the Canadian Pacific Railway Company . . . a post which was declared superfluous after four years. He died as a result of a London taxi door slamming on his finger, causing blood poisoning. At death he was worth $500,000, an end result which should inspire all shingle-splitters. He is buried in Ross Bay Cemetery.

In the Esquimalt neighbourhood, the "Dingle House" (originally called "The Dingle") on Gorge Road which is now the Redwood Park Motel was built by Charles W. "Gasworks" Thomson, a rugged 200-pounder who could smell money as a camel smells water. Thomson's first break came when his ship while rounding the Horn was blown off course in 1859 and made a landfall in an area where there was an abundance of mules.

He found when he arrived in Victoria that the Fraser River gold rush was causing an unprecedented demand for pack animals. Thomson imported mules, broke them in himself on Wharf Street and shipped them to the Cariboo. He then went into the fish business and turned also to farming. He was, in addition, a big realtor and rancher, saw money in gas and in 1862 was made secretary of the Victoria Gas Co. He also found time to import pheasants from Mongolia and thousands of their progeny now breed in the Victoria neighbourhood.

Thomson built Dingle House in 10 acres of land in 1880 and it was one of the show houses of its time. While it was building he lived in "Maplebank," now part of the Yarrow's Shipyard. He died in the Dingle House in 1916.

A near neighbour of Thomson was Sir Frank Barnard who lived just beyond the Johnson Street Bridge in "Clovelly." "Clovelly" was built by A. J. Brideman in 1894 and purchased by Sir Frank in 1899. The Barnards were a family to be reckoned with in Victoria, Sir Frank being brother of George Harry (Senator) Barnard who was mayor of Victoria 1904-05 and in that capacity helped to get the Empress Hotel built.

Sir Frank became lieutenant-governor at the outbreak of World War I and suffered some embarrassment as a result. Mrs. Frank Barnard was a Loewen of German extraction, and threatened demonstrations against her following the sinking of the *Lusitania* led to the posting of military patrols around Government House. The driveway to "Clovelly" was what is now Barnard Street off Esquimalt Road.

The Loewen girls all married remarkably well. Joseph Loewen

built a brewing empire here with a fellow immigrant from Germany, Ludwig Erb (Loewen & Erb) and his six daughters married into the Barnard, Pooley, Prior, Arthur, Jones (realtor), H. M. Robertson and Rogers families. Young Rogers from New York had a letter of introduction to James Angus in Victoria. Angus was brother of the C.P.R. president and through him Rogers discovered that sugar imported from Fiji could compete successfully with the Honolulu product.

The discovery sweetened the lives and bank accounts of both men considerably and laid the foundations of the Rogers' sugar fortune.

The fine homes of the well-to-do coincided with the acceptance of the mercantile community as part of the fashionable world. No longer did Hudson's Bay Company officials, landowners and imported clerics and officials rule the roost. They still had status and were welcomed, of course, but the social leaders were the previously "not in" trading classes. We see this in the list of those present to greet Sir Edmund Barton, Australia's prime minister, when he arrived in 1902. On hand were E. G. Prior, Premier and hardware merchant; Chas Hayward, mayor and funeral director; L. G. McQuade, ship chandler; E. G. McPhillips, lawyer, David Russell Ker, miller, A. E. McPhillips, lawyer, and R. P. Rithet, shipping and sugar merchant and former mayor.

We see the leading businessmen again to the fore at the funeral of Henry F. Heisterman in 1896 . . . not a single Hudson's Bay Company representative or government official honoured as pallbearers who included: R. P. Rithet, Thomas Shotbolt (druggist), C. E. Renouf, broker and merchant who came here from the Channel Islands in 1879 and was a partner in Nicholles & Renouf, hardware merchants; and R. B. McMicking, director of the telephone company.

These instances of the dominance of the mercantile community can be multiplied in the social calendars of the period. For instance the committee formed for the opening of the Mount Baker Hotel in 1893 were all lawyers, politicians, doctors and businessmen. On the committee were: David Higgins, publisher, H. D. Helmcken, J. S. Yates, R. Jones, W. H. Langley, barrister, Allan Cameron,

GOVERNOR FREDERICK SEYMOUR
1820-1869
Like many of his colleagues, he was
fond of cricket.

AMOR DE COSMOS
Lover of the Universe and founder
of the *British Colonist.*

SINGING LOLA

John Tod had four wives, three of
whom were of mixed blood.

PARLIAMENT BUILDINGS
still form, especially with the nearby
Empress Hotel, Victoria's most
impressive landmark.

FRANK MAWSON RATTENBURY
architect for the Parliament Buildings
and Empress Hotel. He came to a
dramatic end.

THE WAR MEMORIAL
the scene every year of Victoria's most
impressive remembrance ceremony.

A TIGHTLY-PACKED C.P. STEAMSHIP
leeaving the harbour with
enthusiastic volunteers in 1914.

HATLEY PARK
now a training centre for future
officers of the Armed Forces.

C.P.R. agent; Arthur G. Smith, barrister and H. B. Haines, an official of the Bank of British Columbia.

The splendid Mount Baker Hotel on 10 acres of grounds on the Oak Bay waterfront had genial Joseph Virtue, former manager of the Hotel Vancouver as host. It was located near the corner of Currie Road and Beach Drive and the grounds stretched well beyond Orchard Street.

The old Oak Bay Boathouse, demolished to make room for the present Oak Bay Marina, was near the front entrance to the Mount Baker Hotel and belonged to the Hotel. The Hotel had a short and financially not too happy life until it burned down in 1902. One reason for its lack of success was that it was too far from town in the pre-automobile age.

The period of the Mount Baker Hotel probably marked the apex of the fortunes of the mercantile community of Victoria.

Politics and business, industry and mining promotion, construction and the lawyer fraternity were all booming. The wealth of the province was funnelled into Victoria. There was no income tax and assessments on property were low. Victoria was a rich man's paradise and offered distinct advantages to "those of lesser breeds." The large homes and gardens provided employment for gardeners, landscapers, furnishers and carpenters, stone masons, French polishers, carriage builders and many other trades.

One firm on Broad Street employed 14 carpenters who could make anything from a cabinet to a staircase and catered exclusively to owners of large homes.

Chapter 11

WIDE-OPEN CITY

THE LARGE HOUSES OF THE RICH and the meaner dwellings of the artisans — the latter often relying on the milk from their cow and home-made preserves to balance the budget — were only two of the contrasts which drew tens of thousands of visitors annually to the capital in the years 1890 to 1910.

The visitor, arriving on well-appointed steamers, could contrast the fine new Legislative Building with a junk-covered waterfront, exhibiting the mud, derelict hulks, deadheads and slime-covered debris of a busy shipbuilding and manufacturing city.

The fine equipages of the wealthy and the handsome "for hire" carriages of top-flight coachmen like the Winters contrasted with the ramshackle contraptions of cabbies, disputing with much bad language, the patronage of disembarking passengers at Rithet's and other wharves.

The visitor could eat in well-appointed dining rooms like that of the Driard Hotel which could seat 350 persons, drink in the Brown Jug or one of the numerous clubs or purchase a quart of Scotch at the nearest grocery store for 75 cents and take it to his room.

He could contrast city dandies wearing spats with businessmen who still came to work riding a horse. A few motor cars were in evidence and also women doing shopping on the new-fangled bicycles, hats and skirts adequately secured in the windy downtown streets. On Saturday night he could join the shopping throng on a regular routine — Yates, Broughton, Douglas Streets and return

taking in the stores of Spencers, Hibbens (at 69 Government between Fort and Trounce), Clays the caterers with their bakery,
delicatessen and sandwiches, W. & J. Wilson and M. W. Waitt, or
go to the newly arrived movies.

People in Victoria were different — easy going, seemingly never
in a hurry, always ready with a smile (as they are today). The
streets were different and a refreshing change from the checker-
board style of American cities.

A *New York Sun* reporter wrote in 1894 that Victoria was the
quaintest English town in North America with no more hustle than
a summer resort, the residents being more idle than the visitors.

Visitors also remarked on the good fellowship which seemed to
exist between all classes. The rich greeted employees on the streets
as their equals and there was a friendly nod for everyone they knew.

But Victoria's way of life also had its critics. An A.D.C. to Lord
Minto, Governor-General of Canada who came here in 1900,
thought Victorians lethargic and impolite. He ascribed their laziness
to the "wet winter months and the hot 'Italian' sun in summer
which drained their energy." He complained that it took him 90
minutes to get from the Oak Bay Hotel to a downtown theatre by
a "noisy streetcar which clanged its bell incessantly." The Savoy
Theatre show, object of his journey, was, he said, "third rate" and
he found residents concerned with class distinctions and the importance of precedence. It was an insult to seat a "lady" next to a
small tradesman's wife, and names of guests invited to social functions were eagerly scanned for any who might have been left off.

Lord Minto's A.D.C. also noted the "ill-treatment of horses,"
which seems curious in view of the large numbers of English —
natural animal lovers — in the city and is in great contrast with the
position today where the Society for the Prevention of Cruelty to
Animals initiated by Dr. R. Hamilton, veterinary surgeon, in 1888,
is one of the most active in Canada.

The critical visitor had, however, a word of praise. He wrote that
he had seldom seen such handsome schoolchildren as in Victoria.
Other Victoria contrasts were top-hatted, frock-coated merchants,
lawyers, businessmen and politicians sharing the sidewalks with
semi-naked Indians peddling salmon, jog-trotting Chinese with

laundry baskets on their heads, roistering red-jacketed sealers, lumbermen and adventurers of many nations.

The visitor could gamble after dinner in posh saloons or go to No. 5 Fan Tan Alley where the Man Hop Cafe served boneless chicken and squashed duck to the silent entry and exit of lottery runners and the click of ivory gambling chips.

Sam, proprietor of the Man Hop, used to shuffle about in thin slippers, a limp cigarette dangling from his lips, demonstrating on request ju-jitsu holds with his large bony hands and with guttural orders to his assistants add to the furtiveness of dimly lit alleys, stairways and dining room.

Victoria's Chinatown in those days rivalled that of San Francisco. Its joss house or temple at 556 Fisgard was reputed to be bigger than San Francisco's. This temple, the oldest in Canada, was removed in 1965 to the Chinese Benevolent Association Building opposite the City police headquarters on Fisgard Street. The Chinese have had difficult times in Victoria. When the first large shipment of coolies (355 of them) arrived in the barque *Quickstar* in 1878 they were driven like cattle to smaller transhipment vessels at the Inner Wharf and pelted and jeered at. The *Colonist* commented: "As their presence in our midst is not desired the welcome they received was not of the most flattering nature."

By 1884 Chinese in Victoria totalled 15,000, equal to that of the white population. Many of them were brought to Canada to build the trans-Canada railroad and were unceremoniously abandoned when construction was completed. But it was a rather pitiless age and people were more concerned with getting and maintaining their own livelihood than with the fate of others. Heeding the outcries of voters, the government first imposed a head tax of $50 in 1885 and doubled it to $100 in 1908. But the Chinese are a patient and persevering race. They built their own school here on Fisgard Street in 1885. It was succeeded by a new school in 1908 and this school is still on its original Fisgard Street site.

The Chinese have made their own unique contribution to Victoria life. Many of the tall and narrow Chinese buildings on Government and Fisgard Streets are a credit to the city architecturally and the

Chinese participate actively in community life, notably through their branch of the Victoria Lion's Club.

It is only in recent years that the Victoria Chinese have lost their own newspaper, which went to Vancouver to serve the large community there. This, however, did not herald necessarily a decline in residents of Chinese extraction, but rather of the older-type unassimilated Chinese. There were for instance in 1967 still 900 members of the Lee family and 400 Wongs in Victoria. Of course, many old practices have necessarily been abandoned. One very much regretted by the Indians was that of putting a feast for the Gods on the graves of newly interred Chinese. The Indians used to watch for these burials, slink up to Ross Bay cemetery in their canoes and rob the Gods of their meal. But sometimes local youths used to get the whiskey first.

Chinese, at one time associated only with domestic services, gardening and laundries, are now found in many branches of commerce as importers and in professions such as insurance, investments, and real estate.

A comparatively recent trend has been their invasion of the corner-store business of which they are tending to get a monopoly.

In addition to railroad construction in earlier years Chinese labour was employed in many industries, notably salmon canning and agriculture. Todd's cannery at Sooke, the huge structure of which still dominates the waterfront, employed many Chinese; so did the West Coast canneries. In Oak Bay in 1879, Lee Dye was farming 193 acres beneath the Lansdowne Slope on what is now Carnarvon Park. He also had a large general store on View Street just above Douglas Street.

In downtown Victoria Ames Holden employed 40 Chinese as shoemakers at the turn of the century in a plant at the corner of Langley and Broughton Streets.

The first Chinese settlement here in 1860 was in the Yates, Fort, Quadra, Cook rectangle. It was from a residential point of view a most undesirable area.

There was a two-acre lake between Yates and Cook Streets, the outlet from which flowed along View Street, across Douglas Street and through the Johnson Street ravine into the harbour. They lived there probably not out of choice but of necessity. In the gold rush days all dry land was at a premium and the Chinese were not in a position to pay a premium. Gradually they consolidated their settlement around Government, Fisgard and Herald Streets, so much so that at the turn of the century the city directory published separate listings of "Chinese and Hindoo" residents.

In this neighbourhood the nervous visitor could see Chinamen, apparently stacked in tiers, smoking their opium pipes. It was one of the sights of Victoria. Opium manufacture and the smuggling of opium to America was a good source of income for many Victorians in these years. Victoria at one time had 14 opium factories and when the Americans put a tariff on opium in 1894 it caused an estimated annual loss of $200,000 to Victoria.

Many opium factories closed down, but the Tai Yung plant behind the City Hall still had 30 or more employees. The intrigued visitor could peer through dirty plate-glass windows at Chinese putting basketball size portions of gum-like opium into huge copper vats for processing. It was said that 50 tons of opium were smuggled into the United States annually from wide-open Victoria and that one leading citizen owned three opium schooners. Victorians saw nothing wrong in the trade. If the Chinese wanted opium they were going to get it, if not from Victoria then from somewhere else. In 1907 newspapers were still advertising "For sale . . . olives, onions, opium" and "Opium direct from China." Federal laws closed all factories a year later.

Another profitable source of income for certain Victorians was the smuggling of Chinese into America. Nearly all smuggling went on from Kingston's Wharf on Wharf Street, which is now a large parking lot. A notorious smuggler was "Pig-iron Kelly," so named because allegedly he weighted his Chinese emigrants with pig-iron so that all evidence could be drowned in an emergency.

Pelting Chinese and pulling their pigtails was a popular pastime with local rowdies. The police seldom intervened because they too resented the fact that Chinese worked for half the wages of whites. On the other hand the Orientals were popular with those who needed servants, the extensive establishments of the times calling for expert gardeners, cooks and other domestics. To their patient skill we owe Victoria's gardens, exceeding in number, size and beauty anything to be found this side of the Rockies. Hatley Park alone employed about 100 Chinese who had their kitchens and dormitories in a separate enclosure in the grounds. A score or so of the old-time Chinese domestics are still to be seen around as retainers or gardener's, but their's is a dying race.

The unfamiliar language, squalid surroundings and racial exclusiveness contributed not a little to Chinese difficulties in Victoria. For example Chinese domestics could be hired only through a downtown Chinese agency. The Chinese tended to deal with their own kind for shopping, clothing and all their needs and seemed to stand in more fear of their own secret societies than they did of the white man's law.

Magistrates used to find court cases involving Chinese most trying. In the 1880's a San Franciscan residing here was charged with procuring a Chinese girl for his own use and when he got tired of her, selling her to a Chinese coolie, disguising the transaction as a marriage between the girl and the coolie. The magistrate heard numerous Chinese witnesses in his efforts to find out whether the marriage was genuine, whether the Chinese husband understood the ceremony, whether the girl's relatives were consulted and so on. The broken English of some witnesses, the consultations in Chinese between witnesses and other ramifications so perplexed the magistrate that when a Canadian doctor came forward to give evidence he involuntarily exclaimed: "Thank God, here is someone who speaks English."

But the Chinese had their difficulties too. Sing Lee, a caterer who went bankrupt, was asked for a list of the people who owed him money. His list included: red shirt man, man come late, cap man, lean man, fat Frenchman, whiskey man, lame leg man, red whiskers, get tight man," which, one may assume, was a fairly representative group of downtown citizens at that time.

Victoria's Chinese now have their own hospital on Herald Street and their own Presbyterian Church. Whatever the merits and demerits of the Chinese way of life it is noteworthy that Chinese youth in Victoria does not seem to have been affected by drug-taking, pot smoking and other excesses so common among white youth in the sixties and police testify that they are the most law-abiding of citizens.

Right up to the present day local hosts considered a visit to Chinatown a "must" for out-of-town visitors, but even more appreciated by visitors was the hospitality of private homes where at the turn of the century they could find the best-dressed and most educated women to be found in the Pacific Northwest. A few of these ladies, now advanced in years, still survive today and one must say that they have a gentleness of disposition and graciousness foreign to our more hectic days.

The visitor looking for "fun" could find many dance halls and in Burne's House on Bastion Square and neighbouring establishments fair and dark companions of many races. That these companions had a wide clientele is shown by the report of a prostitute pursuing and shouting at a young gentleman of Victoria, which cost her a $10 fine. The lightness of the punishment seems to indicate that "money talked" because at the same period, Mrs. Paine, described as "an unfortunate woman," was given six months with hard labour for begging on the street. Presumably she was unable to pay a fine. Victoria's prostitutes came mostly from San Francisco.

The $1 bawdy houses were on Chatham Street. Their chief patrons were dockyard workers and seamen. The better class "$3 houses" were on Herald Street.*

Hacks on Government Street, between the Causeway and Fort Street did a considerable traffic with the higher class prostitutes. The centre of Government Street was a hack stand and a rendezvous for women and their patrons. One of the most popular of houses was "Stella's" on the Gorge waterfront just past the Gorge Hotel. Stella took over the old Loewen home and men used to visit it by canoe.

The City's attitude to prostitution was that Victoria as a seaport had to provide some amenities. Provided licence did not become too pronounced the police did not interfere. In spite of prostitution, or perhaps because of it, Victoria was a much safer place for women

* A woman before the police magistrate in 1970 said she charged $35. Inflation has hit this business as it has all others.

then than it is today. Police had regular contacts with the under-world through their women informants and no crime went unsolved for long. The women knew every suspect character around town.

Burne's House, it may be noted still stands on Bastion Square. Renovated inside and out it is an outstanding example of en-lightened restoration and now houses lawyers and other offices and the noted "Coq au Vin" restaurant. It was built by old-time hotel-man Tommy Burnes around 1893.

Victoria had also much to offer besides the more strenuous activi-ties like dancing, riding, tennis, cricket and garden parties. There was the Victoria Theatre opened with Robert Dunsmuir and Mayor Rithet on the stage in 1885 with everybody who mattered in the audience.

The venture was unfortunately to go broke later in spite of the management efforts of John Austin, its moving spirit, who quit a well paid government job to go into real estate before promoting the Theatre (sometimes referred to as the Victoria Opera House).

Another attraction was movies. Victoria was in 1897 the only place within a thousand miles where the visitor could see the mar-vellous new invention — animated pictures. They were first shown at the Searchlight Theatre on Fort Street, although some people aver that the Trilby in the Duck Building on Broad and Johnson had the first movie projector.

At the Searchlight, Maynard F. Macdonald projected the 25-foot-long film strips, which bore no sub-titles, and the meaning of which he shouted to the audience while hand-cranking the film. Admission price was 10 cents, standing only, and the shows lasted 10 minutes. Performances were continuous and patrons could see two or more shows if they liked, but as the only films were of racing fire engines or ditto passenger trains there wasn't much point. Be-sides there were long intervals between shows while the operator gathered up the strips of film littering the floor and put them in order again.

When Macdonald ran out of fire engine and passenger train film he had to quit as new film was hard to get. He returned to Victoria a year or so later with a 15-minute version of *Cinderella* which he showed on property leased at 637 Yates, where the King Edward

Hotel stood in 1932 and which is the location of the Surrey Block today.

In addition to movies, Victoria was the only city on the Pacific Northwest where vaudeville could be seen. The first vaudeville was staged in the Orpheum (formerly the A.O.U.W.* Hall) in 1900. Interested financially in the venture was Alex Pantages, a former Greek immigrant cook at the Maryland Cafe who made a fortune in the Klondike.

The staff consisted of only three people, Charlie Johnson, prop man, cashier and janitor; Fred Tracy, singer, and Kate Rockwell, actress, singer, dancer and acrobat. Pantages met Kate Rockwell in Dawson when he was operating the Orpheum Theatre there. He fell in love with her and she later sued him unsuccessfully for $25,000.

Kate Rockwell's troupe was followed by that of Madame Sehl and her performing lions. At one performance the report went round that a lion had decided to perform outside his cage. The audience stampeded and the exit being too small they enlarged it by pushing the wall down. That finished the Orpheum and Madame Sehl, but it didn't finish Alex Pantages who went on to become owner of the biggest theatre chain in North America before going broke. The Orpheum Theatre later became the Princess Playhouse and then the Plaza (now the Haida).

During World War I, Mr. Reg Hincks, a well-known local actor, played continuously for four years under Red Cross sponsorship at the Princess Playhouse, raising thousands of dollars for troop comforts. Another feature was the 15-piece orchestra. Gertrude Huntly Green, the famed Victoria pianist, was a frequent performer at the Princess, and Reg Hincks ran pantomimes there from 1908 to 1947.

The Grand Theatre at 50 Johnson Street was also well patronized. The Grand opened originally as the Savoy in 1899 at Government and Yates. It was later renamed the Rio, then the Pantages having been acquired by the Pantages chain in 1907. It was demolished in 1957 and the Imperial Bank now stands on the site.

Variety shows were also staged at the Delmonico Music Hall,

* The initials stood for "Ancient Order of United Workmen." As years went by, wags transformed initials to O.A.U.W.

which could seat 600 people, at 109 Government Street, between Yates and Johnson; at the Royal Savoy next door and at The Trilby in the Duck Block. The picturesque Duck Block building on Broad Street was built by Simeon Duck, M.L.A., in 1892, and now houses the well-known contractors Parker, Johnston and other businesses.

Other popular theatres in their time were The Bijou in a building now the premises of Jeune Bros. on Johnson Street, the Romano on the northeast corner of Government and Johnston and the Totem Theatre now remodelled and used as the McPherson Playhouse.

Talkies which inaugurated the decline of live theatre came to Victoria in 1933 with the film *The Crimson Paradise* (although some say the first talkie was *Sonny Boy* with Al Jolson) being shown at the Dominion Theatre alongside where the Haida now stands. The Odeon Theatre first appeared in the 1948 city directory.

Few people would recognize Victoria from the pictures of the city which appeared in the first years of the century. In front of the Main Legislative Buildings (the two wings had not been built) was a mudflat at low tide. When the tide came in, a local character Bill Nye could be seen in his barrel, weather permitting, using his hands as paddles and scouring the waterfront for junk. Bill Nye was as much a part of the local scene as James Dunsmuir and his yacht *Thistle*, or the well-appointed Alexandra steamers which operated a regular service between the city and San Francisco. Bill Nye used to delight youngsters by writing his name on submerged clamshells. Gunny sack on back and wearing one gold earring he was the city's only rag-and-bone man. He lived rough. When he broke a leg and was taken to Jubilee Hospital the nurses had to rig up a bed of boards because he wasn't used to a mattress.

Fort Street was blacktopped in 1899 and a publicity brochure of the time claimed that all downtown streets were macadamized. If so the contractors scamped the job because a few years later Mr. A. Carmichael told the real estate board that Victoria streets were unpaved, dirty, badly lighted and a sea of mud or dust. Pebbles were still being dumped to fill mudholes at the Bastion Square and Langley Street intersection to give footing to complaining lawyers who had their offices in Chancery Lane and Court Alley.

Generally the streets were notable for their impassibility after heavy rains, but they didn't go far as will be seen from the map illustrating Victoria's growth. Government Street petered out in a trail beyond John Street.

There were many nasty smells, notably of sewage and tanneries and horse sweat and the many sealers anchored in the harbour were themselves no orchids.

A great problem was drunkenness and fighting in downtown streets. Even today this problem continues, but today's Victoria is a Sunday school class compared with the city of 1900 and earlier years. In one year — 1862, the magistrate dealt with 368 drunk and disorderly charges and with 193 of disturbing the peace. U.S. brandy sold at $1 a quart, imported ale 12 quarts for $2.75 and with the average wage at $12 to $30 a week the alcoholic nirvana was within reach of most people. Many of the Fraser River and Cariboo gold-seekers arrived here well-heeled already from the California goldfields.

They could afford to spend freely and did so, tossing gold nuggets on the counter in payment. But Victoria's permanent residents were no Baptists where drink was concerned. The rich prided themselves on their cellars and their absorptive capacities.

Drunkenness in Victoria was no offence. To incur a fine one had to be guilty of obstruction and disturbing the peace. An ingenious plea by a drunk before the city magistrate in the 1880's was that as he was dead out, half on the sidewalk and half in the road, he was obstructing nobody. It gained him an acquittal.

In the same year a man named Eugene Growley was charged with stealing a watch and chain. After listening to accuser and accused the magistrate wearily concluded that both were drunk at the time and dismissed the case. Downtown merchants didn't object to people fighting unless it happened outside their stores, but they often complained to the magistrate about their trials.

The Klondike gold rush scenes in 1898 repeated those of the earlier gold rushes. It seemed to be a point of honour for those seeing each other off to become inebriated. Beer was sold from wagons in Bastion Square notwithstanding plentiful supplies available in 14 saloons on Johnson Street between Wharf and Government Streets and the nearby Boomerang Saloon . . . a brick cottage where the Yates parking building now is ... and Steele's Saloon in the Square itself which boasted at the time of being the oldest licence holder in the city "in its present location since 1869."

The dust, shouting, singing, miners' packs, mules, beef on the hoof, horses, trunks, parcels and handcarts, amid which the occasional hotelkeeper was to be seen anxiously searching for skeedaddlers (those who had quit without paying their bill) provided scenes of lusty and, for Victoria, profitable chaos.

As regards amusement the topers of those days like their brethren today were easily satisfied.

In 1861 for instance a man named Knox won $300 on a bet by walking round a local saloon uninterruptedly for 100 hours. Encouraged by this he challenged a character known as the "Butcher Boy" to a 80-yard heel-and-toe match at Beacon Hill, put $300 on himself and lost it. Rat-killing matches with the use of ferrets were also popular. A favourite location was Eden & Boland's Saloon on Langley Street.

By 1900 sports were still not much more sophisticated. The racing of commandeered garbage wagons by top-hatted, frock-coated young bloods was a familiar downtown sight and tossing in a blanket to sober up a drunk was still high on the list of topers' entertainment.

Drinking kept pace with the city's growth and no class had the monopoly. All people drank heavily as a matter of course, but as they were much more active physically, with walking, riding and dancing being much to the fore, they could absorb more alcohol, and the police had no problems with impaired drivers as a horse could be depended on to find his way home even if his master couldn't.

Ladies were not allowed in bars: it was "genteel" to permit them a quiet drink of brandy brought by their escorts to the coach. But when they could drink indoors they did not lag behind the men. Chronicler Pere Grinator wrote in *The Victoria Home Journal* in 1893: "Drunkenness among women is increasing to an alarming extent. The habit is not confined to the lower and middle classes of society for the story was common property last week that several ladies moving in good society partook too liberally at a Victoria hotel and had to be literally carried home." A quite appropriate prize for a lady in the 1900's was a glass revolver full of rum.

The Driard Hotel at Douglas and View Streets, now part of the Eaton block, although hailed as the finest hotel north of San Francisco was also noted for the heavy drinking of its guests. Mrs. Baillie-Grohman, a visitor in 1897, wrote home that the "Driard is no place for a lady." The Driard was not of very imposing size when it opened in 1862 as the St. George's Hotel. Alongside it was a shack which in 1888 was still renting at $4 a month — this on Victoria's downtown Douglas Street.

The St. George fell on bad times after early gold rushes tapered off and was bought in 1872 by Sosthenes Driard, a pioneer immigrant who later become corpulent and asthmatic. He enlarged and improved it over the years, aided no doubt by several fires which were well covered by insurance.

When the Victoria Theatre was built in 1885 at View and Douglas its upper floors became part of the Driard Hotel. The decline of the Driard began with the opening of the Empress Hotel in 1908.

Another hotel noted for its hospitality was the Dallas built in 1882 and named after Alexander Grant Dallas, James Douglas's son-in-law. Situated on the waterfront opposite the later Ogden Point Docks it was a natural for farewell parties as ocean-going steamers berthed at the nearby Rithet's Outer Wharves. Also passengers could be sure of not missing the boat, the porter undertaking to alert them in time. The Dallas Hotel was demolished in 1928 and became a parking lot for workers at the Victoria Machinery Depot shipways.

Indicative of the growing attraction of Victoria was the Dominion Hotel on Yates Street. For years it had been a narrow two-storeyed structure. In 1889 it was enlarged and modernized and this process was repeated three times in the next 20 years.

The hotel now occupies the same area as it did at the turn of the century except that the adjacent vacant ground became a gas station and is now the hotel parking lot.

Other popular hotels included the St. Francis (formerly called the Oriental) on Yates, now occupied by the Goodwill Enterprises bazaar; the Clarence, where Bank of Nova Scotia now stands, corner Yates and Douglas (it was a favourite with sealing captains); the Grand Pacific at the corner of Johnson and Store Streets, and the White Horse at 68 Humboldt (north side of Humboldt and McClure) near the Roccabella Hotel. A famous hotel and restaurant which survives as a restaurant only today is the Poodle Dog opened in 1885. There was also a Poodle Dog in San Francisco and the name is an anglicization of the original "Poulet d'Or" restaurant. Poodle Dog alley, south from Yates between Broad and Government Streets was the western boundary of the restaurant.

Another new establishment of the period was the Brunswick Hotel, built in 1892. It stood at the southeast corner of Yates and Douglas Streets in the Jewell Block and had 100 bedrooms but only two bathrooms. This must have inconvenienced guests at times. Worth mentioning is the Pacific Telegraph Hotel, largest of its day when it was built in 1871 on Store Street between Herald and Fisgard streets. It had 150 beds and its owner, Italian immigrant Andrew Astrico, was a renowned chef de cuisine and caterer. Taught by experience, he used to advertise "Room and board $6 a week, terms cash in advance."

Not the least of Victoria's attractions was the excellent food available. To those who had lived mainly on clams, salmon and moose-meat along the coast and in the backwoods of British Columbia the menus of Victoria's restaurants must have seemed like a dream from "Arabian Nights." The Poodle Dog as an example featured *Soup* — Julian or Consomme; *Fish* — halibut, flounder, fried tommycod; salad and lobster mayonnaise; eastern oysters or spring chicken a la Maryland; sweetbread patties or welsh rabbit on toast; apple fritters; sherry sauce; *Roasts* — young turkey, prime ribs of beef, leg of mutton; *Vegetables* — browned sweet potatoes, cauliflower, stewed tomatoes, mashed potatoes; *Dessert* — fig pudding, brandy sauce, apple, lemon, cranberry pie; orange jelly. Assorted cakes, oranges, apples, grapes, nuts, raisins; Canadian cheese; black coffee. And the price? Fifty cents (about $5 today).

This was not an exceptional menu. Competition between hotels was keen and the best had unexcelled cuisine and service, the latter including beautiful panelled dining rooms, white linen, cut glass

133

and excellent waiters. The Driard and Hotel Telegraph were outstanding for their food, as also the New England Cafe built in 1860 and demolished in 1892.

One could expect a lot for 50 cents when the Maryland Chop House was offering "the best meals in Victoria from 25¢ up," while The Grotto on Trounce Alley offered FREE hot lunches with beer at 50 cents a glass.

Saloons competed with the hotel restaurants and often it was difficult to distinguish between the two as far as eating was concerned, except that in saloons you weren't allowed to sit. Bars were of gleaming mahogany or black walnut, the spittoons of fine brass, the plate-glass mirrors bevel-edged, the glassware often crystal. Counters were piled high with food of a quality which makes this age of affluence look like austerity . . . slabs of beef and ham, cheeses, sausage, stacks of bread . . . and many saloons offered free food with drinks.

The hefty white-aproned bartenders doubled as a rule as bouncers, but they were generally good-hearted men and generous with the needy. Victoria was still small enough for everybody to know everybody and a good word, or a bad one, could do much to influence custom.

Chapter 12

PAROCHIALISM AND PATRIOTISM

ON THE SUNNY AFTERNOON OF May 25, 1896 conductor George Farr of tightly-packed streetcar No. 106 remarked jokingly to passenger James Townley as they approached Point Ellice Bridge: "If we get over the bridge we'll be lucky." They were his last words. Seconds later the streetcar with 124 screaming passengers plunged from the bridge amid a mass of iron spars and broken beams into the tidal waters below. With conductor Farr perished 58 men, women and children who had been joyously bound for the Queen Victoria Day military fete at Macaulay Point.

Not since the loss of the S.S. *Pacific* which went down in 1875 with 230 of its 232 passengers, after being hit by a collier within a few hours of leaving Victoria, had so many Victorians been simultaneously bereaved. If we today could imagine 600 of our citizens being killed in a single accident it would be mathematically in proportion to the loss of lives in the Point Ellice Bridge disaster.

The accident cost relatives endless grief and the city $150,000 in legal claims. It was caused by a decayed beam in the centre span. The beam had been drilled for inspection four years earlier, but the drillholes were either not caulked at all, or insufficiently caulked. Rot spread from the holes to the entire beam. The beam snapped with the weight of the overloaded streetcar ... it was scheduled to carry only half the number of passengers on board at the time, and the whole centre span collapsed into the water.

It was revealed later that the bridge had sagged when the heavy

135

streetcar was crossing it four weeks earlier . . . hence the conductor's joking remark: "We'll be lucky if we make it."

The bridge which collapsed was the third on the site. The first was built in 1861 and was followed by the 1873 and 1885 bridges.

A temporary bridge was built soon after the tragedy and a new rivetted bridge opened in 1904. This was again replaced in 1957 and many of those who witnessed the 1896 tragedy or were bereaved thereby were present at the opening of the new Point Ellice Bridge.

The Point Ellice Bridge tragedy marred what had been the practically accident-free record of the Victoria Electric Tramways since the first car line was started in 1890 from the Outer Wharf to the Fountain (Humber Green). Gradually the steel tracks were lengthened. The second line to be built ran from the steam plant on Store Street to the Jubilee Hospital and was a tremendous boon for visitors to the sick. The No. 5 cars ran from Victoria West to the Gorge. Lines also ran to the Oak Bay Hotel, to the Willows Inn — a favourite rendezvous for sports fans — from Burnside to Tolmie, Fairfield to Hillside, Cloverdale to the Outer Wharf and to James Bay via the trestle bridge.

The drivers and conductors worked a 10-hour day for 365 days a year and were paid 22 cents an hour.

Pioneer directors of the Company included D. W. Higgins, Andrew Gray, Joseph Hunter, F. S. Barnard and Thomas Shotbolt, the druggist.

Many Victorians recall even today with nostalgia the passing of the streetcars, the last of which ran in 1948. The open, raised platform sightseeing car was as sure a sign of spring as the Tally-Ho horses on the Causeway are today. Guests at the Empress Hotel delighted in watching the quaint cars trundling across the Causeway like noisy toys.

At 5 cents a ride (later raised to 7 cents) the cars were immensely popular for many years with the thousands of passengers who used them daily. In spite of this, many people were not above cheating the conductor by handing their passes out of the window so that waiting friends could board free.

Many citizens complained of the swaying, jogging and jolting on curves and points and the incessant clanging of the driver's bell.

The motorcar doomed the streetcar in Victoria as in all growing cities. The original Company finished up as part of the British Columbia Electric Co., which took it over when tight money hit the North American Continent in 1896. A. T. Goward, who started as a streetcar conductor, became vice-president of the B.C.E. The buses which replaced the electric cars were in turn taken over together with the B.C. Electric Company by Premier Bennett and his Social Credit government in 1962, a measure which caused great controversy.

The drivers and conductors of Victoria's tramcars were better known to city dwellers than the premier or the mayor. The deaths of motorman Harry Talbot and conductor George Farr on car 106 was felt as a personal loss by thousands of passengers.

Close ties which were partly a result of isolation knitted together the permanent residents of the community and these ties were reinforced by intermarriages. The marriages between Priors and Works, Rogers and Angus's, Barnards and Loewens had their counterparts among the Smiths, Browns, Dickinsons and Joneses on the lower social scale.

Some newcomers found this clannishness of Victorians rather irksome ... which is the complaint of many newcomers, especially those from the prairies ... today. A sidelight on some of the grumblers was given by Mrs. Baillie Grohman, a visitor in 1897, whose husband engineered great mining developments in the interior. She stayed at Mrs. Doane's boarding house opposite the Cathedral, where the Tyrrwhit-Drakes, Creases and others called on her.

She wrote in her diary: "I could never understand a lot of Englishmen saying as they do that they do not like the Colony and it is a dull place. There's plenty going on. The Navy is in Victoria the greater part of the year and there are dances, tennis parties, picnics, boating parties up the Arm and the sea, and country drives on a duckboard. Added to this is the lovely scenery and fine weather and beautiful wild spring. The families are mostly English or Scottish."

Mrs. Baillie Grohman also got from landlady Doane a "Who's Who" of Victoria. According to Mrs. Doane there were people of "good class" and "no class."

Mrs. Doane presumably was considered "no class," but she hit back, telling Mrs. Grohman that lots of women giving themselves airs were second-raters, married to schooner captains when "it was easy to get her man and women were scarce." Also, said Mrs. Doane, many of the so-called ladies had Indian blood.

No doubt many of the newcomers felt as they do today that Victoria was somewhat claustrophobic. Residents had to get out of the city occasionally to appreciate all it had to offer, but in the 1890's there were many fewer alternatives than there are today. The S.S. *Charmer* ran once daily to Vancouver, a town with merely 19,000 people. For those with more time and money the American-owned S.S. *H. F. Alexander* and other ships of the Pacific Steamship Co. ran once a week to San Francisco. These ships were subsidized by the Federal government and the *H. F. Alexander*, the crack steamship, could make San Francisco in 1½ days.

But the grumblers were a minority. Most people had never left Vancouver Island and had no possibility or desire to do so.

For those with business interests the shipping arriving in Victoria provided endless opportunities for cultural and commercial exchanges. All visitors could be assured of a warm . . . and if they had money or influence . . . a still warmer welcome. The reception given to Dr. Webb in 1889 was almost vice-regal. Dr. Webb, whose father-in-law was Wm. Henry Vanderbilt, arrived here after a cruise to Alaska and was escorted personally by militia colonel E. G. Prior and Robert Ward, president of the Board of Trade, to Craigflower Bridge.

An elaborate system of tip-offs, messages from agents in ports of departure and even on the ships themselves kept local realtors and other businessmen well posted regarding passengers and their means. It is to be feared that many who thought they were coming to a quiet, uncommercialized British city, different from go-getting San Francisco or Vancouver, were rather bewildered.

Most welcome of all were British visitors and the most avidly read items in the local newspapers were those revealing where they were staying and who was paying them visits.

The importance of visitors could be gauged from the calibre of their visitors. The preference given to Britishers was evidence of a trend. In the last two decades of the nineteenth century Victoria became overwhelmingly pro-British.

The great architect of this sentiment was Princess Louise, daughter of Queen Victoria who arrived in 1882, accompanied by her husband, Governor-General the Marquis of Lorne. Her arrival gave much needed encouragement to a city still dubious of its future. In fact many at the time of her visit thought there wasn't much of a future. It was by then known that the trans-Canada railroad would definitely terminate in Vancouver. The sealing, canning and manufacturing industries had not acquired the importance of later years and the drydock project was bogging down in a conglomerate of cement and corruption.

Princess Louise by her very presence restored confidence just as the proximity of a brigadier or other "red tab" in the firing line gives confidence to the scared private soldier.

Victoria went all out to show its appreciation. These "all-out" efforts are portrayed, not very flatteringly, by Margaret Ormsby in *British Columbia — a History*. She writes: "The merchants, householders and the civic authorities entered into a tense competition to demonstrate the fact that Victoria was au courant with Gothic revival. Hideous monstrosities made their appearance: the arch at Point Ellice Bridge intended to typify the city gates was supplied with two tiers surmounted by parapets. But its circular pediment bore the slogan: 'Loyal Hearts and English Homes.'

"A massive and imposing castellated structure was erected by the City Council, and Fort Street boasted a pseudo-Tudor arch with two hexagonal towers and parapets, as well as a centre arch surmounted by an embattled gable — all this in imitation stone. 'Victoria Welcomes Queen Victoria's Daughter' said one placard.

" 'Union is strength,' declared the other.

" 'The Orient greets the Occident,' announced the Chinese arch. From the balconies of their shops furriers draped bear skins with 'Welcome' letters in rawhide and a show window in David Spencer's shop displayed a circular headed screen surmounted by a crown in scarlet and blue fringed with evergreens."

Princess Louise came for two weeks and stayed for three months in Victoria. Storekeepers proudly announced her patronage and the privilege of "purveying" to her. She was very popular with all. Black was her favourite colour and Victorians became accustomed to her black shawl and bonnet or black-figured silk dress with dolman as she shopped on Government Street. The Princess saw nothing undignified in inspecting 15 varieties of Pendray's locally manufactured soap, Brackman-Ker's oatmeal, Goodacre's dressed beef and other not very glamorous exhibits at the Beacon Hill exhibition.

Nor did beer shock her. She went with her husband to see one of the town's master brewers in action. They found the master brewer Arthur Bunster in shirt sleeves chopping wood to heat the brew . . . which is evidence that industry in the early 1880's was on a rather modest, do-it-yourself basis.

The object of the royal visit was to investigate and encourage industry in the province. It was because her husband pursued so indefatigably this aim and was constantly touring the Mainland that Princess Louise was left so much on her own. But her presence in itself gave great stimulus to local dressmakers, clothiers, the carriage trade and caterers. She gave a dinner for Mr. Justice Gray, Mr. Justice Walkem and Mayor and Mrs. Shakespeare and other guests in Cary Castle (Government House). To console the non-invited she held a "drawing room" in the James Bay Assembly Chamber (in one of the Birdcages). She also gave a garden party at Government House, attended bazaars and other functions, was guest of honour at a Union Club dinner and visited St. Ann's Academy, the High School and the Royal Jubilee and St. Joseph's hospitals. So popular was the Princess (and desperate the Colony) that Premier Beavan even asked whether she could be the Queen of a separate Vancouver Island. This revealed a rather lamentable lack of knowledge of British monarchical tradition.

The Empire-mindedness which the Princess inaugurated increased with the increasing prosperity of the 1880's and 1890's. Indeed, Victoria's patriotism exceeded anything to be found in the Mother Country. Local newspapers constantly referred to Victoria as a "Watchdog of Empire" and the *Colonist* editorialized that "Victorians hoped to be forever loyal subjects of the Queen."

Citizens fondly assumed that Victoria was a vital base for the Royal Navy when, in fact, it was a holiday base where officers and men could recover from their tour of duty in tropical South American waters. In Victoria they found fresh English complexions, the English language — much purer than in many parts of England — English gardens and sports and English homes. Indicative of the growing enthusiasm for things British were the Queen Victoria birthday celebrations of 1892. They brought out the biggest crowds in the history of the annual celebrations. Ex-mayor R. P. Rithet was out with his family in his launch *Hollybank*; Captain John Irving took a party around in his new "naptha" launch and the Arm (Gorge) was crowded with other happy parties. The steamers *Dale* and *Badger* with passenger-carrying scows in tow plied from the foot of Johnson Street. Canoes, skiffs, sailing craft, Indian dugouts . . . anything that could float was in service for the regatta.

There were fireworks displays in the evening, a scow carried the magnificent band of one of H.M. warships and serenaded the holiday makers; every little cove along the Gorge had its picnic party. Diving competitions were held near the Point Ellice Bridge and crowds watched men walking the greasy pole, and the Indian canoe races. But the water regatta was only part of the celebrations. In Beacon Hill Park Royal Navy ratings took part in tug-of-war competitions and soccer games. Horse races consumed a large part of the afternoon, and various games of skill and chance were staged by visiting showmen. The day climaxed with a military full-dress parade and a grand concert in the evening. Victorians did not get many holidays — six days a year, namely the Queen's birthday, her succession (June 20), Coronation Day, Good Friday, Easter Monday and Christmas Day — and they made the most of them.

To be accepted in Victoria society meant being a British patriot and Colonel E. G. Prior, commander of the volunteer Militia Coast Artillery Brigade typified the sentiments of his times. He told the 34th annual dinner of the Sons of England in 1908 that he hoped Canada would soon have conscription with millions of young men "willing and ready to uphold the honour of our dear old flag, under which and for which our forefathers fought and bled, and of the King of whom we are all so proud." The enthusiastic singing of "Land of Hope and Glory," "The Maple Leaf Forever" and "God Save the King" terminated the proceedings.

Prior may have been more of a fire-eater than some of his contemporaries. One imagines that the highlight of his life was when
he was permitted to accompany the 1885 expedition as a volunteer
on the staff to restore quiet and confidence to the Skeena River
Indians above Port Essington.

The battery landed and deployed its guns, but no shot was fired.
The provincial constable expressed confidence that the object of the
expedition had been achieved.

Rather embarrassingly, the warship which was supposed to bring
the expedition back forgot to keep the engagement and Prior and
his men had a less glamorous return voyage as passengers on the
C.P.'s *Princess Louise*.

The Hon. E. G. Prior, as he became known, was a Yorkshireman
who built up the big hardware business which once stood at the
northeast corner of Government and Johnson Streets. It then moved
across the road and in 1969, the B.C. Hospital Insurance offices
were on the location. Prior was premier for five months, November
1902 to June 1903, and lieutenant-governor 1919-1920.

In Prior's days there had been no world wars, nor had the nuclear
bomb been invented to make people doubt the wisdom of law
backed by the Royal Navy.

If there had been a few more Priors in Victoria's early days this
city, instead of being south would be north of the border with the
United States. Douglas himself, as Royal Governor, had wanted the
Royal Engineers and Royal Marines to capture Puget Sound and
push on to the Columbia River in 1861. His object was to safeguard
trade for Britain by securing the Columbia River as boundary, but
Whitehall discouraged his patriotic zeal and told him to hold his
hand.

Victoria's pride in Empire coincided with a tremendous increase
in Empire trade. Many large vessels called here regularly on their
way to Vancouver and those from the Orient brought Japanese
silk, Chinese tea, Chinese immigrants and businessmen, globetrotters
and Indian Army people who chose the all-Empire route via Canada
to the Home Country. The Canadian Pacific "Empress" liners were
the pride of Victoria.

The service from Japan and China was inaugurated in 1893 in

an all-out effort to capture the booming silk trade. The effort was successful. By transhipping in Vancouver to railcars, for which the route across Canada was specially cleared, Japanese silk could reach Britain before that sent in ships via the Suez Canal. The white hulls and yellow funnels of these magnificent liners arouse nostalgic memories today. They could steam continuously at 22 knots. The first liner, the *Empress of India,* was followed by the *Empresses of China, Japan* and in 1913 by the crack liners of all, *Empress of Russia* and *Empress of Asia.*

The Japanese, for reasons of national prestige, felt they should share the trade and their steamers named mostly after their ports of call: *Seattle Maru, Yokohama Maru* and others were visitors here. Other regular lines whose vessels called here included the Royal Mail, Blue Funnel, Holland-American, Canadian-Australian and Canadian Mexican line, the latter with one ship S.S. *Lonsdale.*

Government and Wharf Streets were busy as beehives with agents, skippers, brokers, ship chandlers and other businessmen buzzing in and out of the offices of the steamship and railway companies (including American) who did business there.

There was in addition an extensive coastal trade as the seaway was the only direct communication with Nanaimo (the Malahat Drive was not built until 1912) and the West Coast. C.P.'s *Princess Patricia* made the first trips to Nanaimo followed by the *Princess Mary,* part of the latter now being the Princess Mary restaurant vessel.

The growth of Vancouver and Seattle and the advent of motor car and air transport helped to speed Victoria's decline as a port. This was at one time a matter of deep regret, but in recent years there has been a reaction to the idea of ever growing ports and cities. This reaction has been caused by the growing awareness of pollution and the belated realization that centres can grow too large for efficient administration.

Chapter 13

INDIAN SUMMER

ALTHOUGH CITIZENS DID NOT REALIZE IT at the time, the period 1900 to the outbreak of World War I was Victoria's Indian summer. Never again would the city have such a busy industrial complex.

On the surface nothing was changing. Mrs. James Dunsmuir gave extravagant parties at "Burleith." Expensive and rare automobiles made their appearance in city streets. The Board of Trade and its closely associated members including the Todds, Wards, Rithet, Cuyler Holland, Wilsons, Renoufs and Turners were as active as ever and just as party and banquet conscious. Racing, soccer and cricket dominated the sports field. Nobody who really wanted work needed to be without a job. The prosperity was not, of course, continuous. The year 1908 was especially poor, but Victoria had had setbacks before, notably in the prosperous 1890 decade when from 1893 to 1898 a financial panic in the States caused many bankruptcies and amalgamations in Victoria.

By 1910 the American investment in British Columbia totalled $65,000,000 and it was to be expected that when America sneezed Victoria would catch cold.

But the coming trouble for Victoria was more deep-rooted. It was not due to the war clouds in Europe. The devastating effects of World War I were no more envisaged in Victoria than in say London or Brussels and indeed Victoria did not suffer too badly if at all. The coming trouble was not due to labour. Labour was causing

144

in British Columbia as in the rest of the world some apprehension. But labour unrest seemed to be directed more at competing imported Chinese and Japanese labour than at the social order. As far back as 1886 a Working Man's Political Association had been formed and had put up candidates in Victoria and Nanaimo, but politically it had made little headway. Disrupting strikes occurred in other parts of the province involving the C.P.R. and the Kootenay mines. The most serious of all was the 1913 strike of Nanaimo miners who seized the town temporarily but were speedily subdued by specially dispatched militia units.

Victoria with its more patriarchal economy was spared these labour upsets. To be a socialist in Victoria was to be a social outcast.

Victoria's fundamental economic troubles were to stem from the rapid growth of cities like Vancouver and Seattle. She was being rapidly overtaken in population as the following figures indicate:

	Victoria	Vancouver	Seattle
1870	7,886	no figures	1,107
1880	5,925	no figures	3,533
1890	16,841	18,829	42,837
1900	20,219	27,198	80,671

One of the first to see where the future lay was David Russell Ker of the Brackman-Ker Milling Co. This company which was to become famous for the quality of its milled products throughout North America started in a modest way with Brackman's grist mill at Shoal Bay, Saanich. David Russell Ker, one of pioneer Robert Ker's four sons (see page 115) became a partner in the firm in 1882 at the age of 20.

In the 1890's the firm built a new mill near the Outer (Rithet's) Wharf at the entrance to Victoria Harbour, processing local and imported cereals. David Russell Ker aroused much criticism among commercial circles when he started a Vancouver branch in 1894. But he was more far-sighted than his contemporaries. Brackman-Ker finished up not as a Victoria organization but with three mills on the Mainland and 14 grain elevators in British Columbia and the prairie provinces.

David unfortunately did not live long enough to see the full results of his foresight. He died in 1923 after a long illness at the early age of 60 and the business and social contacts to be made at "Kershaugh" at the northeast corner of Yates and Fernwood, where he lived with his wife, a daughter of pioneer librarian Henry Heisterman, were sorely missed. Outside "Kershaugh," he built the first boulevard on Yates Street and the fine maples he planted are still there. In his lifetime, besides founding the Ker family fortunes, he headed the Board of Trade, the Agricultural Society and raised the funds for the new Y.M.C.A. building on Blanshard Street

He is also credited, particularly by Senator Harry Barnard, Victoria's mayor at the time, with getting the Empress Hotel built in Victoria. In contrast with Brackman-Ker was the fate of the Albion Iron Works. They were originally founded on Discovery Street by Jos. Spratt in 1861, but by 1890 covered 3½ acres, a whole city block, bordered by Pembroke, Store, Chatham and Government streets and employed 230 men. Directors of the reorganized company registered in 1882 were the well-known Robert Dunsmuir, R. P. Rithet, Robert Ward, J. Trutch and Jos. Spratt. In these works were built the railcars for the E. & N. Railroad, pipes for the Victoria and Vancouver waterworks, engines and boilers for most vessels on Puget Sound and colliery engines. One of the biggest jobs was the repair of H.M.S. *Amphion* at a cost of $150,000.

The Company had a monopoly of stove manufacture in the Pacific Northwest and from its stove showrooms at 515 Pembroke, now a lumber warehouse, most houses in B.C. obtained their stoves. Alas for a great industry. The last remnant of the Albion Iron Works disappeared in 1953 after purchase by Eastern interests. It was stated that wages in Victoria no longer justified manufacture here.

Gone too, swallowed up in amalgamations or transferred to the Mainland, are nearly all the other large concerns of that era. We no longer have M. R. Smith & Co., biscuit manufacturers, who started here in 1859 supplying the Royal Navy with 3,500 loaves a day and whose factory at 120 Niagara Street, James Bay, was a mainstay of employment there in the early 1900's. Gone are J. H. Todd & Son who owned the Beever and Richmond canneries... the largest in the world, also a wholesale grocery, and managed their operations from large Wharf Street offices. So highly thought of was the senior J. H. Todd, who was also a Victoria alderman, that flags were flown at half-mast on his death in 1892.

The sash and door industry meant millions of dollars to Victoria at the turn of the century. The pioneer was probably D. O. Stevens who in 1863 was operating Steam Sash & Door at the corner of Government and Wharf Streets, adjacent to the James Bay bridge.

At the turn of the century the Victoria Planing Mills (J. Muirhead and J. G. Mann) employed 100 men. The Shawnigan Lake Lumber Co. had two acres on Discovery Street between Store and Government Streets, whose manager for 30 years was Victoria resident T. Elford. A reorganized company still occupies the same site today.

Lemon Gonnason occupied an entire block on the waterfront at Orchard and Government Streets for the manufacture of sash, millwork and lumber. This firm finally went out of business in the 1950's when a fire destroyed their plant.*

Jacob Sehl, who came to Victoria in 1858, manufactured furniture at his three-storey brick built factory on Laurel Point. His nearby mansion, where British America Paint now have their plant, was a landmark for ships entering the harbour. Sehl started furniture manufacture in 1879 and in the 1890's was running with associates a two-storey retail store at 66/68 Government Street, called the B.C. Furniture Co. His plate-glass windows were a sensation in Victoria.

The largest mill in Victoria was owned by the Sayward interests. It occupied a two-storey block on Store Street north of and adjacent to the present Capital Iron & Metals. Downtown the Sayward interests built on Douglas Street in 1910 the Sayward Building, said to be Victoria's first multi-storey office block. This block, one of Victoria's finest office structures, is now owned by members of the Ker family.

William P. Sayward was a California "forty-niner" who arrived in 1858 and started his first mill at Shawnigan Lake in 1861 and the Shawnigan Lumber Co. in 1868. Many of the huge stumps

* Ocean Cement now has the site.

147

between new growth in the area are reminders of the Sayward milling operations.

Gone too are the Pendray (Victoria) soapworks started in 1875 at the corner of Humboldt and Douglas Street (opposite the present Humboldt Street liquor store). At one time the works turned out 40,000 pounds of soap a week.

Their "electric soap," 20 bars for $1, was a good seller. They moved their works to Laurel Point about 1900 in keeping with the general trend of industry towards that area. Pendray's soapworks installed Victoria's first telephone from their plant to Jeffrey's store at the corner of Government and Yates Streets. But shortly afterwards on May 15, 1,880 telephones came into use generally and within three weeks the Victoria and Esquimalt Telephone Co. had 50 subscribers. Directors of the Company included Rithet, A. A. Green the banker whose former home is the Art Gallery, E. A. McQuade, of the pioneer ship chandler family and Captain J. D. Warren. R. B. McMicking was president, and the first telephone company office was in Trounce Alley. The increase in telephone subscribers gives a good indication of Victoria's growth.

In 1912 there were 5,110 telephones; in 1922 13,223. The next eight years to the beginning of 1931 showed an increase of only 4,037 telephones bringing the total to 17,270.

The Telephone Company really came into its own in the "retirement city" period ... 1950 to 1970. In 1940, for instance, there were 20,154 telephones, in 1950 34,506, in 1960 63,051 and by 1970 there were 100,544 phones. Illustrating the drift to the suburbs were the figures for Gordon Head — 214 phones in 1940 and 8,360 on January 1, 1970.

In addition to Brackman-Ker, Victoria at the turn of the century had another large cereal firm — Victoria Roller Rice & Flour Mills — who had two buildings, one of four storeys on Store Street. One of them is now used by Capital Iron & Metals. The 1,000-ton ship *Thermopylae* was in constant shuttle service bringing rice from the Orient to the Company's wharf to be milled and re-exported as flour.

Headquarters of the important sealing industry (see page 155) was the Victoria Sealing & Trading Co. on Discovery Street. Captain

William Grant who came to Victoria in 1882 was managing director. In 1912 the offices were at 303 Bay Street and Grant's house was next door.

Grant came from Granville, Cape Breton. He became a skipper, lost his ship in the American civil war, then blockaded the River Plate with three vessels to aid the Argentina government. Later his ship the *Thomas E. Kenney* foundered in the Atlantic and he and his wife and two sons were picked up by a passing schooner.

In addition to Sehl's furniture factory, Victoria had John Weiler's plant. John Weiler started his factory in 1862 on Government Street. In 1879 he built a block at the corner of Fort and Broad (51/55 Fort Street). Five years later he built a factory on Humboldt Street, and in 1891 a four-storey factory of brick next door and at the turn of the century employed 65 men.

His name is commemorated in two downtown office blocks. Other undertakings included six breweries, among them the Silver Spring Brewery started by Frederick Tate in 1898 and Loewen & Erb (Phoenix Brewery) who were turning out 4,000 barrels of beer a year and had the practical monopoly of up-island trade.

The first brewery in Victoria was started in 1858. Loewen & Erb bought it out in 1870. There were in addition shirt and overall manufacturers (T. B. Pearson & Co.), bookbinders, boot and shoe makers, carriage builders, engineers and many shipyards. The most notable shipyard was the British Marine Railway Co. on the eastern shore of Esquimalt Harbour. Wm. Fitzherbert Bullen, founder of the Company, arrived here in 1884 and was with the Albion Iron Works for many years. In 1897 he established a branch also in Vancouver. British Marine turned out four ships for the Canadian Pacific Steamship Co., including the S.S. *Maquinna* and repaired several warships. Wm. Fitzherbert Bullen married Annie Amelia Bushby, daughter of Judge Bushby and granddaughter of Sir James Douglas. He died in 1921, seven years after selling out to Alfred Yarrow, and was widely acclaimed as one of the founders of the Victoria shipbuilding industry. Other shipyards at the turn of the century included the Star, Union, Clyde, Foot & McDouglas, Jones, McIntosh and Robinson yards. If one wonders how they kept busy, official figures for 1891 give the answer. In that year 1,349 vessels (excluding B.C. coastal ships) arrived in Victoria and 920 of them were from overseas.

The centralization in Victoria of government, finance and manufacture, enabled fortunes to be made in the retail and brokerage world. One of the oldest firms still in existence is the Hickman Tye Hardware Co. Mr. T. H. Tye came here from Britain in 1863 and with partners formed Matthews, Richards & Tye. Later he bought out his partners.

The firm did very well out of the Klondike gold rush and the opening up of mining in the interior.

Mines, logging camps, shipping and canneries needed immense quantities of provisions. Along Wharf Street in 1903 were J. H. Todd & Son, and Wilson Bros., wholesale grocers whose building later was on Chatham Street.

Turner Beeton & Co. (wholesale drygoods, Big Horn brand shirts and fire and marine insurance brokers) were at 90 Wharf and also at No. 71 opposite Rithet & Co., general brokers. J. H. Turner of Turner, Beeton and Company was associated with J. H. Todd in the fish canning and general merchandising business, operated with him the Victoria Produce Market and had a four-storey brick building at Government and Yates Streets. Turner was mayor of Victoria from 1879-81. His partner, Beeton, appointed himself British Columbia agent-general in London. There was some controversy about this. Anyway it was a happy combination for Beeton (and later his partner Turner who also became agent-general) were able to channel enquiries about investment in the province and direct people with capital direct to Turner Beeton & Co.

Businessmen of those times considered it quite fair to use public office for private gain. Their reasoning was that they were giving the government something, i.e. their knowledge and expertise . . . and it was only fair they should get something in return.

Also on Wharf Street with warehouses and quays were Rithet & Co. at street numbers 104-6 and 118.

Robert Ward, one of Victoria's most enterprising businessmen, had his offices in the nearby Temple Building which he had built to the design of the well-known architect McClure.

The Temple Building now houses the Liquor Control Board.

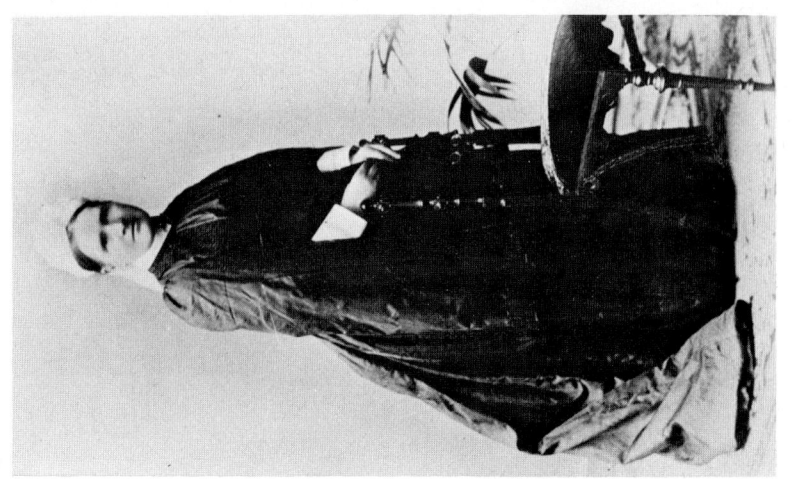

ROBERT DUNSMUIR

MRS. ROBERT DUNSMUIR

CRAIGDARROCH CASTLE
— a promise fulfilled.

SUCCESS, TURN OF CENTURY STYLE
Motorcars, newest prestige symbol,
with horses and carts outside
R. P. Rithet & Co.'s premises on
Wharf Street.

THE DRAWING-ROOM
at "Hollybank," the Rithet home.

RECEPTION IN STYLE

The Hon. E. G. Prior receives at "The Priory."

THE VICTORIA THEATRE
and renovated Driard Hotel (both
now incorporated in Eaton's).

JOSEPH DESPARD PEMBERTON
He laid out the townsite.

THE PUBLICITY-SHY PHILANTHROPIST
Thomas Shanks McPherson.

GONZALES

The former Pemberton home,
situated on the corner of Gonzales
and Rockland.

Ward, a clean-shaven, determined looking Englishman, married a daughter of Mrs. Edward Hammond King (see page 52) and his home "The Laurels" on Rockland Avenue is described on page 109. Ward was broker, insurance agent and dealt in general supplies, import and export. He was also president of the Board of Trade when they opened their new building on Bastion Square and presided at the sumptuous banquet in the Driard Hotel lasting until 4 a.m. which marked its completion. Ward and his family suddenly left Victoria for Britain in the early 1900's, never to return.

Prominent ship chandlers of the time in addition to McQuade's (P. McQuade came here in 1858 from Albany, N.Y.) were E. B. Marvin & Co. Their building was next to McQuade's on Wharf Street (No. 74). Marvin had many adventures getting here. His ship was wrecked in a storm in the Pacific, losing its mast. In one of the gold rushes he canoed alone on the Fraser River from Fort Hope to Quesnel.

Such experiences were by no means uncommon. John Teague, a Cornishman, mayor of Victoria 1894-95 and the architect responsible for the Royal Jubilee and St. Joseph's hospitals and the Oriental Hotel, booked passage from San Francisco to Victoria. He was landed at Whatcom on Puget Sound and had to get here in a "plunger." During the Cariboo gold rush he walked 9½ days on six pannikins of flour. During the last three days he had nothing to eat at all. John Teague eventually became navy storekeeper and his $12,000 home in Esquimalt is now the Admiral's House. Admiral's House saw many gay parties in the 80's and 90's, and became the home of George Phillips, British naval architect stationed here from 1905 to 1917.

Prominent retailers in the early 1900's included Thomas Shotbolt and D. E. Campbell, druggists. Campbell at 66 Fort Street marketed his own specialties ... Campbell's sarsparilla blood purifier, Rose Leaf face powder, Japanese hair tonic.

As though fearing the effect of these revelations on the reader, a trade directory of the time added that he was very popular.

Lawrence and Goodacre had taken over the Queen's Market of the defunct Mayor Harris and with it the navy contract. Other prominent merchants of the time included Nicholles & Renouf, general hardware, 61 Yates; the Victoria Vinegar and Sauce Works run by J. H. Falconer, a Scot; the Victoria Steam Bakery; the Ledingham & Christie Carriage Works at 97 Cormorant and their competitors, the Brayshaw Carriage Factory at 17 Broughton, Brayshaw having come here from New Zealand. Also worth mention are Braden & Stamford, civil engineers, who employed 30 men and put in electric lighting and waterworks in Port Angeles and many other cities.

In the retailing field David Spencer began to expand at the turn of the century. Spencer arrived here from Wales in 1864 and at first went into business with Wm. Denny. In 1891 his store at 65 Government Street was 240 feet long and had a frontage of 66 feet — enormous for those years although only the width of a house lot.

Notable commercial buildings which went up at the time were the Duck Block on Broad Street . . . Simeon Duck, who arrived here in 1859 and died in 1905, was a pioneer blacksmith and carriage builder before he became M.L.A. and Minister of Finance; the Jewell Block and the Wilson-Dalby Block. The Jewell Block, named after Henry Jewell, was where the present Metropolitan Stores and National Trust are at Yates and Douglas.

The opulence of the City Hall today is in great contrast to the skimping on municipal administration customary in the times of our fathers. The City Hall got an addition in 1890 and this followed a rather disgraceful episode when the chairs of the mayor and councillors and office furniture were auctioned off to satisfy a creditor.

Also seized and sold were the corporation seal, a stone crusher, two horses and a wagon and four dump carts . . . representing probably the total fixed assets of the City of Victoria. J. W. Carey, mayor in 1884 when the episode occurred, seems to have been a rather pig-headed man. He was an old-timer, having arrived in 1856 and very self-important. A previous City administration had incurred a debt of $875 with lawyers Drake & Johnson. The new councillors, headed by Carey, approved the signing of a cheque in payment, but Carey refused to sign it. He had some grudge against Drake & Johnson, but what the grudge was records fail to show. The upshot was that the sheriff, acting on the orders of Drake & Johnson, seized the City's assets. A crowd of 700 people attended the auction and a number of leading citizens thought it a dreadful disgrace. The auction had begun when D. W. Higgins, acting for a group of public-spirited merchants, offered the sheriff a cheque in payment of the debt if he would stop the bidding.

The sheriff agreed to this, but meanwhile much of the property had been sold. Mayor Carey, obstinate as usual, refused to accept the unsold City property and refurnished the City Hall with furniture hired from Weilers. The *Colonist* promised he would never get in office again and the next election proved them correct. Rithet succeeded him.

An outstanding building of 1899 was the Exhibition complex and race track at the Willows fairground. Its main roof was 56 feet high surmounted by octagonal towers rising to 100 feet with an open cupola. The open balcony was 75 feet from the ground and afforded a splendid view. The building with its 20,000 square feet of floor space, two staircases to the galleries and its fountains was a justifiable source of pride. Near to it was the best race track in the Pacific Northwest.

The Exhibition Building appears to have replaced that of the B.C. Agricultural Association built in 65 days in 1891.

Before that fairs and exhibitions were staged in the Fair Building at Beacon Hill Park although in the 1860's Victoria's first fair was held in Market Square between Broad and Broughton Streets and followed up with a sumptuous dinner at Ringo's Restaurant.

Also at the turn of the century Victoria got a new Government House. Cary Castle burned down in 1899 and Lieutenant-Governor McInnes lost $3,000 of his personal effects in the blaze. The new Government House built in 1905 lasted until 1957 when the popular Lieutenant-Governor Frank Mackenzie Ross, a former Scot who won the Military Cross in World War I, was burnt out, also with the loss of valuable personal effects. The present building replaced it in 1959.

The first public library, made possible by a Carnegie grant, was opened by the Duke of Connaught in 1891. It stands today at the corner of Yates and Blanshard Streets and architecturally compares favourably with the 1951 addition built on to it.

One of the fruits of Confederation was the construction in the 1890's of a new Post Office.

It superseded the Post Office on the southwest corner of Yates and Government Streets, an area which during the Hudson's Bay Company's regime was occupied by so-called government buildings and later in 1873 was the location of the Adelphi Saloon, the Bank of North America, the *Colonist* and Barnard's Express offices. It was in this Post Office that Noel Shakespeare, Postmaster, used to call out the names of those for whom mail had arrived following the arrival of a ship.

The 1890 building now houses, with additions, the Customs and Excise branch, corner Wharf and Government Streets. The Post Office moved in 1952 to the fine new Federal Building on Government Street at Yates. The inter-city postal service was at the turn of the century considerably better than that of today. House delivery (two deliveries a day) was begun in 1888. Four postmen then covered the whole of Victoria as compared with 158 today. Twice daily deliveries ceased except for downtown in 1954 and Saturday deliveries were cut out in 1969. An exceedingly rare stamp is the $2\frac{1}{2}d$ stamp issued in London in 1859 for use in Vancouver Island and British Columbia.

The early years of the century were notable above all, for the construction of the Empress Hotel, one of the city's greatest assets. The decision to build was a very bold one because when the announcement was made by the Canadian Pacific Railway Co. in 1905 there were already ominous portents for Victoria on the economic front.

One of them was the decline of the great sealing industry, heralded by a sharp drop in sealskin prices in 1897. Sealers' wages were a main source of revenue for hotels, rooming houses, eating houses, saloons and the general retail trade. City ship chandlers fitted out not only Victoria-based sealers, but those from Nova Scotia, Newfoundland and U.S. Pacific ports which chased the seals to Alaska.

Victoria shipyards were building many vessels financed by U.S. capital. But generally speaking the entire sealing industry was Victoria-controlled. Fifty-seven vessels were fitted out here in 1897 and the seal catch eight years earlier was valued at $247,170.

The decline of this cruel industry had many causes. The main cause was the rapacity of the sealers themselves. U.S., Japanese, Russian and Canadians harvested the pelts in such quantities that the market was swamped. At the same time the number of seals began to diminish and the Americans were alarmed at the depredations of Canadian and U.K. sealers.

There is no doubt that vessels operating out of Victoria were inhuman and wasteful in the extreme. Seals could be speared or shot, and shooting was easier. It was estimated that for every shot seal retrieved, two went to the bottom. Also, at sea it was impossible to distinguish the males which were greatly outnumbered by females. It was reckoned that every female killed on her way to the breeding grounds led to the loss of two seals . . . mother and pup.

When the U.S. purchased Alaska from Russia it granted the sealing monopoly to the Alaska Commercial Company. The seal breeding grounds in Alaska and the Pribiloff Islands were as a consequence put off bounds to Canadian vessels. They therefore resorted to open sea or pelagic sealing, killing the seals on their way to and from the breeding grounds. The open waters of the Behring Sea were well beyond the three-mile territorial limit and in these waters Victoria sealers reaped their richest harvests.

The United States government was alarmed by these inroads and declared the whole of the Behring Sea to be territorial waters. They began seizing Victoria and U.K. registered vessels. Some 19 such vessels had been seized by 1890.

Britain protested for herself and Canada against these seizures. An international court rejected the U.S. claims.

But the court at the same time so limited the sealing season, ostensibly in the interests of conservation, that Canadian vessels could not operate profitably in view of the distances between port of departure and the sealing grounds.

The U.S. was ordered to pay Victoria sealing interests $463,454 compensation for seized vessels, which was less than half the amount claimed.

In spite of the fact that Victoria and British vessels were now practically out of the business, seals continued to decline in numbers as Japanese and Russian sealers continued their operations in the

Behring Sea, which was nearer to their home bases. The result was the 1911 Pelagic Sealing Treaty, whereby the U.S., Russia and Japan agreed to limit hunting and turn over a proportion of the proceeds of pelt sales to Canada in return for complete abstention by Canadian vessels from sealing.

But the matter was now of academic interest to Victoria. The industry had been practically bankrupt since 1898 and but for the Klondike gold rush which occurred that year Victoria would have experienced very bad times. The Klondike gold rush obscured the long term effects of the loss of a lucrative industry.

The Klondike gold rush also helped to obscure the fact that the completion of the Esquimalt and Nanaimo railroad in 1886 was not an effective substitute for a trans-Canada railroad terminating in Victoria, illogical though the latter would be from a national point of view. This venture of Robert Dunsmuir and his American associates was not justifying itself. The extraordinarily expensive route through most difficult country and the absence of large populations or resources all mitigated against it. The C.P.R. took it over in 1905 and today there is talk of discontinuing the service altogether.

The Indian summer was coming to a rapid end marked by serious financial crises in the United States between 1900 and 1912 which affected seriously Victoria's mining and industrial interests. They led to many liquidations and amalgamations.

Most serious of all, however, was the accentuating disparity in populations. Victoria's 31,140 inhabitants in 1911 compared with 100,401 in Vancouver and 237,194 in Seattle. Instead of queen, Victoria had become a very minor princess.

Chapter 14

SOCIAL LIFE AND SOCIAL CONSCIENCE

WHILE VICTORIA WAS IN THIS PERIOD of industrial and mercantile decline the elements of its population were changing rapidly.

The city was invaded at the turn of the century and in the next decade by Englishmen, many of them remittance men and many others who were ex-Indian army officers. Invariably they joined a club, that period being the heydey of the men's club from which women were rigidly excluded. A favourite then as today was the Union Club, foremost business and political club of Victoria.

The Union Club is one of Victoria's venerable institutions, its first meeting having been held in 1879 over Van Volkenburgh's butcher shop, now the site of the Poodle Dog Cafe, in premises vacated by the Mining Exchange. The Club moved to premises on Douglas and Courtney Streets opposite the Strathcona Hotel in 1885 and the move was a source of considerable annoyance to the nearby St. Andrew's Presbyterian Church.

Many English members of the Club were great dog lovers and parked their pets outside the Club premises. This led not only to many disputes between members and between dogs as to rightful parking spots, but while their masters were enjoying themselves inside the Club, the dogs gave vent to their boredom by fighting and continuous barking.

Sermons and prayers lost something in solemnity when punctuated by this chorus of tethered canines, but church protests were of no avail. The canine parking problem, like that with cars today, was apparently insoluble.

The dogs also contributed to inter-Club friction because some members got into the habit of feeding their pets with kitchen leftovers and sometimes with food snitched from the dining tables. Occasionally a member would wonder whether his clean plate was a result of efficient washing up or efficient licking.

The Club was also noted for the heavy drinking which accompanied the many political, business and social contacts made there. Drunkenness became too much for some members. Patience was finally exhausted when a member accused of continuous inebriation appeared before the committee in a drunken stupor to answer the charges. An example was made of him and he was expelled.

The Club's reputation was also sullied by dark hints of prostitution. Two "madames," no doubt prompted by traffic density, had their premises near the Club. Mistress Jennie Morris had a brothel at Courtney and Douglas where Woodward's later built a store and which is now an executive block, while Alice Seymour ran a rival establishment facing the Club where the Strathcona Hotel now stands.

It was rumoured but never proven that an underground tunnel enabled discreet access from the Club premises to one of these establishments.

In the easy going ways of those times, the Club was continuously in debt. Many members seemed to regard it as a philanthropic institution and postponed settlement of their accounts indefinitely. There were also complaints on a semi-permanent basis of the food, stench, flies and, in winter, chilly rooms. Cooks were hired and fired like film extras in efforts to satisfy complainants.

The club did not remain immune from the real estate fever which swept Victoria from 1905 onwards, reaching its climax in 1914. It acquired from Senator MacDonald for the fancy price of $50,000 in 1908 the old Badminton Club at the junction of Gordon and Humboldt Streets, demolished it and erected its present premises on the site. This accentuated rather than improved its financial predicament. The Club was later sued by the City for non-payment of taxes and members were shocked to read in the *Vancouver Daily Province* that the land on which their club stood had been sold to a third party. Attempts were made from time to time to pare expenditure by amalgamation with the Pacific Club; but they came to nothing. But somehow the Club survived. The list of its presidents, the first being Sir Matthew Baillie Begbie, is a Victoria commercial Who's Who. Every premier, not excluding Premier W. A. C. Bennett, has been a member; it has been racked by political controversy and many Cabinets have been made and unmade in the Union Club.

The heavy drinking at the Union Club induced a number of English gentlemen to sponsor a club where they could enjoy tea and crumpets without the shoulder-slappings, snores and hiccups of effusive topers. They took over the Chancery Chambers on Broad Street built by lawyers for offices and founded the British Public Schools Club in the mid-twenties "to assist any public schoolboy except financially." It didn't pay its way and the reason for this was quickly divined by perspicacious George (the Joker) John Patton, a generous, club-footed ex-Esquimalt tavern keeper. He obtained a liquor licence for the premises, took the Club over in 1936, broadened the membership base and left in 1950, having apparently made a good thing of it. The Club still operates and its name, savouring of class distinction and a bygone world, brings faint smiles to the lips of those who pass the premises.

Rival of the Union Club was the now defunct Pacific Club whose last premises were the B.C. Cement Building at the northeast corner of Wharf and Fort Streets.

The B.C. Cement Building was erected by Californian Tommy Golden who made money in the Barkerville gold rush, went broke with the "Brown Jug" and later became insane.

When built in 1863 the building cost $3,000 (about $30,000 today). In 1865 Tommy Golden put a saloon downstairs and rented the upstairs to the Oddfellows. It was later owned by Donald Fraser, correspondent of *The Times* of London, a position which carried almost diplomatic prestige. In the economically dark days of 1870 a fire broke out in the building. It was insured for $5,500 and the enquiry revealed that the fire occurred after the Chinese caretaker had been told to "take the night off." The puzzling verdict was that "the fire was neither accidental nor on purpose."

The Pacific Club was the successor of the Victoria Club formed in 1885 with premises at Fort and Broad Streets (the *Victoria Times* building). The Victoria became the Pacific Club in 1894 and was the first tenant of the Pemberton (later the Yarrow) Building on Fort Street. The Pacific Club directors, imbued with unwarranted optimism, decided in 1964 to move to larger premises and took over the whole of the B.C. Cement Building. Within a year the Club was bankrupt and many members lost heavily as a result.

The Pacific Club was more of a sporting club than the Union and was noted for its excellent billiard players.

Downtown Victoria in 1910 was becoming generally somnolent, seedy and rundown. The situation wasn't improved by a disastrous fire in 1910. The fire left the entire frontage on Government Street empty and debris-infested for decades. It demolished all except one building in the area bounded by Trounce Alley, Government, Fort and Broad Streets, including the Five Sisters Block at the northeast corner of Fort and Government Streets, site of the Hudson's Bay Company bakery in Victoria's earliest years.

Only the *Times* building survived.

David Spencer, the city's most go-ahead retailer, seized the opportunity to buy up the partly damaged Driard Hotel and Victoria Theatre for $370,000 giving Spencer's (now Eaton's) frontage on Douglas, View and Broad Streets. A result of the fire was to bring View Street through to Government Street. *The Times* of London reported that the blaze had destroyed "half of the City of Victoria" and damage was estimated at $1,000,000. Firemen were handicapped because water pressure decreased as the blaze increased.

Victoria has had several large blazes and they all occurred during periods of economic depression, a fact which must have seemed significant to the insurance companies. And firefighting was not very efficient. In the earlier decades firefighters were hampered not only by bad roads and poor water supplies, but also by rivalry. Victoria's first firefighters were members of the Union Hook & Ladder Company formed in 1860 whose motto was "We strive to serve" and who had their headquarters within the Hudson's Bay Company enclosure at Fort and Bastion Streets. They made use of the fire engine bought by James Douglas for $1,600 in 1858.

But two rival companies speedily came into being, namely the Deluge Company chiefly composed of Britishers and the Tiger Company, chiefly Americans. National pride and firefighting zeal often vented themselves in the sabotaging of the efforts of the rivals, a favourite method being to disconnect the rivals' hoses.

Firemen were also greatly hampered by sightseers who considered fires free entertainment and by the fact that fire engines had to be manhandled when the going was too rough for horses. As to the state of the roads, Fire Chief Thomas Watson was thrown from his fast horse and buggy and sustained cuts and burns even before he reached a fire in 1907. When a venerable old lady like Mrs. Blinkhorn could be pitched from her carriage at Fort and Government Streets and lose her only remaining tooth it does not speak well for road maintenance.

Victoria's early firemen were enthusiastic and bibulous. Their bull horns, mouthpiece removed and stopped with a cork, were often used for mammoth libations at social functions and on May Day which, for some unexplained reason, became in Victoria "Firefighters' Day." Sometimes the Firefighters' Day parade would be led by a band from the Royal Navy. Volunteer firemen in their gorgeous uniforms . . . scarlet shirts trimmed with black velvet, silver helmets, shining belts and black pants outshone President Nixon's Capitol guards of today.

Generally the firemen assembled first outside the homes of the mayor, aldermen, lieutenant-governor and other benefactors to receive verbal and liquid homage to their good citizenship. Then they paraded downtown. Most saloons along Government Street felt custom-bound to help quench the seemingly insatiable thirst of the volunteers, some even installing barrels on the sidewalk. Many saloon keepers must have thought eventually that fires would be less expensive than fire brigades because there were 70 thirsty firefighters in the Deluge Company, 65 in the Tiger Company and another 60 in the Hook & Ladder crew and they drank not only on Firefighters' Day but during the rehearsals for several days prior to it.

The post of fireman, not surprisingly, was much coveted. There was no pay . . . a member even paid to join . . . but the liquid and other fringe benefits such as periodic benefit concerts were substantial.

For decades after Victoria's incorporation, the City turned down repeated efforts by firemen to have the honorary honour converted into a taxpayer-supported effort, but finally in 1886 City Council agreed to a part-paid, part-volunteer fire service. The force consisted of 26 men — three firemen at $16.25 per month, three at $60 a month and 18 at $14 per month. Firemen were expected to be on duty 24 hours a day, seven days a week with time off for meals.

Double shifts were not instituted until 1918. Even allowing for the greater value of money in those days, firemen today are considerably better off. They averaged in 1970 $679 a month plus fringe benefits; fire protection exclusive of the municipalities was costing nearly $1,000,000 per annum. But at the same time firefighting methods and firemen's training and equipment have greatly improved and become more costly. We no longer have whole areas burnt out like the fire on July 3, 1907, which destroyed everything within the perimeter of Government, Chatham, Store and Herald Streets and rendered 250 families homeless.

The blaze consumed the disused Albion Boiler Works, the Indian Mission, an old soapworks, St. John's schoolroom, the Calvary Baptist Church with its 150-foot steeple and the brothels on Chatham Street. Hundreds of people had to stack their belongings in Central Park until they could find substitute accommodation. Damage was estimated at $75,000 and the firefighters said they would have been more successful if the three-hose steam pumper had been used, but unfortunately it had settled through the floorboards of its sheds through neglect.

Only three years before, in 1904, another fire devastated the industrial area. It started in the Albion foundry and burned out a large part of the Government-Pembroke-Blanshard Street zone. Another big blaze was that of 1883 which burnt out Cormorant Street with a loss of $50,000. Pandora Avenue from Government to Store Street was then called Cormorant Street.

The institution of a paid firefighting service coincided with the realization that the population was outgrowing many other long-established voluntary services. A case in point was that of hospitals.

Victoria's hospital history began in the 1850's when the Reverend E. Cridge of the Victoria District Church opened his back door one morning to find a sick man had been left in his garden. It was a parishioner's way of reminding the minister that he was expected to minister to the physical as well as spirtual well-being of his flock. The minister took care of the patient in the parsonage and immediately asked Royal Governor James Douglas for money to build a hospital. Douglas made a modest grant and in 1858 Victoria's first hospital came into being. It was a pioneer effort . . . a mere cottage at Yates and Broad Streets given by Mrs. Thomas Blinkhorn whose husband managed the farm at Metchosin. Patients speedily outgrew the capacity of the cottage and were very soon transferred to a small building in the Songhees Reserve with Dr. Trimble as supervisor.

It was named the Royal Hospital and catered only to male patients. Four years later, in 1864, the cornerstone was laid of a female infirmary on Pandora Hill beyond Cook Street, well away from the nearest dwellings. The building was due again to the indefatigable Mrs. Blinkhorn, Mrs. Harris, wife of the first mayor, the Rev. E. Cridge and Mrs. R. Woods. Mrs. Woods, it may be noted as a matter of interest, was the wife of Richard Woods, registrar of V.I., who built one of the first houses in the Gorge. It was called "Garbally," which is Welsh for "The House on the Hill," and was situated on a rise on Garbally Road.

A matron was appointed for the Female Infirmary whose salary varied with the number of patients. In 1869 the Royal Hospital was amalgamated with the Female Infirmary and in 1890 the Royal Jubilee Hospital was opened on its present site at the junction of Cadboro Bay Road and Richmond Avenue by H.R.H. the Duke of Connaught.

It was very much smaller than the present complex, had its own farm and kitchen gardens and was expected to manage on a very stringent budget. The Royal Jubilee cost $55,000 and had 50 ordinary and 50 paying patients. First directors were John Davies, J. Stuart Yates, James Fell, E. A. McQuade, Alex Wilson, Wm. H. Chudley, Mr. Justice Crease, Wm. C. Ward, C. E. Redfern, Charles Hayward and Thos. R. Smith. The Jubilee, when built, was away from everything. There were only five dwellings between what is now the Oak Bay Junction and the hospital. Beyond the hospital to Cadboro Bay was mostly farm and waste land.

An isolation ward was put in in 1891 as a result of the smallpox epidemic of that year. Victoria was no stranger to smallpox. At Holland Point, named after George Holland, a passenger on the S.S. *Beaver* in 1836, there is a granite memorial commemorating a smallpox victim of 1872.

The quarantine station in those days was the nearby disused Nias farmhouse. But the 1891 outbreak was the most serious Victoria had encountered. The first victim was M. W. Waitt, father-in-law of the late Herbert Kent, who, it was alleged, contracted it in Vancouver. Victoria was panic stricken. All who could afford it made tracks for Seattle and San Francisco. The less privileged fled their homes and lived in tents outside the city. Infected houses had to be marked with yellow flags. Many homes were empty for years.

The Royal Jubilee Isolation Hospital was in the vicinity of the present D.V.A. hospital, but in 1893 a contract was let for the erection of a City isolation hospital replacing the temporary building. One of the buildings of the City isolation hospital is now used for storing garden equipment. With the growth of population new wards were added ... the Strathcona (1904), Children's (1906), T. B. Ward, now the Medical Pavilion, in 1910, nurses' residence (1909), maternity (1916) and new nurses' home (1930).

In 1940 the central block was erected and soon afterwards a psychiatric unit added. The new wing was built in 1961 after the razing of the old administration building and the Royal and west wings opened in 1963. The latest addition in 1970 has been a $625,500 laboratory, a great advance on the bare room with sink and tap which was the laboratory of 1887.

The beginnings of St. Joseph's were equally modest. The first St. Joseph's cost $13,800 and was opened in 1876. It resulted from the combined efforts of Dr. Helmcken, Bishop Demers and the highly respected Sister Mary Providence. In 1888 St. Joseph's expanded into a second building which cost $33,000. A third $38,500 addition followed in 1893 and in 1900 the School of Nursing was inaugurated, followed by the Humboldt Street annex (1908) and the

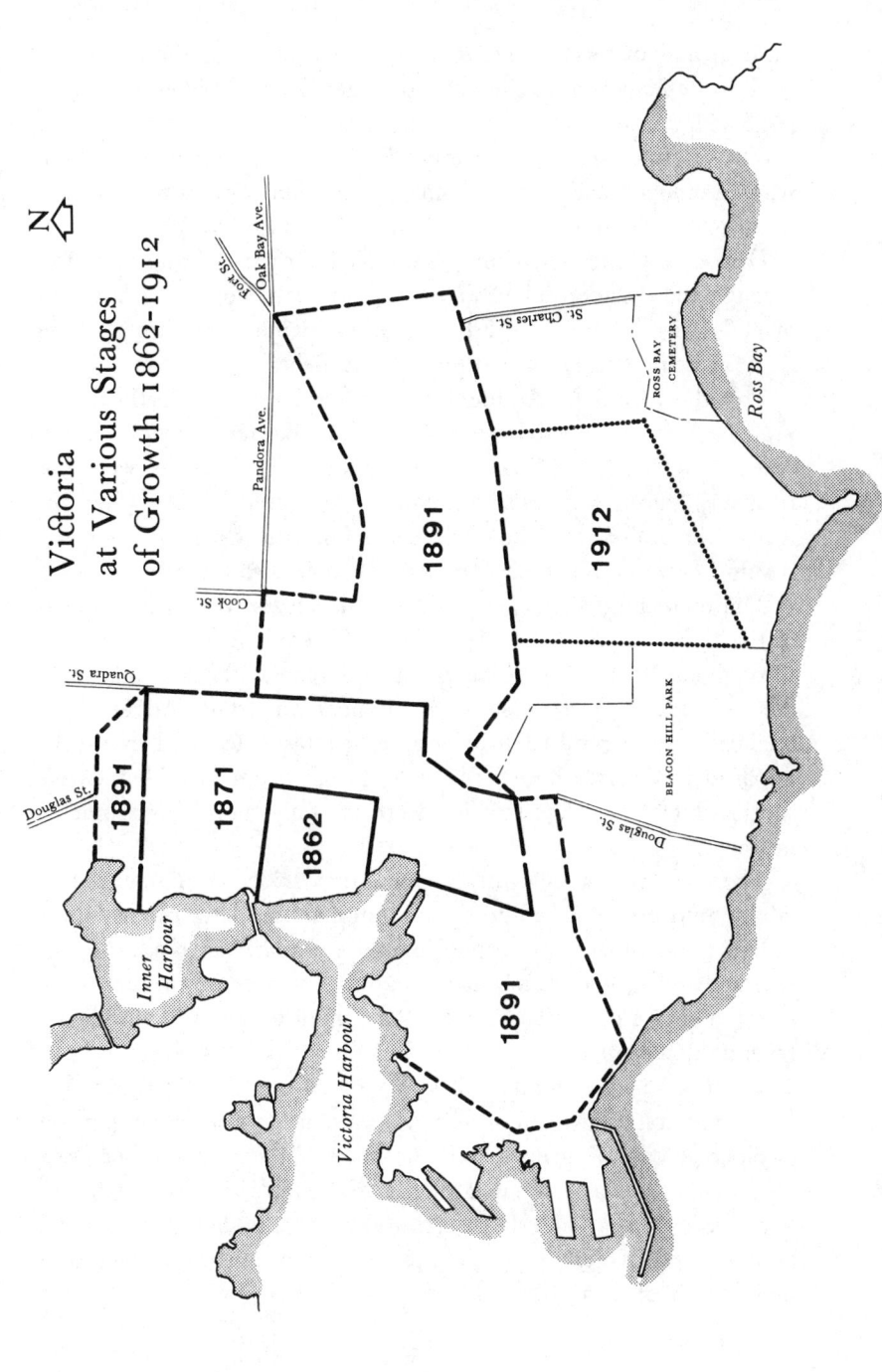

Victoria
at Various Stages
of Growth 1862-1912

N

1891

1912

1871

1862

1891

1891

Fort St.

Oak Bay Ave.

St. Charles St.

ROSS BAY
CEMETERY

Ross Bay

Pandora Ave.

Cook St.

Quadra St.

Douglas St.

Inner
Harbour

Victoria Harbour

BEACON HILL PARK

Douglas St.

surgical and maternity unit in 1927. The annex for the treatment of T.B. patients was in the old world garden of Vernon Villa (see page 50).

The original wing of the Gorge Road hospital, opened in 1887, was "Ashnola," the former home of Captain and Mrs. Northing Snowden, a daughter of Mr. and Mrs. R. Dunsmuir.

Hospital administration problems have not changed much through the decades. The modest "no patients, no pay" institution of 1864 was described by Edward Mallandaine, a publisher at the time, as being "sadly overburdened with debt."

Providing funds and amenities for hospitals became the social urge for Victoria's public-spirited women. Bazaars, sewing circles, tea parties, home cooking sales and other staged events were the mainstay for the hospitals' recurring urgent needs. From 1890 onwards, the annual Hospital Ball was a function which every citizen wishing to retain his fellows' esteem felt bound to attend.

The financial problems of Victoria's hospitals were compounded in the 1960's by three factors . . . two of them common to hospitals throughout North America and one peculiar to the city. The two common factors were costs of equipment and staff. Advances in medical science resulted in ever more sophisticated and expensive apparatus. Victoria had come a long way from Dr. Helmcken's surgical kit of the 1850's which were the only surgical instruments in town.

The organization of nursing and other skilled and semi-skilled labour into unions immune to the anti-combine laws resulted in a considerable increase in hospital employees' material standards, but was also reflected in much increased costs of treating the sick. The rising costs were a great concern to administrators and provincial revenue departments.

The third factor compounding Victoria's hospital problems . . . a factor not common to most cities . . . was the increasing proportion of older people living here, large numbers of them from other parts of Canada. It was estimated in the mid-1960's that one in every five citizens was an elderly person and that their claims on medical facilities were largely responsible for the acute shortage of beds and increasingly onerous hospital costs.

Another factor was the increasing incidence and cost of treating mental illness. In Victoria's earliest years mental patients were housed in a building on Laurel Point at the entrance to the Inner Harbour.

This, like the location of the Old Men's Home suggestively overlooking Ross Bay Cemetery was a most inhuman arrangement. Ships entering the Inner Harbour used to fire a cannon to salute the Hudson's Bay Company fort which was deafeningly acknowledged by the gun from the bastion. According to the supervisor, patients not already up the wall used to climb the wall when the building shook to the gunfire. Superintendent of the women was Flora Ross from San Juan. In San Juan she was married to Paul K. Hubbs who, according to Dr. Helmcken was "an ignorant hoodlum who thought that an American should be boastful and a bully." His ill treatment of Flora Ross made her leave him.

Patients were few in number because only those who were dangerous were confined. Today's trend is for mental illnesses which our forefathers had to get over "as best they could" to be treated as seriously as physical illness. An outcome of this trend is the Eric Martin Psychiatric Institute, named after a former provincial Minister of Health and opened in 1970, adjacent to the Royal Jubilee Hospital. It cost $7,275,000 and can handle 232 in- and many out-patients.

The growth of the social conscience in the 1890's is also evidenced by the resuscitation of the Y.M.C.A. and the founding of a Y.W.C.A.

It is startling to note how little was done in Victoria for women in distress although as a busy seaport, where seamen contracted marital and other obligations with the lightheartedness typical of that roving profession, many women must have needed help. It was not until 1897 that a committee of the Church of Our Lord succeeded in starting in Victoria a branch of the Young Women's Christian Association. The beginnings were modest . . . lunches were prepared for needy women and girls in the homes of the volunteers and served at the Central School. The Y.W.C.A. then rented rooms on Government Street, then in a flat over the store of Thomas Shotbolt, the druggist, on Johnson Street, then in the old Protestant

Orphans' Home on Rae (now Courtney Street). But these proved to be more than teething troubles. Owing to lack of funds and interest the branch had to close down completely.

In 1906 the Y.W.C.A. started up again in an upstairs room at the corner of Fort and Government Streets, moved to the old Denny house on Pandora, then went back to the Courtney Street annex. In fact the moves of the Y.W.C.A. would have kept a moving firm in business if there had been much in the way of furniture. Subsequently the Y.W.C.A. was housed in a cottage at Quadra and Caledonia Streets, in a building at Douglas and Humboldt, in the old Union Club building on Douglas, in two flats in the Stobart (now Standard Furniture) Building and at 920 Blanshard. The branch's perambulations came to an end with the building of the present combined men's and women's branches opposite the Law Courts towards the cost of which philanthropist McPherson contributed $200,000. Now largely an activity centre, the Y.W.C.A. incurred the gratitude of many citizens normally outside its scope for its good work in the depression years and in entertaining troops during the two World Wars.

The Y.M.C.A. also had its teething troubles, but they seem to have been less severe than those of its sister organization. The Y.M.C.A. made an early start in 1859 with an organizational meeting under the chairmanship of Colonel R. C. Moody, Royal Engineers. It was apparently dormant in the depression years which followed the early gold rushes, but in 1875 Thomas Trounce became president and regular meetings began to be held in the Fardon Building and the Omineca Building on Yates Street before it again faded out. The Y.M.C.A. was next heard of in 1884 when a meeting was held in the Humboldt Hall with the object of "forming" a Y.M.C.A. Among the most active sponsors were B. W. Pearse, Surveyor-General, Walter Walker of the fuel firm and John Meston whose name is perpetuated in an auto-body firm downtown today. Reading rooms were rented successively at Adler's store on Fort Street, Government and Bastion Streets and in Spencer's Arcade building. The latter was burnt out in 1887 and with it the Y.M.C.A.

In 1889 the Y.M.C.A. was in the upper storey of a building at the northwest corner of Broad and Trounce Alley, which now houses the Christian Science Reading Room and was there intermittently for 20 years. At times, like its female counterpart, it went completely out of business and on one occasion the furniture was sold to pay the rent. Its revival really began in 1903 when it was put on a firm basis in the same Fort and Broad Street premises and then thanks to the efforts of David Russell Ker and others, the cornerstone of the substantial building at Blanshard (recently demolished) was laid in 1910. The Y.M.C.A. benefitted from the McPherson donation (see page 224) for the erection of the new combined Y.W.C.A.-Y.M.C.A. centre in 1965. The new building cost $1,300,000 most of which was raised through the efforts of former Victoria mayor Hugh Stephen.

The Salvation Army which arrived here in 1887 got a rather hostile reception at first. The "Soldiers of the Cross" were greeted with remarks such as "Why don't you get a job?" "When are you going to do some real work?"

But when the lassies arrived with their tambourines, public relations improved considerably. The girls were much admired, although whether it was solely due to their tambourine performances is problematical. The first Salvation Army men had a barracks in an abandoned skating rink on Fort Street, between Douglas and Blanshard Streets. They then rented the old Methodist Church, Broad and Pandora, the old Y.M.C.A. quarters at Broad and Trounce Alley, then premises on Cormorant Street popularly known as the "Salvation Ark." In 1947 the new Citadel on Pandora Avenue was built and in 1963 a new Harbour Light building at 516 Yates.

The Salvation Army gained great popularity during World War I, not only because of its Three Services Centre for troops in the Duck Building on Broad Street, but also because it shared the hardships and hazards of life at the front with its troop canteens. It is Victoria's most enduring charitable institution.

In this period the Protestant Orphanage at 2691 Cook Street also came into being, helped by a $30,000 gift from city philanthropist George Taylor. The centre is now known as the Bishop Cridge Centre for the Family.

With increasing concern for general welfare arising out of the growing prosperity of the 1890's came also increasing concern for education.

Royal Governor James Douglas did not differ from the Scots of the homeland in the importance he attached to education. He wrote to London in 1853: "We are now erecting a schoolhouse and expect it will be ready at the end of summer." The school — Craigflower School — was not in fact opened until 1854 and is considered to be Canada's first school west of the Great Lakes. In 1859 a school was built in Victoria itself. It was the Colonial School, a whitewashed log house on what is now the playground of the Central School. The master and his family occupied two-thirds of the building. A cosmopolitan gathering of Scottish, Jewish, German, French and English children were taught in the remaining third.

A healthy walk through swampland and forest to reach the school from Blanshard Street where the city ended, enabled the boys to withstand better the caning which played an important role in education. The Royal Governor sent his son James to the Colonial School.

Almost at the same time Miss Langford, an unmarried sister of Captain Edward Edwards Langford, started at Colwood a Young Ladies' Academy.

First principal of the Craigflower Boys' School was Charles Clark and first teacher was Charles Bailey, a young man who taught children on the ship which brought him here.

These and all other schools of those years were private schools in that the parents were expected to pay a fee for their children. The fee at the Colonial School was $5 a year or about $50 today. But many other private schools sprang up and received no help from the colonial administration.

J. Silversmith opened in 1859 a "select day school" for boys and girls from five years up. This was followed by Mrs. Petitbeau's boarding and day school for young ladies on Fort Street. The school does not appear to have lasted long because Mrs. Petitbeau was on the staff of the Collegiate School soon afterwards.

The zeal for imparting education in those early decades may have been due not so much to desire to further learning as the desire of the promoters to get a living. Mrs. Wilson Brown, for instance, announced in 1860 the opening of Church Bank House "Academy for young ladies where instruction will be given in English and useful and ornamental parts of tuition, the use of globes, etc."

In the same year St. Luke's opened the Cedar Hill School as a church school. Almost simultaneously Mrs. Cridge, wife of the Dean of Christ Church, started her school for girls on Kane Street which ran from Douglas to Quadra Streets. One wonders with a permanent population of only 600 how so many schools could function. When Mr. J. Jessop opened what he called the Central School in 1863, it was one too many. This school was on Fort Street between Douglas and Blanshard, and had accommodation, according to its opening announcement, for 150 pupils. It appears to have closed down for lack of support in 1866 and the present Central School, it is believed, borrowed the name.

In 1866 the lush gold rush years were over and Victoria was feeling the economic pinch. This was not evident at the beginning of 1863 which is perhaps the reason why Victoria got its first "free school" in Esquimalt. But by 1867 the position of this school was so poor that the Victoria Amateur Dramatic Club staged a benefit performance to raise funds for the teacher's salary. There appears also to have been a "free school" in Saanich because in 1864 the School Board resigned after making a final payment of $94.81 to Mrs. Butler who had taught a full year without pay.

School building in the next few years was practically non-existent with a static and sometimes declining population. In 1869 a South Saanich School was opened at White and Vyaness Roads, consisting of one room. In 1872 all Victoria public schools were closed for lack of funds.

A great leap forward educationally was the construction in 1876 of the Central School. This was a substantial brick building, in great contrast to the one-room efforts of earlier years which the principal was expected to heat and clean up out of his or her modest salary. Indeed the Central School may have been an over optimistic effort because in 1879 a $3 poll tax on all grown men was imposed to meet school costs which were running at $42.70 per pupil in the city. At that nearly half of the children played "hookey." Out of 720 registered pupils in 1883 the daily average attendance was 410.

An economy campaign resulted by 1887 in the costs per pupil being reduced to $19.48. The Central School served Victoria well and was not demolished until 1954, the solidity of its construction causing many headaches to the demolition contractors.

An entirely "New World" feature of Victoria was that its economy progressed so fitfully. In good years optimism abounded and school building went ahead. These were succeeded by bad years when everything came to a halt. In 1887 Victoria's economy was taking a periodic turn for the better. For the first time residents began to feel that they had a permanent settlement and not a temporary lodgement in the wilderness. This was reflected in school building. Among schools which went up were the Kingston Street or James Bay Ward School in 1883, which served until 1955 and the Spring Ridge School, or Fourth Ward School at Chambers and Gladstone Streets, whose headmistress used to buy boots for needy pupils and send the bill to the parents. Spring Ridge School had 55 pupils and the teacher principal, Miss L. Horton, was paid $70 a month. The school was closed in 1943. By 1894 Victoria's school population was 2,500 and the North Ward school was erected, followed the next year with the South Park School on Michigan Street. The North Ward School site was sold to the Victoria Press in 1969 and the school demolished. The Strawberry Vale School went up in 1893.

But Victoria was still delightfully rural. The first Esquimalt High School was a three-room building and looked like a large house. The principal, C. K. Kelly, related at the opening of the new Esquimalt High School that "people used to come to the door and try and sell me crabs and things. It was hard to convince them that I was just a poorly paid teacher."

The cornerstone was laid in 1901 of the Victoria High School which later became the Girls' Central and is now the Central Junior High at Fernwood and Yates Streets. It was built at a cost of $436,000, opened with a staff of six and remained Victoria High until 1914, when the present High School opened. H. L. Smith was with Vic-High for 41 years, for 21 of them as headmaster.

Other schools built in the early 1900's included the Victoria West Elementary (1908), Cloverdale (1917), Sir James Douglas, Quadra, Oaklands, Margaret Jenkins (1915), George Jay, Burnside, Beacon Hill, Bank Street, Oak Bay High (1929), Willows (1920), Monterey (1914), Mount Douglas High (1931) and Mountview (1932).

Victoria College was started in 1903 and was for two years affiliated with McGill University. It consisted of a two-room wooden building on the Victoria High School grounds. The prestige-conscious teachers used to put on cap and gown when going from the High School to the College. Victoria College ceased to exist in 1915 when the University of British Columbia opened, but started up again in 1920 at Craigdarroch Castle. It was then moved to the Normal School (junction Richmond and Lansdowne) and is now part of the University of Victoria.

Universal education as we know it today was not in the mid-nineteenth century highly desired. Those who wanted to educate their children preferred private to "free schools."

Popular with pioneer parents was the Collegiate School, a church school founded by Bishop Hills in 1861. The premises it used on Church Way were those of a former congregational church (probably negro) which had quarrelled with Christ Church over alleged colour discrimination. Fees were $8.00 a year. Robert Ker's sons used to paddle from their "Ferniehirst" home in the Gorge to the Collegiate School, tying up their canoes where the Crystal Garden now stands. The Collegiate School was burned out in 1882 and the School moved to premises near St. Paul's in Esquimalt. In 1912 it moved into the central of three buildings on Rockland Avenue at the former Ward home, "The Laurels." The other two buildings were occupied by St. George's and University schools. The Collegiate School closed down in 1929.

Mount St. Angela, 923 Burdett Street, was in 1866 the home of the Girls' Collegiate School. The building was then known as Angela College after its benefactress Mrs. Angela Burdett-Coutts. Angela College became a hotel in 1908 and in 1959 was sold to the Sisters of St. Ann, who renamed it Mount St. Angela.

In the 1890's Victoria's most prestigious private school was Corrig

College. It had 80-feet frontage on Niagara Street and 60 feet on Douglas Street facing Beacon Hill Park. The site is now marked by Corrig Manor Apartment house. Corrig College could accommodate 125 boys and pupils included many Americans who wanted their sons to be brought up the British way. Corrig College advertised extensively. The promotion-conscious administrators claimed unblushingly that Beacon Hill Park was part of the school "grounds."

Corrig College enjoyed the patronage of lieutenant-governors and premiers and was the alternative to sending boys to England to be educated as was the fashion among the well-to-do at the turn of the century. Corrig College was the Victoria equivalent of Eton or Harrow, and J. W. Church, M.A., and his assistants were reckoned the cream of instructors. The school was claimed by its principal to be the oldest of its kind in the province. It dated back to the 1860's when it was conducted by archdeacons Woods and Hogg in the old archdeaconry. It then moved to Ross Bay under the supervision of C. J. Brenton and afterwards to Vancouver Street. Many of the province's most prominent men of the 1900's were pupils of Corrig College.

Sports played a large role in the curriculum, cricket and soccer matches with Royal Navy teams being prestige events. With changing traditions this College also came to an end.

But Victoria also had a large Catholic community and the Roman Catholics were first in the field with education. Father Lamfritt, a French Oblate priest, was teaching here soon after he arrived in 1849.

By 1865 the Roman Catholics had a girls' school on View Street and a boys' school on Humboldt Street where St. Andrew's Roman Catholic Church was also located. But pride of the Roman Catholic educational efforts was St. Louis College, founded in 1864, which was attended by many future notable citizens. But the same fate befell St. Louis College as Corrig College, the Collegiate School and other traditional institutions. St. Louis College closed in 1968 and its principal, Brother John Clarkson, left Victoria to return to Ireland. Bishop de Roo commented that closure was "part of the widespread upheaval affecting society through North America and around the world." The building is now used by the newly formed St. Andrews Elementary School.

Public education came in for criticism during the 1929-35 depression years. There were no jobs for young people and critics alleged that they received too much academic and too little practical education.

It is interesting to note that the same criticisms were being voiced in 1970 which saw many thousands of young people without work. The effect of the 1929-35 depression was to decrease the number of students and Victoria had fewer school pupils in 1939 than it had 10 years earlier. In the same period the number of teachers fell off by 15%.

In post-World War II years the surge in school population was responsible for a tremendous schools-building programme. Among the new schools erected was the S. J. Willis High School. This school, built in 1959, is on the site of the old Hillside Jail, which had 66 cells measuring 6 feet by 9 feet; many criminals were buried in quicklime beneath the exercise yard. The youngest prisoner was a boy of 10 and the oldest was Danny Creigan, aged 90. The City records were at one time stored in a tunnel beneath the jail. The jail burned down in 1912.

The post-World War II building programme led to a burdensome increase in educational costs. The municipalities lost control of their schools with the formation of the Greater Victoria School Board. By 1970 educational costs of $22,959,239, 68% of which represented teachers' salaries, were absorbing more than half of most municipal budgets as compared with 27% for the City of Victoria in 1939. The largest short term increase in educational costs was in the period 1960 to 1970. The cost per pupil rose from $346.17 in 1960 to $617 per pupil in 1969. In January 1969 the Greater Victoria School Board controlled 32,155 pupils, 1,240 teachers, 402 other employees plus 289 instructors in the adult education programme. Greater Victoria schools numbered 57.

But for Victoria's private schools the public schools would be coping with many more pupils and the cost to the taxpayer would have been proportionately greater.

St. Margaret's School for Girls was first located at 913 Cook

Street. It was founded by the Fenwick sisters who drowned with 19 other people when the S.S. *Iroquois* foundered on Easter Day 1911 — a tragic end to an Easter excursion. In the following year a new building was erected at Fort and Fern Streets, replaced in 1970 by the new school in 30 acres near Blenkinsop Lake.

Norfolk House School for Girls was founded by Miss Julia McDermott and Miss Dora Atkins in 1913. For many years before 1931 the school was in the cul-de-sac formed by Granite and Amphion Streets. J. D. Pemberton's "Gonzales" home was used as dormitory until it was demolished in 1952 and afterwards a home at 620 St. Charles became the dormitory. Today the School is a day school located in 5½ acres at 801 Bank Street which was part of the Pemberton estate, the principal being Miss A. W. Scott.

St. Michael's on St. Patricks Street was the first private preparatory school in Oak Bay. It was conducted by Mr. K. C. Symons at the corner of Roslyn and Windsor Roads. The School is now managed by the founder's sons, K. W. and E. J. Symons.

Glenlyon, also a boys' preparatory school, was begun in 1913 in a rented house on St. David Street, and moved to its present location, the former Rattenbury home in 1935. St. Christopher's, a mixed school at Currie Road and Newport Avenue in Oak Bay started in a flat over a grocery store on Newport Avenue.

But Victoria's most famous private school is University School on Mount Tolmie, the oldest boys' residential school in the province. It was founded in 1906 as a result of the amalgamation of three boys' schools . . . one on Belcher Avenue, one at the corner of Oak Bay Avenue and Richmond (now Richmond Court Apartments), and the third on Rockland Avenue. Principals of these schools were J. C. Barnacle, the Reverend W. W. Bolton of St. Paul's, Esquimalt and Captain R. Harvey of Vancouver's Queen's School. In 1908 the School moved to its present many-acred grounds. Many of Victoria's most respected citizens attended University School and know its vice-principal W. R. G. Wenman and the late J. J. Timmis, headmaster from 1948-1970.

The School has produced some outstanding Canadians, among them L. Dana Wilgress, Col. C. C. I. Merritt, V.C., and Sir Charles Loewen, Adjutant-General of the British forces in World War II.

Chapter 15

TOURISM — THE NEW INDUSTRY

THE GROWING IMPORTANCE OF VANCOUVER and consequent decline in Victoria's importance was causing concern in the early 1900's to businessmen and others for whom Victoria was the one and only "Queen City."

Alternative sources of revenue had to be found if Victoria was to survive. As a result of their efforts the Empress Hotel came into being and laid firmly the foundations of what has been Victoria's most important industry ever since, namely tourism. Not that Victoria was until then a stranger to tourists. The city had always been a mecca for ranchers, politicians, businessmen and all who wanted a few weeks amid naturally beautiful and man-made civilized environment to offset the roughness of nature in the raw. But travel had become easier. Other attractive communities were springing up this side of San Francisco. Victoria had to have something special.

Like everything undertaken by the Canadian Pacific Railway Co., the Empress Hotel was conceived on a grand scale with a view to permanence. The magic transformation of the waterfront caused by the construction of the hotel is inconceivable to Victorians of today. The site now graced by the hotel and its extensive gardens was an odoriferous slough and garbage dump for the city. The slough was filled with silt dredged from the harbour to create footage on Government, Humboldt and Bellevue streets. The James Bay wooden bridge was removed and the Causeway built.

Instigators of the $1,600,000 project were Harry Barnard and

David Russell Ker. So keen was Barnard on the project that he became a city councillor and then mayor in order to further it. The hotel was opened in 1908. The north and south wings were added in 1911 and 1928 respectively and whole complex cost $13,000,000. Harry Barnard, son of Francis Barnard, inherited his father's business acumen.

Francis Barnard, it will be recalled, founded Barnard's Express services which monopolized freight and passenger services during the Cariboo gold rush when freight on a ton of merchandise from Victoria to the Cariboo was $825. His son Harry was the typical businessman-politician of the era. He owned property all over town and his brother-in-law, J. Mara, was the most powerful man on the Mainland, politically and financially. He was interested in mines and initiated transport companies in Kamloops and Revelstoke. Mara lived with his brother-in-law on part of the "Duvals" estate on Rockland Avenue, his address being 750 Pemberton and the Mara home and coachhouse still stand at the rear of "Duvals," both converted into apartments. Harry Barnard's friends included the Rithets, Dunsmuirs, Pooleys, Wards, Trutches, Kers, Macdonalds (senator), Creases, Turners and others whose connections embraced everyone worth knowing from San Francisco to Victoria and Vancouver to Ottawa and London.

Harry Barnard induced the C.P.R. directors to see the potentialities of Victoria as a tourist resort and transit stay. Canadian Pacific S.S. Co. were already running a regular service from Vancouver to Victoria, later at the instigation of Captain Troup to embrace (in 1928) the triangle run — Vancouver, Victoria, Seattle. The Empress liners were also bringing Victoria to the attention of world travellers.

Before C.P.S. became interested, the American-owned Canadian Pacific Navigation Co. operated a service daily to Vancouver. C.P.S. bought them out and so improved the traffic that they aroused the envy of American interests. In the early 1900's the Americans tried to "muscle in" on the service and at one time C.P.S. reduced the return fare to Seattle to 25 cents. Passengers got the added thrill of competing steamers racing to reach port first, but the Canadian Pacific steamships always won.

178

The Empress Hotel was incomparably superior to any hotel in Victoria, well provided though the city was with first class hotels. With its additions it had 570 rooms, most with bathroom. No money was spared to give the interior decor an atmosphere of dignified luxury. It was a bad day for many of the city's hotels when the Empress started operating. They were already feeling the pinch of slackening demand, the Klondike gold rush having been their last bonanza. The collapse of the sealing industry and departure of captains and crews deprived them of a most profitable off-season income.

Competition between hotels for business was so intense that C. G. Harrison, who was operating the Driard under some difficulty following a fire, complained bitterly that touts told disembarking visitors the Driard "had been burned out." Harrison said he didn't mind fair competition but this was a bit too much.

The Empress quickly monopolized most of the prestige trade. To stay at the Empress put the hallmark on respectability. Its banqueting rooms and assembly conveniences made it the social centre of Victoria, and its managers were as well known as the lieutenant-governor himself. Through the years managers were Stewart Gordon, Col. B. H. Humble, H. Jackson, A. Benaglia, T. Coles, W. Winpross, B. F. Quail, J. E. Evans, H. J. Wilson, the famous Kirk Hodges, manager for 21 years, a flower enthusiast who started the Empress nurseries and initiator of the Empress Golf Week, Thomas Chester, Cyril Chapman, Les Parkinson, O.B.E. and now Louis Finamore.

Equally well known to most people was maitre d'hotel Zanichelli, who joined the staff in 1927.

Dancing being one of the favourite local recreations . . . more so in past years than today . . . Billy Tickle and his Saturday night "Toe-Tappers" were an institution. Billy Tickle from Cumberland played for 32½ years at The Empress and gave his last performance in 1960.

Famous guests who have stayed at The Empress include the Prince of Wales (1919), Winston Churchill, Lord Jellicoe, King George VI and Queen Elizabeth and the King and Queen of Siam with 56 attendants and 556 pieces of baggage.

Princess Margaret was a guest before her marriage. Her visit was marred by an unpleasant incident. An ambitious but rather brash girl reporter from Toronto pretended to have been accepted in the Princess's intimate circle. She wrote a report on how "she got together with the girls, they kicked off their shoes and discussed make-up and the Princess put a call through to her boy friend Group Captain Peter Townsend." There had been much talk in London of the Princess's friendship with the Group Captain, who was a divorced man, and the Princess was understandably annoyed at the report.

She issued an angry official denial of the whole story and the reporter was denied the privileges accorded to other press representatives.

The Duke of Edinburgh has addressed several gatherings in The Empress, the last being the joint meeting of Canadian Clubs in 1969.

As an institution which many cities envied but could not emulate, The Empress came in for good-humoured sarcasm in other cities. The afternoon tea and crumpets in the lounge where staid dowagers allegedly listened to Billy Tickle's chamber music was the subject of many witticisms. The most famous was the cartoon by the *Vancouver Sun*'s Norris when one afternoon a shot was fired through the ceiling of the lounge. Shooter was an amateur hold-up man who after robbing a room guest was making his escape. The dignified imperturbability of the dowagers and retired colonels as they go on sipping their tea while incredibly eyeing the hole in the ceiling and the masked gunman was one of Norris's funniest cartoons.

After World War II the Empress Hotel and the Canadian Pacific steamships suffered from militant trade unionism. Strikes made the ferry service to Vancouver unprofitable. It was abandoned, but the C.P.R. triangle service in summer was maintained. With the service to Vancouver the night boat, on which it was freely rumoured cabins were shared more often by unmarried than married couples, also was withdrawn. The Empress also suffered from new concepts of travel, including the use of trailers, and a different class of travelling public.

NORRIS CARTOON of wild west gunman's hold-up of Victoria's Empress Hotel, reconstructed from all available data and eyewitness accounts... *courtesy Vancouver Sun*

A motor hotel was established and in 1968 it was frenquently announced that the Empress would close down. But instead the owners decided on a $3,000,000 modernization programme. Increased parking facilities cut down the area of the beautiful lawns and gardens. There was talk that even what remained of them might be used for a convention centre. Whatever the future the Empress Hotel has been a boon to Victoria architecturally and economically. Since its inception more than 700,000 guests have stayed there.

An even greater attraction from a numerical standpoint have been the Butchart Gardens. The 25 acres of carefully tended gardens attract more visitors each year and in 1969 were visited by about 250,000 people.

The gardens were the happy inspiration of Mrs. Jennie Butchart, whose husband Robert was a pioneer of the Saanich Inlet cement industry. His first limestone crushing mill was on the site of the Gardens, about 15 miles from Victoria and he quarried limestone in the immediate vicinity. Mrs. Butchart decided to create beauty in the despoiled quarrying area. Mr. and Mrs. Butchart at the turn of the century brought in hundreds of tons of soil and many thousands of plants. The plants, protected from winds by the towering quarry walls, thrived in their new location. Mrs. Butchart called her gardens "Benvenuto" and before Victoria grew to its present size the gardens were open free of charge to any visitor and available for charitable functions. The King and Queen of Siam and Eleanor Roosevelt were entertained at "Benvenuto."

Robert Butchart died in 1943 and his widow in 1950. Meanwhile, however, Ian Ross, a grandson, had taken charge. He still further embellished the gardens, increasing their area, installing illuminations and a beautiful fountain. But with increasing labour costs the gardens in the post-war years did not find it easy going. In 1939 they were offered to the Provincial Government for the nominal sum of $1, but the government refused the offer.

The gardens are Victoria's most genuine and outstanding tourist attraction besides being a great amenity for local residents. Especially in the 1960's they stood in pleasant contrast to the numerous, sometimes phoney attractions created to exploit the tourist. Still almost hidden among the trees at one end of the gardens can be seen the smokestacks of the mill to which Butchart Gardens owe their origin.

Another innovation pleasing to tourists and residents was first seen in 1913. In that year cluster lights replaced the old lamp standards. Hanging flower baskets were added soon afterwards and gave the city a pleasingly unique atmosphere.

The cluster lights were not popular at first and were known as Morley's Folly after A. J. Morley, the mayor of 1913.

The Empress Hotel, the Butchart Gardens and the fine homes and gardens of the well-to-do began to change radically the character of the City. Gone was the drive of the 1890's. The energetic businessmen-politicians began to fade into the background. In their place a new type of resident emerged ... more interested in the amenities of living than making a living. The Empress Hotel got its quota of permanent guests, some of them well-heeled elderly ladies who could obtain there all the benefits of comfortable living without the headaches of household management.

Remittance men in knickerbockers and brogues found Victoria a place where their pound sterling went a long way, Canada being a tax free country.

Here they could enjoy at a fraction of the cost in England their golf, racing, club and social life and watch cricket, croquet and other spectator sports like racing, hockey and soccer.

Many Americans began to live here, some of them U.S. citizens of British descent who still had a nostalgic affection for the Royal Navy and the Union Jack.

Victoria's old-established successful families like the descendants of the Barnards, Dunsmuirs and Rithets now had time and money to spare. Some of them like Jack Rithet, son of the famous R. P. Rithet, speedily spent a lot of what their fathers had made. Jack, who lived at "Gisburn" on Rockland Avenue, lost $30,000 on a baseball park he promoted on land where the Crystal Garden now stands.

The Willows race track was a great attraction. There in 1913 was held a 60-day race meet which was not surpassed until the British Empire Games came to Vancouver in 1954. The Sidney

"Sandown" races in the 1960's were very small in comparison with the former events at the Willows course. The Willows was also famous for its athletics.

The 1913 meet featured many athletes from San Francisco, Portland, Seattle, Vancouver, New Westminster and Medicine Hat who had taken part in the Olympic Games in Stockholm the year before. The U.S. cruiser *West Virginia* was in port for the occasion. Hal Beasley was Victoria's hero of the series, winning the 100-yard dash in 9.8 seconds, equalling the then world record. Rugby was another popular sport. New Zealand's "All Blacks" met the pick of Victoria at Oak Bay (now Windsor) Park in 1914. Among the Victoria team were the Gillespie brothers, Grant brothers, Carew Martin and a fleet young three-quarter, Peter Ogden. A heavy tackle grounded Ogden and he died on the way to hospital.

Lacrosse also attracted large crowds. Vancouver promoter Con Jones sponsored a team with headquarters at Oak Bay Park. Among amateurs who turned pro to play with the club were Byron Johnson (later premier), Joe Dakers and "Cotton" Brynjolfson.

The year 1909 saw the opening of the Victoria Lawn Bowling Club at Beacon Hill Park, its first president being W. Oliphant (after whom the street is named). The club produced in 1911 its first singles champion in R. E. Dunn, who later became president.

The Victoria Hunt Club staged capital runs in Colwood and Cadboro Bay. The James Bay Athletic Association, formed in 1881 primarily as a rowing club, had its boathouse at the foot of Menzies Street. Cricket was popular both as a spectator and participatory sport. The Maple Leaves, Junior Columbians and Royal Navy teams played regularly at Beacon Hill and fans were fond of recalling that the first cricket club in Victoria, the Pioneer Cricket Club, was formed in 1858 with Thomas (later mayor) Harris as president.

In 1911 Victoria got its first introduction to what has since become a local passion . . . hockey.

The first artificial ice rink in Canada was built on Epworth Street and Cadboro Bay Road, now the site of Cranmore Court Apartment. Builder was a Nelson lumber magnate, Joseph Patrick, who with his two hockey-playing sons, Lester and Frank, decided to popularize the sport here. They spent $10,000 on the six lots and

$110,000 on an arena which could accommodate 4,200 spectators. Their faith was justified. More than 1,000 skaters, some of whom had never skated before, turned up on opening day, Christmas Day 1911.

Until the Arena was destroyed by fire in 1929 it saw many great events, the greatest of which was the Stanley Cup final between the Montreal Canadiens and Lester Patrick's Cougars. In four games the Cougars triumphed. It was the only time the Stanley Cup had been won by a Vancouver Island team. At this Arena was played the first professional hockey game west of Toronto and the first professional hockey game ever played on artificial ice — on January 2, 1912.

Contestants were the Victoria Aristocrats and New Westminster Royals. Hon. T. W. Paterson, Lieutenant-Governor, faced off the puck. The Aristocrats lost 8-3.

Before the season ended arrangements had been made for the first attempt to inaugurate a world series for hockey, similar to that in the United States for baseball. Lester Patrick brought an all-star team from the East to play the All-Stars from the Coast League. The Coast All-Stars won the series. The next year, when the Aristocrats won the Coast League title, Quebec, the eastern champions, came here for the playoffs.

By 1914 this competition had advanced to the stage where the Stanley Cup was put up for competition between the Western and Eastern champions. The Aristocrats again being coast champions went to Toronto and played and lost in the first world series. It may be noted that while Joseph Patrick could claim to have pioneered professional ice-skating, where roller skating is concerned the Indians were 50 years ahead.

In the 1860's a syndicate of Indians started a roller-skating rink on the site of the present E. & N. Station. They built the roller track in the middle of a large "store" they erected. This store, according to contemporary reports, was the scene of "extraordinary carousals by day and orgies by night."

After the burning down of the Arena in 1929 Barney Olson, who later bought the Strathcona Hotel, came on the scene. During the Second World War he converted the Horse Show Building at the old Willows Fair Grounds into an Arena and the greatest amateur hockey ever seen in the West was played there with Army, Navy and Air Force teams.

Victoria's increasing appetite for sport resulted in 1893 in the formation of the Victoria Yacht Club (now R.V.Y.C.) with G. A. McTavish as its first commodore and first moorings at the foot of Kingston Street.

The Yacht Club started with 100 members compared with nearly 900 today, and at one time had moorings at No. 12 Wharf Street near the James Bay Rowing Club. It moved to its present location in the Uplands in 1912, the site being that of a former slaughter house.

Proliferating sporting activities towards the end of the nineteenth and beginning of the twentieth centuries evidenced that Victoria had emerged from the hand-to-mouth economy of the pioneers. There was the Baseball Club with its home field in the Oak Bay Park in the 1890's and which featured Hal Chase as one of the greatest first basemen of all time. Baseball made headway in spite of the cynicism of English-orientated sporting fans who considered it an effeminate game. One of the local boys was Bernie Schwengers who could play any position and was a terrific hitter. He later became Canadian singles tennis champion and member of the Canadian Davis Cup team.

Oak Bay Park also had the honour of staging the 1913 Lady-smith-Nanaimo soccer final. Oak Bay was chosen because the fans were too partisan to permit of play in either Ladysmith or Nanaimo.

Golf in Victoria began as early as 1887 with the nine-hole course of the United Services Club at Macaulay Point and the Victoria Golf Club came into play in 1893.

The turn of the century saw the advent of the motor car. It was a hobby for the rich and sporting fraternity. Most people had to be content with bicycle, tramcar, cab or horseback. The first auto here belonged to Dr. E. C. Hart who covered five miles from his home on Cadboro Bay Road to Macaulay Point in 17 minutes in 1903. The city's second car is believed to be that of A. E. Todd — a steam auto purchased from the White Sewing Machine Co. of Cleveland. David Russell Ker (of Brackman-Ker) got a French

Tonihan in 1903 and in 1904 a Rambler. Reason for the purchase of the Rambler was that the Tonihan wouldn't go.

By 1905 the car-owning fraternity had 17 members.

Among them were A. E. Todd, Dr. Hart, Captain Troup (of C.P. Steamships), R. P. Butchart, David Boscowitz, David Ker, T. B. Brayshaw (Brayshaw's carriage works) and Thomas Plimley, who operated a bicycle shop. R. P. Butchart paid $4,500 (at today's equivalents about $30,000) for his "Thomas Flyer" in 1906. It was reported to be capable of the "fantastic" speed of 40 m.p.h. and the *Colonist*, announcing its arrival added that Seppell & Troup, the Victoria Garage, "are putting it in running order." Lumberman J. A. Sayward had a 12 h.p. Franklin with polished brass mountings . . . a luxury which caused admirers to gape. Most of these men were the charter members of the Victoria Automobile Club, now incorporated in the B.C.A.A. and Canadian A.A.

In 1905 David Russell Ker and Captain Troup shipped their cars to Cobble Hill (the Patricia Bay highway was not built until 1912), motored to Nanaimo where they picked up friends from Vancouver and continued on to Comox.

A year later the Victoria Garage Co. imported for tally-ho (excursion) purposes a car to seat 25 people.

Beach Drive then as now was the favourite local excursion for motorists, but the surface of the Drive was very different. It was narrow, sandy and potholed so motorists probably did not find the 6 m.p.h. city speed limit too onerous.

Victoria's oldest road transport company, C. & C. Transportation Services started up in 1900. Owners were Cameron and Caldwell (C and C); many years later the concern was bought by Rawlings and Rhodes, both of whom were killed on a flight over Nitinat Lake in 1960. After brief ownership by the Nordal family, C. & C. became part of Vancouver Island Coach Lines in 1969.

But Victoria had a great deal to offer besides outdoor activities for residents of modest means. Many of the city's newer residents came from the Orient where they had been accustomed to domestic servants. The Chinese here enabled them to maintain their living standards at only slight additional cost.

To maintain such standards in England on their retirement income would have been most difficult. At the same time they could enjoy educated society among people of British descent whose views on Empire coincided very much with their own. Their wives could afford to have their own dressmakers. The cost of living was moderate, there were many good family hotels like the Roccabella at Humboldt and Blanshard where one could stay for a month or a year amidst pleasant surroundings. Rents were low. A good house and lot in the Rock Bay area could be bought for $875.

Indeed for such people Victoria, in spite of or perhaps because of the fact that it lacked the aggressiveness of larger cities was a very pleasant place in which to live.

Chapter 16

THE GREAT LAND BOOM

IN THE SUMMER OF 1912 a strang malady assumed epidemic proportions in Victoria. It attacked the poor and the rich, the educated and the uneducated. The virus was spread by top-hatted, loudly-dressed young men, whose Pierce-Arrow, Peerless and Packard automobiles, the newest symbols of opulence, were parked outside clubs like the Union, Pacific, the Camosun in the Central Building and outside real estate offices all over town. They injected the germ of desire into thousands of people who until then had been more or less content with their modest stations in life.

What attacked Victoria was the biggest wave of land speculation in its history.

The importuning of pedestrians by these salesmen who portrayed with more enthusiasm than regard for truth the fortunes to be made by buying land was backgrounded by the hammering of carpenters, the shouts of carters with their heavily laden drays and the tumble of falling masonry as old buildings gave way to new.

Working people pledged their salaries and wages. Many thrifty elderly people invested their life savings. Craftsmen, labourers, civil servants, merchants, bank clerks . . . all classes of citizens saw the promise of El Dorado and were prepared to back financially their illusions. Many of the realtors themselves were infected by the speculative enthusiasm and invested (and lost) heavily. Fortunes were made by the few who sold out in time. But for many hundreds of ordinary citizens, who supplemented modest incomes with garden produce and home-made preserves, the speculation was a disaster. The quick fortunes were not realized. Victoria did not become overnight a city of 250,000 people as the optimists forecast. What gave rise to the madness?

It was a province-wide phenomenon. Prince George was to be the Chicago of the North, Prince Rupert the Liverpool of the Pacific and Victoria the "first and last port" on the Pacific coast.

Victoria's optimism was based partly on the fact that the Panama Canal was nearly completed. When on completion the Royal Mail in 1913 announced a regular monthly service via the Canal to Victoria it seemed to herald the beginning of a new era in sea transportation.

But the speculative boom was mostly caused by railroads. Railroads had a fascination for our grandparents incomprehensible in this later automotive and air travel age. Ordinary people who had been confined to areas within walking or a tramcar ride of their homes found their travel horizons extended to an unimaginable degree. They could explore in comfort hitherto inaccessible regions ... forests, lakes, meadows and mountains. New worlds were opened up. A day's excursion, the limits of which in pre-railroad days, were the racetrack at Willows Park, or a trip to Macaulay Point would be extended to Sidney or any other part of the Saanich Peninsula.

The plodding horse was to be replaced with mechanically-hauled, smooth-running carriages. Exposure to wind and weather would belong to the past. The revelation hit people like a bombshell. This marvellous invention would enable populations to multiply and the countryside to be covered with homes and factories. Many hitherto inaccessible natural resources would be brought into world markets.

The impact of railroads on the ordinary citizen was far greater than that made by the discovery of the Americas by Columbus. Railroads affected the lives not of the minority of seafarers, traders and world-travellers, but of everybody in their vicinity, from cottager to millionaire. Small wonder that they were regarded as the road to the millenium. One had only to think of what they had achieved for Britain, then the greatest industrial power in the world.

Land sale promoters produced charts which showed railroads lacing the province like a spider's web. The environs of Victoria including Deep Cove and Sidney were portrayed as future vast dormitories for commuters. The C.P.R. trans-Canada railroad and E. & N. Railway were already in being. The Grand Trunk Pacific was being extended from Edmonton to Prince Rupert. The Pacific Great Eastern had been given a charter and financial guarantees, and around Victoria no fewer than three railroads were planned, or perhaps one should say "promoted," additional to the E. & N. Railway.

The first was the well-known "Cordwood Limited" from Victoria to Sidney. It affords an illuminating example of the intertwining of business and politics so characteristic of the period. Directors when the Company was incorporated on April 23, 1892, were Robert Irving, whose "Gisburn" residence on Rockland Avenue was a showplace of the time; Julius Brethour, a powerful North Saanich farmer-politician and his brother Henry.

There was a four-year delay in getting the railroad into service while efforts were made to sell the operation to the C.P.R., but nothing came of them.

In the meantime a fourth figure had arrived on the scene. He was J. White, a Toronto politician, temporarily out of office, who had much experience of behind the scenes negotiations. He came to Victoria as representative of the Toronto & B.C. Lumber Co., which was desirous of obtaining concessions in the province and thought White would be useful to them. He was introduced to the Brethours, a company was formed and a lumber mill built in Sidney. The mill stood in several acres of land, covering the entire waterfront and was leased by the Brethours at a rent of 10 cents an acre per annum. The mill was awarded the contract for supplying the railroad with ties and was put in charge of White's nephew. When the railroad was finally built the nephew become Sidney agent and Samuel Brethour Victoria agent.

A year after formation of the V. & S. Railroad Company in 1892 control passed to a consortium consisting of the Great Northern Railway, A. W. Guthrie, a U.S. financier, and T. W. Paterson, a public works contractor who later became Liberal member for

North Saanich and lieutenant-governor of the province. The Great Northern Railway issued bonds for $300,000 to finance construction and by some extraordinary behind the scenes moves the City of Victoria and the Provincial Government were induced to guarantee the 5% interest on the bonds. They continued to pay this interest until 1913 when "Cordwood Limited" went into receivership.

The railway never made any money, but Samuel Brethour and T. W. Paterson obtained what was said to have been a most profitable contract for supplying the railroad with cordwood.

First public run of the Victoria & Sidney (V. & S.) railroad was on April 5, 1896. The service was received rapturously. The 16½-mile run took 30 minutes, but as time went on punctuality became of ever less account. It was understandably popular with passengers who did not have to foot the bill personally for its deficits. At weekends the carriages bulged with trippers. It was a leisurely railroad . . . two trains a day, frequent unscheduled stops to deliver messages and parcels . . . sometimes to enable passengers to gather mushrooms or wild flowers. Other unscheduled stops were due to mechanical difficulties such as the piston parting company with the cylinder and flying into the bush, or failure to made a gradient. It was always interesting to speculate how many tries the engine would make to conquer the gradient at Royal Oak. The route was from the station on Blanshard Street, where the entrance to the Hudson's Bay Company parking area now is, via Royal Oak, Beaver and Elk Lakes, Keating and Saanichton to the Sidney waterfront.

It helped to convert the Saanich Peninsula from an area of farm and logging operations to partly residential territory. The railroad ceased operation in 1922.

The V. & S. railroad, as mentioned earlier, went into receivership in 1913. In the same year the second Peninsula railway was started, namely the B.C. Electric Company's inter-urban line to Deep Cove. It ran from Douglas Street, via Burnside Road, Tillicum, Strawberry Vale, Wilkinson Road, West Saanich Road and Tod Inlet to Deep Cove, the terminus being approximately at the site of the present Deep Cove Chalet.

The inter-urban made its last run on October 31, 1924 and the track was lifted the next year. The advent of the automobile was partly responsible for its demise.

But realtors did well out of both railroads. Their large advertisements extolling the Saanich Peninsula and forecasting a densely-populated future filled the newspapers. It was said that every lot alongside the tracks of the V. & S. and Inter-urban railroads was sold before the rails were laid.

In spite of the failure of these two railroads yet another Saanich Peninsula railroad was built. The Canadian National Railways began in 1917 a 15½-mile extension of their line from Victoria to Patricia Bay and Sidney, with freight connection from Sidney by the S.S. *Canora* to Vancouver, abandoning the extension after severe losses 18 years later.

As a result of railroads and tramways, mooted and operating, houses were in the early 1900's going up everywhere, not only in Sidney but in Esquimalt, Saanich and in Oak Bay which had been previously a reserve for the summer homes of the better-to-do. The Greater Victoria muncipalities were incorporated in these years, Esquimalt in 1912, Oak Bay and Saanich in 1906. The banks were equally optimistic about Victoria's future. The evidence of general growth was there for everyone to see. In the period 1890 to 1914 — mostly after 1900 — new buildings transformed the downtown area.

The still standing granite-faced Bank of Montreal building was erected in 1897 at 1200 Government Street, on the site of the former house of Mayor Harris. Other buildings of the period included the Sayward Block, the Union Bank (now Royal Trust) Building on Government Street, the Central Building on View Street, the Metropole Hotel, the Belmont Building, the Pither & Leiser Building (1904) which now houses the Recreation Department of the Provincial Government and the Bank of Toronto and Campbell buildings. In 1911 the Stobart and Pease Building was erected on Yates Street. It was acquired by the Standard Furniture Co. in 1959, while almost next door to it the Dominion Hotel put on a new wing. The Jones Building on Fort Street was also built in 1911.

More reassuring than any other building was the construction in

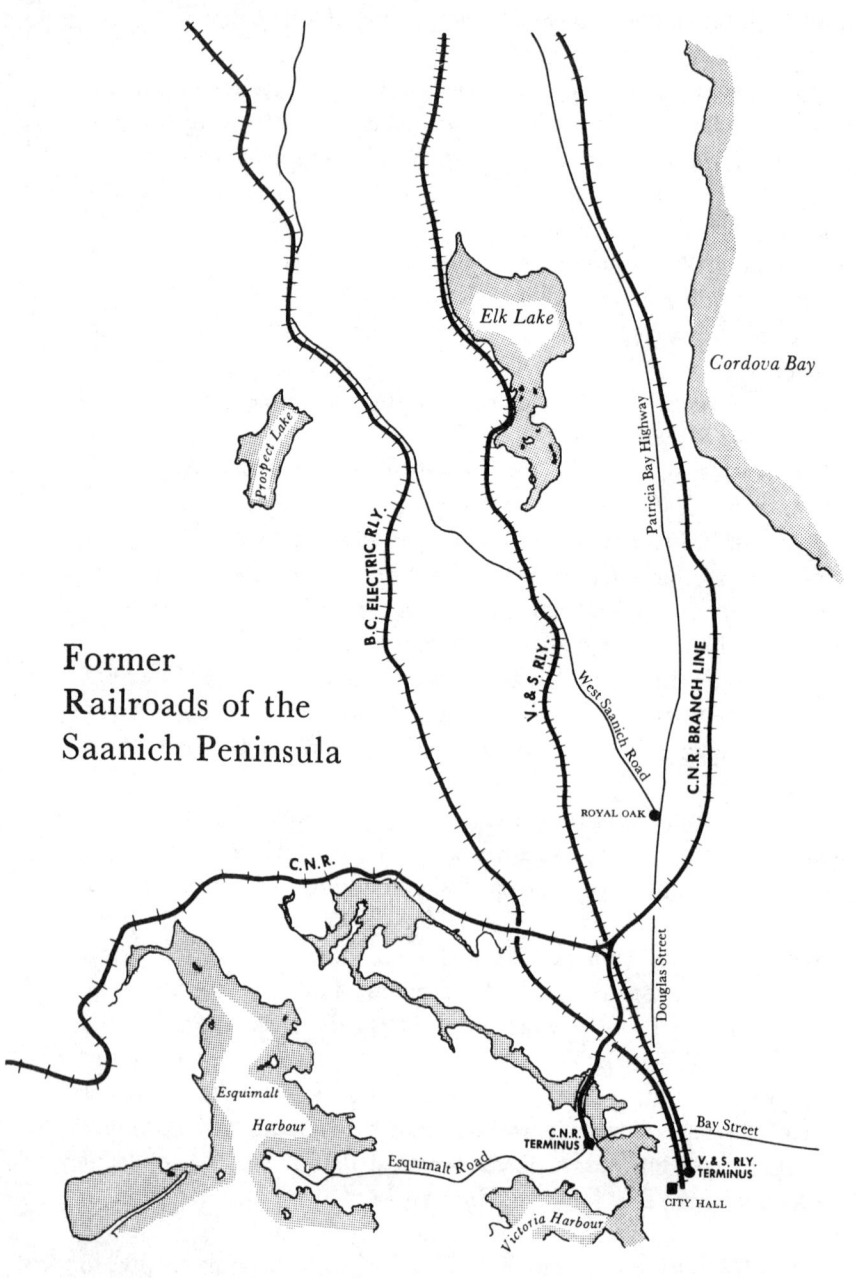

Former
Railroads of the
Saanich Peninsula

Elk Lake

Cordova Bay

Prospect Lake

B.C. ELECTRIC RLY.

V. & S. RLY.

West Saanich Road

Patricia Bay Highway

C.N.R. BRANCH LINE

ROYAL OAK

C.N.R.

Douglas Street

Esquimalt
Harbour

Esquimalt Road

C.N.R.
TERMINUS

Bay Street

V. & S. RLY.
TERMINUS

CITY HALL

Victoria Harbour

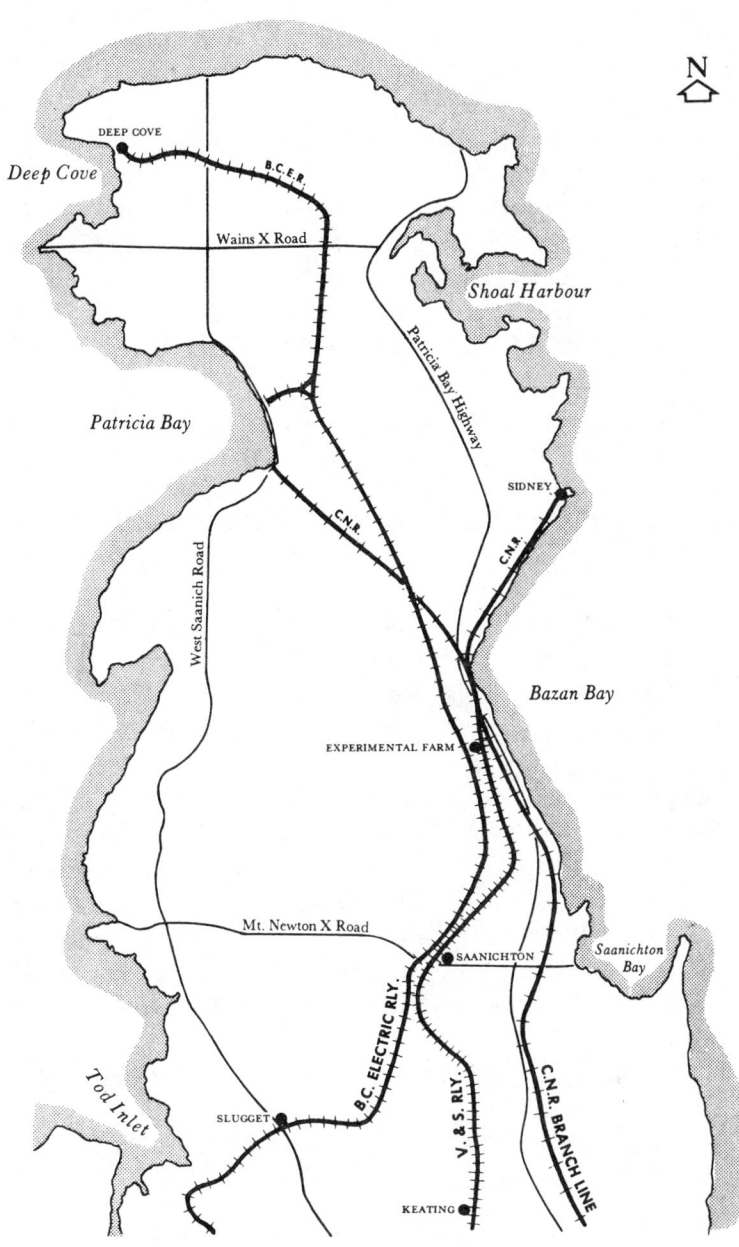

N

DEEP COVE

Deep Cove

B.C.E.R.

Wains X Road

Shoal Harbour

Patricia Bay Highway

Patricia Bay

SIDNEY

C.N.R.

C.N.R.

West Saanich Road

Bazan Bay

EXPERIMENTAL FARM

Mt. Newton X Road

SAANICHTON

Saanichton Bay

Tod Inlet

B.C. ELECTRIC RLY.

V. & S. RLY.

C.N.R. BRANCH LINE

SLUGGET

KEATING

1913 by the Hudson's Bay Company of their department store on Douglas Street on the site of St. John's "Iron" Church. If this great Company, founders of Victoria, had such confidence, who was the small speculator to have doubts?

The prominent citizens who attended the gala opening of the Royal Theatre in 1913 seemed to embody the stability which arises from tradition and well-founded optimism. They included Mr. and Mrs. J. Matson of the *Colonist* publishing family, Mr. and Mrs. Henry Croft, Mr. and Mrs. Hickman Tye, James and Mrs. Dunsmuir, Mr. and Mrs. R. Elliott, Hon. and Mrs. Wm. Templeton, Dr. and Mrs. M. Robertson, Hon. and Mrs. D. M. Eberts, Hon. W. and Mrs. Bowser, Hon. W. R. and Mrs. Ross, Mr. and Mrs. Gavin Burns, Mr. and Mrs. Charles Lugrin, Simon Leiser, president of the Board of Trade, A. E. Todd, Andrew Wright, agent for the developers of the Uplands estate, and Fred Pemberton.

The proscenium arch which they so admired at the inauguration of the Theatre is still the finest example of alabaster work in Victoria and an enduring tribute to the city's craftsmen of those days.

Both the Parliament Building and the Empress Hotel had by 1913 put on additional wings.

Hatley Park (Royal Roads), Craigdarroch Castle, "Burleith" and scores of substantial homes on Rockland Avenue and on Lampson Street testified to the solidity of local citizens. Built around this time were the dwellings of Judge Harold Robertson at the northwest corner of Rockland Avenue and St. Charles Street, J. Wilson at 811 St. Charles Street, and of Bert Todd almost next door (No. 841). Todd sold his dwelling to the Dunsmuirs who changed the name to "Westover," a small town in northwest Virginia for which Mrs. J. Dunsmuir had great affection. The stables of this residence in Shasta Place, now converted to a dwelling, still bear the name "Westover."*

At No. 1005 St. Charles Street is the former home of Simon Leiser, wholesale grocer, while No. 628 of the same street was built by James Ogden Grahame, son of the James Allan Grahame who married Mary Work. The home at 582 was built by architect

---

* The present No. 841 is the spot where stood the entrance gates leading to the large house "Westover" built by Bert Todd above what is now Shasta Place.

Rattenbury for Mrs. James Dunsmuir's granddaughter Elizabeth Harvey and husband George Allan Kirke. It is one of Victoria's outstanding homes.

Maud Street was graced with "Illahie" built by Charles Todd, son of J. H. Todd, while 1035 Belmont (now the Camosack Apartments) was the site of the Mr. Justice Martin's home.

The building boom also saw the erection in 1912 of the "Alcazar" apartment block on Fairfield Road, a very solid construction.

Only a year earlier the industrial area of Victoria was doubled by the acquisition of the Songhees Indian Reserve. The Songhees were persuaded to move farther back into Esquimalt and under their Chief Freezy, whose favourite attire was tall hat and long coat, were paid $434,000 for giving up their land. The Indians may have wondered where the process would end. Around the 1860's they were swarming in the Johnson Street ravine and Roderick Finlayson had the Indian (Johnson Street) bridge built to encourage them to cross over to the other side of the water. The $434,000 they were paid in 1912 was much more to their liking than a rickety bridge, but the unexpected windfall may have proved too much for King Freezy; soon afterwards he overturned his canoe while drunk and was drowned.

It was not only the Indians who did well out of the sale of the Reserve lands. Sam Matson of the *Colonist* publishing family put in a bill for $75,000 for services rendered and lawyer H. D. Helmcken a bill for $30,000. They were much criticized at the time. The total cost of moving the Indians was $700,000, including $212,500 spent on the Reserve. Never were so few moved at so great a cost.

The industrial and social solidity seemed to be backed by equally solid natural assets. In 1906 the province had produced two-thirds of the total mineral production of all Canada. Capital and miners flowed in from all over the world to exploit the new lead, copper, coal, iron ore, silver and timber discoveries. The U.S. investment in B.C. in 1910 was $65,000,000 and the investors were world-renowned organizations. The fantastic salmon-packing industry fascinated not only United States', but British capitalists. No less than 1,200,000 cases of salmon were packed in one year of the decade.

Federal building contributed to the boom. The Ogden Point docks (named after Peter Skene Ogden, an early Hudson's Bay Company official) were begun in 1913, largely owing to the advocacy of Senator Harry Barnard. They were to enable the largest liners afloat to bring thousands of visitors and settlers here. They were completed in 1917 at a cost of $2,260,000. The Dominion Astrophysical Observatory completed in 1914 was being built and also the Gonzales meteorological station.

Provincial government and municipal spending was also at an all time high. Luney Bros. were given a $300,000 contract to build the Mt. Tolmie normal school, named after pioneer Wm. Fraser Tolmie. New sewers were put in all over the city including the extension of sewers on Boyd and Menzies Streets to low water, thus removing the pestilential odour prevalent at times in that area. Trutch and Shelbourne Streets were put through in 1912.

Victoria itself got the biggest facelifting in its history. In the space of two years . . . from 1910 to 1912 the city was transformed from what a resident described as "an unpaved, dirty, badly lighted city" into the "best-paved, best-lighted and best-boulevarded city in North America." Fifty miles of roads were put in.

There was work for every able-bodied man and the busiest bees of all were the realtors. Everywhere were the large signs of Baron Alvo von Alvensleben who controlled a large part of the $5,000,000 Germans had invested in the province. The Baron also owned six large logging camps and a large acreage of timber land. In the Kaiserhof Hotel (now the site of the Kent Apartment Hotel, corner Blanshard and Johnson Streets), where German businessmen gathered, more German than English was spoken and more German beer and sausage consumed than beef or local ale.

These were facts which some citizens remembered to the Kaiserhof's disadvantage when the *Lusitania* was torpedoed by a German U-boat, taking down with her 14 passengers from Victoria, including Lieutenant J. Dunsmuir.

Hundreds of men raided the Kaiserhof, drank all the liquor, wrecked the interior and threw the furniture into the street. They then went to the German Club, smashed it up and threw the piano out of the window. The German Club was on the second floor of the building which now houses the offices of C. & C. Transportation and Nelson & Harvey, customs brokers, at 902 Government Street. Next to be raided was Simon Leiser's wholesale grocery at 524 Yates Street.

All this happened on the Saturday and the mob were threatening the Phoenix Brewery on Government Street when the militia were called in. On Sunday night Mayor A. E. Todd read the riot act in two parts of the City. Among the troops called in was a unit commanded by Lieut. Robert H. B. Ker, who was later one of the first Canadians to join the Royal Flying Corps. The temper of the militia was very aggressive. They regarded the rioters, among whom were many rowdies, as slackers and draft-dodgers. They were prepared to handle them roughly, but the threat of military intervention was enough. There was no more trouble.

Subdivisions were created all around Victoria. One of the largest was the Garden City subdivision near Burnside which dropped to the Colquitz River and then rose to Carey Road. Panama Flats subdivision was a little farther out. It had a habit of disappearing under water in winter and was no doubt well suited for the nautically-minded.

Beyond Oak Bay were the Cadboro Lawn and Queen's View subdivisions. The Dunsmuirs were selling off Craigdarroch lots at $5,000 apiece. The View Royal subdivision went in.

Speculators were comforted by the interest of British capital in Victoria. In the 1880's substantial investments in real estate here and in the Cariboo were made by London publisher Thomas Dixon Galpin who owned the *Illustrated London News*, the *Sphere* and the *Tatler*.

Relatives F. W. and H. V. Galpin had homes north of and on Rockland Avenue adjacent to that of A. J. C. Galletly, manager of the Bank of Montreal.

In London, Thomas Dixon Galpin was one among many hundreds of rich men. In Victoria he seemed like a Croesus. Galpin bought a block on Government Street, the Occidental Hotel (former Royal Hotel) and many other pieces of property. He also bought out Alsop & Mason, realtors, and called his new firm B.C. Land and Investment Agency. This Company still exists and operates in the same building at 922 Government Street (corner Government and Broughton Streets) as the original firm occupied in 1863. It is probably the oldest firm in Victoria's real estate and insurance sphere.

Thomas Galpin had his firm managed by P. R. Brown, who later founded P. R. Brown & Sons, Ltd. Other associates of Galpin were Arthur Wolfenden and Cuyler A. Holland, whose home on Rockland Avenue is mentioned on page 112.

B.C. Land & Investment was Victoria's principal marketer of lands during the 1900-14 boom. At one time it owned or controlled half of the land in the Victoria area.

This land included the McTavish estate comprising most of James Bay, the Douglas estate which included most of Fairfield (500 acres from Heywood Avenue to Ross Bay Cemetery and from Rockland to Dallas Road, including the 33 acres of Government House grounds for which the Province paid a rental of $40.50 per annum).

Fairfield came into its own in 1912. Hundreds of houses were built on what had been a swamp drained by a stream which emptied into James Bay near the Reformed Episcopal Church.

Cook Street ended where the land began to drop and beyond was a garbage dump where old beggars used to scratch around. Popular with neighbourhood children was a rhyme:

> Old Mother Hubbard fell in a ditch,
> Picked up a penny, thought she was rich.

Fairfield became one of the most popular residential areas and 60 x 120 foot lots were selling for $5,000 in 1912 compared with $400 six years earlier.

Other 1912 prices ... a 48 x 140 uncleared lot at Fort and Foul Bay Roads: $3,600; a 46 x 100 foot lot on Faithful Street $3,000; business lots on North Park $7,200. The asking price for 1½ acres Quadra at Cloverdale, right in the bush, was $12,000. This included land for which James Douglas had paid the Indians one cent an acre and which he had difficulty in reselling at $1 an acre in the colony's early years.

Downtown land prices were equally fantastic. On Douglas Street,

Fisgard to Hillside, the land sold at $500 per foot. Downtown corner lots went for $15,000. Senator J. MacDonald sold "Armadale" in 27 acres in James Bay for $1,000,000 and the Balmoral Hotel sold for $500,000.*

It is difficult to say who profited most by the boom, the big landowners or the speculators who sold out in time. One of the biggest landowners was Joseph Despard Pemberton who owned a large part of Oak Bay, the Gonzales district (including Gonzales Heights) and Fairfield (see map). Fairfield Road was put through in 1857.

Joseph Despard was an outstanding example of an immigrant who combined an official position with an eye for future land values. He had to wait a long time but made his fortune in the end. Like so many of our pioneers he came from Ireland where opportunities were few in the depression which followed the hunger years.

With Joseph Despard opportunities may have been fewer than average because his grandfather, a mayor of Dublin, had 18 sons and three daughters. Such large families were a main cause of the starvation which followed the failure of the potato harvests. Pemberton arrived here in 1851 as a surveyor for the Hudson's Bay Company and after undertaking on their behalf many dangerous missions in the Interior, bought in 1858 a five-acre plot, the nucleus of his Gonzales estate, known then as Pemberton Farm.

Joined by his sister in 1856, Joseph Despard went to England, got married and lived with his wife in a 30-foot by 20-foot log cabin on the north side of Fairfield Road. The site is believed to be that of the garage now operating at St. Charles and Fairfield Streets. His nearest neighbours were Mrs. Isabella Ross, Victoria's first woman landholder, and Royal Governor Kennedy who came out on the same vessel as Pemberton and his wife.

Isabella Ross was widow of Charles Ross who supervised the building of Fort Victoria and purchased a large acreage on Ross Bay which eventually became the Hollywood subdivision. Part of the land was purchased by the City in 1876 to create the Ross Bay Cemetery.

As the Pembertons' fortunes improved so did their dwellings. They first built "Glenville" in 13 acres overlooking Ross Bay.

* A 1912 dollar would be equal to $10 today.

"Glenville" when it fell to pieces was bought by John and James Douglas, grandsons of Sir James, who put up homes on the same site — at the end of Masters Road, high on the rocky hilltop.

An M.L.A. and a member of the First Executive Council, Pemberton was influential politically and businesswise. He was appointed Surveyor-General and in 1883 began building his famous "Gonzales" home amid 1,200 acres which included what are now the Victoria Golf Club links. He did not get on too well with Royal Governor Seymour. Some people say it was because Seymour, in contrast to Pemberton, favoured New Westminster as the provincial capital. Others say they feuded over a tax incident. Apparently at one time, Pemberton was 16 months in arrears with his taxes and was dunned by the sheriff. He objected to the sheriff gaining access to his house on several occasions by what he called "tricks."

But his appeal to the Royal Governor to stop the "persecution" brought no response. Seymour, like other royal governors, held no high opinion of legislative realtors.

Joseph Despard was a great benefactor of the city he loved. The Royal Jubilee Hospital, the Union Club and many schools owe a great deal to his bequests. Always cheerful and a fine horseman, he fell dead from his horse near what is now the Oak Bay Junction in 1893. He had suffered with his heart for some time and his death occurred during a paper chase. One son, Frederick, built "Mountjoy," 617 Foul Bay Road, burned down in 1953, but the garden walls can still be seen, and the name "Mountjoy" is perpetuated in Mountjoy Avenue which adjoins the Mountjoy estate.

Six years before his death Joseph Despard established with his son Frederick Bernard the firm of Pemberton & Son, later to become Pemberton Holmes. Frederick Pemberton put through Oak Bay Avenue at his own expense. It was a move of enlightened self-interest as the road also gave better access to the Pemberton holdings.

The potentialities of Oak Bay as a residential area were seen as early as 1891 when the Oak Bay Land and Improvement Co. was incorporated with 3,000 shares of $100 each. Shareholders included Major Dupont of Victoria, two big timber operators and John Paterson of New Westminster.

French capital represented by the Credit Foncier promoted the now beautiful Uplands development in 1912. But strangely enough for those times it made heavy going. Full page advertisements in that year were asking $2,500 to $5,000 a lot but there were no takers and for many years there was only one resident, Andrew Wright, in the Uplands. His home at 3175 Beach Drive is now that of Hubert Wallace.

The subdivision was planned by the Olmstead brothers of Chicago. By 1923 the developers owed Oak Bay Municipality $79,000 for taxes. When the municipality tried to foreclose it discovered that all the taxes were in default except those on lot 1. Lot 1 covered all roads within the Uplands estate. If the municipality had foreclosed it would have had no readily available access to the property.

Today, of course, the Uplands is reckoned to be Greater Victoria's finest residential area, but early records of its transactions and of land deals in Oak Bay generally were reduced to pulp when the basement of the old Municipal Hall, corner Hampshire and Oak Bay Avenue and now the location of the Bank of Nova Scotia was flooded in 1955.

Biggest owners of property in Oak Bay were the Hudson's Bay Company, who owned 1,118 out of the municipality's 1,922 arable acres; next came John Tod (407 acres), Wm. Henry McNeil (200 acres), Joseph D. Pemberton (188 acres) and Isabella Ross (10 acres). The single-storey dwelling of John Tod, a Hudson's Bay employee, still stands at 2564 Heron Street in Oak Bay. Its low doorways and undulating floorboards are typical of the carpentry of the 1850's. John Tod's acreage included Mary Tod Island. Mary married John Bowker and her home still stands in Bowker Place, which was on her father's property. The fine trees along 1900 block Beach were planted, it is believed, by John Bowker.

Mary Tod Island is sometimes called Jimmy Chicken Island. An Indian named Jimmy Chicken lived on it at one time.

Whether he was so named because he kept chickens, sold chickens, looked like a chicken or was "chicken" is not revealed in Oak Bay's history. Nor does Jimmy Chicken appear in any national biographies. In any case he must have had a very pleasant location with an island all to himself until Rattenbury, son of the architect, whose house (now Glenlyon School) was on the mainland opposite, built a swimming pool there, the remains of which can still be seen.

John Tod is often referred to as a Hudson's Bay "factor," but people seem to have been rather free with high-sounding titles in the early days. In fact John Tod was very disillusioned with the Hudson's Bay Company. Like most of our pioneers he came from a poor family, lost his job in a Glasgow grocer firm and enlisted with the fur company for £20 a year (about $1,000 a year today). In his diary he refers to some of the hardships he suffered including meals on the emigrant ship which at first consisted entirely of porridge (without milk or sugar).

The captain improved the diet only when some passengers swam ashore rather than endure it any longer. He served in several very unpleasant Hudson's Bay forts (or warehouses) before coming to the coast and frequently complained of the slow promotion in the Company's service. He had four wives at different times, but little is known of numbers one, two and four who were Indian. His third wife was from Wales. He bought his land in Oak Bay from the Company and ploughed up 100 acres which included Willows Farm. Rumour has it that some very lively parties occurred in his Heron Street home and that there was a tunnel from the house to the beach through which he smuggled in Chinese who at that time were subject to a head tax. His hardships and four wives do not appear to have done him any harm for he lived to the ripe age of 88, dying in 1882. Bowker Creek used to be called Tod's stream.

Wm. H. McNeil, who owned 200 acres with Shoal Bay as the shoreline, was captain of the Hudson's Bay Company S.S. *Beaver*. He had a large farm running to the shore, which used to be known as McNeil Bay. Isabella Ross, by the way, who owned 10 acres, was a daughter of McNeil.

The map in annex shows the boundaries of these properties imposed on a current map of Oak Bay. North of Oak Bay, McKay owned all of Ten-Mile Point and W. F. Tolmie, whose farm was at Cloverdale and North Quadra Street, owned 1,000 acres bounded on the northeast by Mt. Tolmie, joining with the Work property on Hillside.

It is a significant fact that politics, the civil service or dealing in real estate have always played leading roles in Victoria's business life. The reasons are not hard to seek. Except in the periods of the first gold rushes and of the industrial era (from about 1888 to 1905) it was difficult to get a living or make money any other way. For a few years, canning, lumber, sealing, shipbuilding and brokerage offered big opportunities. Then these trades and industries, except for lumber, passed out of Victoria control and selling land and property to each other or to newcomers was one of the few alternatives and least risky methods of making a living, or a fortune.

From the earliest years everyone who could manage it speculated in land. Indeed one can say that a factor which induced the Hudson's Bay Company to establish a settlement here was partly prompted by prospects of appreciation in land values. At one time, Parliament could do no business because the legislators were absent on real estate deals. Victoria's first independent realtor was W. Backus, an American, whose office started in 1853 was a dozen steps from Fort Street northwards along Wharf. When the gold-seekers came, he knew where the business was to be found and set up his office in the El Dorado Saloon on Yates Street. By 1860, Victoria had eight real estate agents. Government Street was realtors' row and on it or nearby were the realtors W. A. Harries, J. J. Cochrane, Selim Franklin, J. B. Timmerman, Leopold Loewenberg, W. Hackus, Wight J. Copland and James A. McCrea.

When the first gold rushes ended, many lot owners who had hoped for an appreciation in prices found themselves, to use a current expression "holding the bag," with unsaleable lots on their hands. At the same time, taxes on their unsold lots were accumulating.

Faced with the sequestration or forced sale of their property these lot holders, who included many legislators, were desperate. A law was introduced extending the period for payment of taxes to give them some relief. But what was relief for the lot holders meant disappointment for those who hoped to buy their property at very low prices. Among such opportunists were De Cosmos (the Friend of the Universe) and his friend McClure. They saw their chances of a quick fortune disappearing. After a 24-hour filibuster they managed to kill the measure.

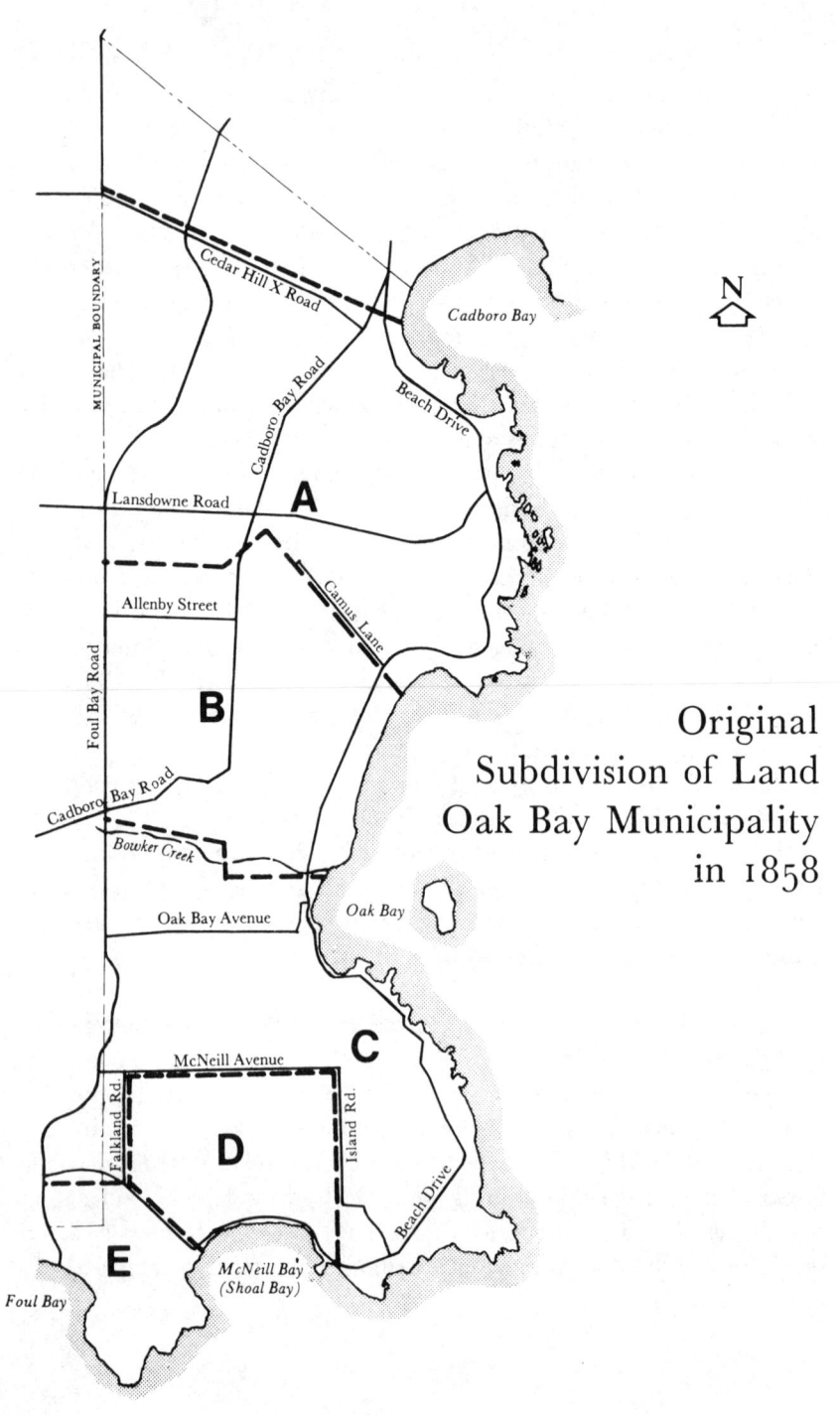

N

Cadboro Bay

MUNICIPAL BOUNDARY

Cedar Hill X Road

Cadboro Bay Road

Beach Drive

Lansdowne Road

A

Camus Lane

Allenby Street

Foul Bay Road

B

Original
Subdivision of Land
Oak Bay Municipality
in 1858

Cadboro Bay Road

Bowker Creek

Oak Bay Avenue

Oak Bay

McNeill Avenue

C

Falkland Rd.

Island Rd.

D

Beach Drive

E

McNeill Bay
(Shoal Bay)

Foul Bay

Amid the spasmodic ups and downs the next substantial increase in real estate values began in the mid 1880's when the population was increasing rapidly and streetcars were introduced. This was a period of booming construction when many of the fine homes went up on Rockland Avenue. So attractive was the realty business that in 1888 Captain Tatlow gave up the position of private secretary to the lieutenant-governor to go into real estate.

Then came the great boom from 1905 onwards. By 1914 there were 300 realty firms in Victoria, for a population of 46,000.

Outstanding realtors of the time included F. O. Richards, whose half-page advertisements substituted for news on the front page of the *Victoria Times* and Beaumont Boggs, whose fine home "Maplewood" overlooking the Gorge at 133 Catherine, testified to his success. This residence was in 1968 owned by Mrs. Violet Warren, widow of tugboat captain F. J. D. Warren. Realty advertising was the largest single source of revenue for Victoria newspapers. British Columbia trade directories bulged with the advertisements of realtors.

But all good things have an end. British capital was the first to become alarmed at the size of the speculative bubble its interest had helped to create. British capitalists began quietly to liquidate their investments. Other outside interests followed suit. Lots fell in price only fractionally at first, but then panic set in. Everybody wanted to sell and there were few buyers.

Some who held on grimly to their land investments were able only in the 1960's to realize the prices they had paid 50 years previously and those prices with dollars halved in value.

The immigrants did not arrive by the tens of thousands as the realtors had prophesied. Instead of being the "first port on the

---

A   UPLANDS FARM

B   TOD PROPERTY

C   PEMBERTON HOLDINGS

D   McNEILL ACREAGE

E   ROSS ESTATE

Pacific," Victoria was overhauled and left behind by Vancouver, Seattle, Portland and San Francisco. By 1911 Greater Victoria's population was still only 45,699. It had taken 10 years to double itself, an average increase of only 2,000 people a year . . . and no justification at all for the phenomenal increases in the asked for price of land.

War clouds were on the horizon. Conservatism, retrenchment and uncertainty were in the air. In 1914 the unkempt condition of Douglas Street, with its burned out shells, the Hudson's Bay Department store standing derelict with no windows, were ominous reminders that the good times were coming to an end.

Prostitutes were as plentiful as beggars in downtown streets. Even the members of the respected businessmen's clubs fell behind with payment of their dues. Property entries disappeared from books until the entire assets of many companies vanished "like snow in sunshine." By 1917 Victoria's 300 real estate firms of the boom days had declined to 97 and many of these existed in name only.

In the circumstances, the outbreak of World War I was a boon to many . . . to doctors without patients, lawyers without briefs, brokers without clients, and above all, the war was initially a boon to many married women, especially wives of realtors. Many of these women, for the first time since marriage, began to receive regular monthly cheques. Their husbands were now in the Armed Forces But with some the state of comparative affluence was short-lived. In a regrettably large number of cases army pay became all too soon a widow's pension.

Real estate sales, measured by volume, did not begin to boom again until the 1950's. The growth then was not in Victoria itself, but in the environs.

By 1970 there were around 700 registered real estate salesmen in Victoria, not including the many non-registered who bought and sold property on their own account. Among the new salesmen were many who used real estate as a means of supplementing a pension. In real estate as in every other branch of business, competition in the 1960's became ever more intense in spite of an increase in the average home value to $25,000 and multiple listing sales of (in 1969) $40,239,000.

But there seemed no end to the growth. Premier W. A. C. Bennett in 1958 foresaw the time when every family in the province would own three homes. Realtors, at the same time, were freely forecasting a Greater Victoria population of 300,000 by 1980. While Mr. Bennett's prophecy may have intrigued men with polygamist inclinations, it was very unrealistic for the many who owned single-family dwellings and found it increasingly burdensome to maintain them in the face of ever increasing taxation of the homeowner.

Chapter 17

THE DOLDRUMS, PROHIBITION
AND THE GREAT DEPRESSION

FROM THE COLLAPSE IN 1914 of the great land boom until the outbreak of World War II Victoria was economically in the doldrums.
The population was static. Between 1921 and 1931 the city gained
a mere 300 people and the position in the environs was not much
better. For a community with a declining industrial complex whose
prosperity depended on a continued influx of people with means or
marketable skills, this was a serious matter.

One effect was to cause ambitious young men to leave a city in
which they had no future and to seek their livings elsewhere. Another was to endow the city with a preponderance of pretty, eligible
girls . . . a situation like that in Eire today where so many young
men find it hard to make progress and emigrate to England.

Victoria, after the first excitement of World War I had subsided,
was a very sleepy town indeed.

It was so quiet that a cougar, presumably of a studious nature,
was shot on the steps of the Public Library in 1926. Citizens joked
that at some hours of the day a cannonball fired down Yates Street
would endanger only the bobby-helmeted policeman on traffic duty
at the Douglas Street intersection.

But a static economy does not necessarily imply social somnolence.
In the field of sports the 1920's saw the triumphs of boxer Jimmy
McLarnin, soccer player Dave Turner, Torchy Peden the cyclist,
Dr. Jack Wright, tennis ace and basketball wizard Norm Baker.
They were conversation pieces for the many who loved to meet and
gossip.

The "Gay Twenties" also meant gay parties: the more leisured sometimes went to two parties in one day. Dancing, tennis, whist and boating were great favourites. Socialites moved in tightly-knit groups and it was very important to be seen in the company of and to invite the "right" people.

Everybody knew and talked to everybody and it was a common, smiling complaint that shopping was difficult because of the gregarious nature of citizens. An expedition downtown to Spencer's or the Hudson's Bay Company store could easily resolve itself into a half-completed shopping list and a pot of tea, a piece of "Golden Rod" cake and chit-chat at Clay's, the caterers.

But it was a very good era for the housewife. Housewives enjoyed service of a standard incomparably better than that they enjoy today. Tradesmen could not easily replace a lost customer and their politeness amounting almost to servility, was on a par with the punctuality of deliveries to customers' homes. Especially important to retailers was the patronage of the old families and the newer middle class. Many among the latter were retired Imperial Army men from India, ex-officials of the customs service in China and widows in good financial standing.

They accounted for a large proportion of those of British birth who doubled their numbers in the 20 years to 1931.

Keeping the goodwill of the more prestigious families sometimes meant barter deals. Towards the end of the century, Mrs. J. D. Pemberton paid an account with cabbages; three dozen eggs in lieu of cash settled the amount owing by another customer, while Mrs. Arthur Bunster, the brewer's wife, tendered beer in settlement of her account.

Refrigeration and the supermarket were unknown in the early 1920's. Cheese was cut from 25-pound slabs, sugar scooped from a bin, bacon bought by the piece or sliced before the customer's eyes at the counter. Victoria abounded in well-stocked specialty shops, among the more prominent being the delicatessens of Mrs. E. J. Dale, M. S. Harvey and Mrs. J. J. Johnson, all on lower Fort Street; the florists Ballantyne's, Brown's Victoria and Layritz nurseries, and A. J. Woodward & Sons (still today in 600 block Fort Street). Outstanding stationers and booksellers were Barber & Holdcroft (who recently closed down), Horseshoe Book, Macey Abell & Co., Sweeny McConnell, Victoria Book & Stationery and T. N. Hibben.

In the furniture business leading merchants were J. Bartholomew & Sons in the 1100 block Fort, Home Furniture, then at 712 Fort, Smith & Champion, the Weiler Furniture Co., and Standard Furniture Co., while in the "fancy goods" category the Persian Art Store, Green's Jewelry Store and the Needlecraft Shop were much patronized.

Women bought their hats from any of 11 milliners of whom only three are still in business today, namely: Crown Millinery, Miss Frith and Malleks Ltd. The footwear field was led by Maynards, Hawkes, Munday and the Old Country Shoe Store.

But Victoria was still very much a man's town. Men had not only the clubs to themselves but also 30 cigar stores and eight shoeshine parlours. The cigar stores included the Collender stores on Yates Street, the Columbia, Empire and Horseshoe stores, E. A. Morris, still today at 1116 Government Street, and Two Jacks Dope two blocks along (at 1313).

Among the most popular restaurants apart from the Empress Hotel were the White Lunch at 554 Johnson, the Poodle Dog, the Strathcona, New England Hotel, 1312 Government Street and the still popular Old British Fish & Chips on Broad Street.

A large salmon could be picked up from the Outer Wharf fishermen for 25 cents. Most people used the streetcars, a far less expensive method than the motorcar of getting around. Domestic labour also was cheap and abundant. A Chinese would often work for and live with one family from boyhood to his death. There was little competing advertising to cause the frantic rush for "bargains." Through the decades Victorians had become accustomed to very "genteel" forms of advertising, in striking contrast to those of today.

While today the public considers price all important, up to around 40 years ago to mention prices in advertising would have been considered rather vulgar.

Going back to the earliest years Janion & Green in 1860 were somewhat hesitatingly advertising sugars and groceries with no mention of prices in a small two-inch-square advertisement in the *Colonist*.

In the same year Lester & Gibbs, the coloured grocers at Yates and Waddington Streets, announced in an equally minute advertisement that they sold self-raising flour, bacon, firkins of Hope butter, Java and Rio coffee, black tea, crushed sugar and Worcester sauce. By 1870 advertisements were calling attention not to prices, but to connections. Fredk. Reynolds, Family Butcher, announced merely that he was "Purveyor by arrangement to H.M. Royal Navy," Van Volkenburgh & Co., that they were "Purveyors to His Excellency the Marquis of Lorne and Royal Highness Princess Louise." They gave no address, but climaxed, or anti-climaxed their imposing introduction in very small print with "geese, turkeys." Merchants did not hold sales, but "auctions." Lumley Franklin announced that he would auction at his sales room on Yates Street "an assortment of wines, groceries and liquors," and C. T. Millard (Wharf Street foot Yates) "salt beef, butter, codfish, dried peaches, cheese, soap, split peas, oatmeal, peaches and jellies."

Food advertising coincided generally with the arrival of ships. The Hudson's Bay Company, then on Wharf Street, announced: "NEW GOODS ex PRINCESS ROYAL" and listed sugar, tea, pickles, sauces, cheese and salt.

Janion & Rhodes announced "Ex ALPHA" Scotch oatmeal, new currants, figs and table salt.

Even in 1912 The Farmers' Exchange, a downtown store, were advertising food items with no indication of price. This reticence was on its way out in the Gay Twenties. Kirkham's Grocery on Fort Street probably started the new trend with a large quarter page advertisement in 1922 giving items *and* prices. The Hudson's Bay Company, which opened its present department store in 1921 after it had stood empty for seven years, took a succession of full page advertisements in the daily papers, competing with Spencer's, the only other large regular advertiser, for prominence.

The notable feature of their full page advertisement is that food and prices are buried in a small square in the corner. They quoted: "Marmalade —4 lbs. $1.00; Tea 60 to 80¢ a lb; coffee 65¢ in lacquered tin; pastry flour 49 lbs. for $2.75; Wesson's cooking oil 15 oz. 50¢; butter 48¢; potatoes 10 lbs. 25¢."

Food was astonishingly expensive. A good wage in those days would have been $100 a month. Compare that with a below-average wage of $500 a month today, multiply 1921 prices by five and we get: Marmalade 4 lbs. for $5. Tea $3 to $4 a lb.; coffee $3.25 a lb.; butter $2.40 lb.; potatoes 12½¢ lb.

This too was at a time when people walked a lot and were hearty eaters. And yet old-timers maintain they not only ate well, but could put money in the bank too.

People did not have to spend on automobiles, oil heating, refrigerators, electric washers and driers; houses too were, for the ordinary people, much smaller.

An advertisement in those times asking for carpenters on an out-of-town job offering $3.00 a day less board $1.25 indicates the large proportion of the budget which went on food.

In the "Gay Twenties" two upheavals occurred which shook society to its foundations. One was prohibition, the other the great depression.

Nothing else could have changed so drastically the appearance of downtown Victoria as prohibition. Saloons were banned from 1917 to 1921. Eighty hotels and saloons, including the Brown Jug and its 50-foot-long bar, largest in the West, the Dallas Hotel and Cliff House opposite the rifle range at Clover Point were forced to close. Very few proprietors were as fortunate as those of the Angel Hotel on Langley Street who were able to sell the site for the Federal Government Building.

Most of the 109 hotels and saloons, deprived of their bar revenue, became rundown and some like the Occidental the abode of prostitutes. Victoria's appearance was transformed as one hotel after another came under the wrecker's hammer but the ghosts of old downtown Victoria can still be seen on lower Johnson Street in premises like those of the American Hotel at 533 Yates, now used as a food warehouse.

Naturally enough, Victoria's considerable brewing interests fought prohibition fiercely. Their dislike for the Reverend John Gibson Inkster of the First Presbyterian Church, one of the most influential

KER-HEISTERMAN WEDDING

Left to right, back row: Col. Richard
Angus, Mrs. Tisdale, Miss Gertie
White, B. S. Heisterman, L. E. Erb,
Miss Lily Erb (Mrs. J. Wilson),
Robert J. Ker, Mrs. Bagster Seabrook,
Mrs. Geo. Haynes, Miss Sylvia
Heisterman (Mrs. R. E. Brett), Miss
M. Erb (Mrs. Biggerstaff Wilson),
David R. Ker, Bagster Seabrook, Mrs.
L. E. Erb, Mrs. Seabrook, Mrs. J. H.
Todd, J. H. Todd, Mr. Henry
Brackman, Thos. Arnot Ker, Albert
Haynes. *Second row:* Miss Mable
Haynes (Mrs. Arthur Kappele of
Vancouver), Harry Austin, Annette
Seabrook, Mrs. David R. Ker, Mrs.
Robert Ker Sr., Mrs. H. F. Heister-
man, H. F. Heisterman, Mrs.
Alex Munro (mother of R. P. Rithet).
Front row: Walter Ker, Henry
Heisterman, Miss Olive Heisterman,
Miss Verna Heisterman (Mrs. Arthur
Smith of Vancouver), Tod Aikman,
Dr. G. H. (Bud) Haynes.

THE BROKEN SPAN
of Point Ellice Bridge after the
streetcar disaster.

KERSHAUGH
at Yates and Fernwood, home
of David Russell Ker, had the first
sidewalk on Yates Street.

KLONDIKE HOPEFULS
drawing supplies from E. Saunders'
store at 41 Johnson Street.

THE JACOB HUNTER TODD FAMILY
Mai Todd (Mrs. Hebden Gillespie),
John L. Todd, Miss J. H. Todd,
Rose Ellen (Nellie) Todd (Mrs. Alex
Gillespie), Albert E. Todd.

THE FORMER VICTORIA COLLEGE
now Adult Education building.

SHOAL BAY
was a favourite Sunday excursion
for pioneer motorists. In leading car
is Captain J. W. Troup and in the
second Mayor A. E. Todd.

A CHARMING STUDY
of Mrs. Joseph Despard Pemberton.

of temperance advocates, was intense. Cartoons appeared portraying a clergyman with a complexion like a rhubarb pie arm-in-arm with the bootleggers who would profit by prohibition.

The author is indebted to Herbert Anscomb, who was in the prohibition years prominently associated with brewing interests, for much of the information which follows. Herbert Anscomb came here from Maidstone, Kent, in 1911, worked for the Victoria-Phoenix (now Lucky Lager Breweries) and Victoria owes to his ability one of its oldest surviving industries, the Growers Wine Company. He was Victoria's youngest mayor (1929-31), reeve of Oak Bay 1925-27, co-premier in the John Hart and Byron Johnson governments, a Leader of the Opposition and at times Minister of Finance.

The brewers were unfortunate in that Premier Wm. Bowser (1915-16), who was inclined to prohibition was succeeded by Harlan C. Brewster, a Baptist and total abstainer. Bowser limited liquor sales. Brewster, British Columbia's first Liberal premier, banned them altogether.

There can be little doubt that Brewster's fanatical anti-alcoholism was partly due to the abuse of liquor in Clayoquot where he served some time as a bookkeeper. In Clayoquot meals were not served, but "poured."

The government lost little revenue by banning liquor. Liquor revenue was derived mainly from licence fees and in Victoria these went to the city. Brewing interests were especially annoyed because Bowser, as attorney-general, had ordered all hotels to have guest rooms in order to stop pseudo-hotels from selling liquor. When the brewers, who were interested in many hotels, complied at enormous expense, Brewster came along and with him prohibition. The brewers were given no compensation.

One of the Reverend Inkster's main arguments was that grain used for brewing liquor could be used to feed the poor, but he did not explain how the poor were to pay the farmer for his grain or whether they were interested in a grain diet.

When the ship in which Inkster was voyaging to New Zealand was mined and he was rescued, brewers were rather sorry.

Prohibition or no prohibition Victorians loved their drink and circumvented the law by devious ways. Many ordered liquor in Alberta and took delivery at a local warehouse. Alcohol could be obtained on prescription from drug stores and citizens developed a plague of colds calling for the prescription of Double "O", or Old Orkney whiskey. There was a tremendous increase in home-brewing and wine-making.

As people were going to get their drink anyway, Premier John Oliver's government (1918-27) decided to compromise by going into the liquor business itself. The first government liquor store was on Yates Street west of the Dominion Hotel. Government liquor stores were popularly known as John Oliver's drug stores. The government's venture into the liquor trade has proved most profitable. Liquor in the 1969-70 fiscal year yielded $61,000,000 in profits.

After the repeal of prohibition, sale of liquor by the glass was permitted by local option only. In 1931 Victoria turned down this option. The result was a run on taverns outside the city limits where beer could be obtained. This resulted in considerable traffic to taverns in Esquimalt and others outside the city area, notably Six-Mile House, Four-Mile House and John Day's Ship Inn.

The restoration of more civilized drinking amenities was a long process. When saloons were again allowed customers had to sit down and drink. Before prohibition they had to stand. The saloons were also provided with separate lounges for women. This recognition of women's right to equal treatment with the men is said to be due to a Victorian "Sylvia Pankhurst," who walked into the Balmoral Hotel (the site now occupied by Canada Permanent at Fort and Douglas Streets) and demanded to be served.

It was not customary for women to enter saloons and the barman refused to serve her. The woman sued, her case eventually came before the Supreme Court and it was ruled that a woman was "a person" within the meaning of the legislation.

Victoria got its first cocktail lounge in 1954 in the Strathcona Hotel. Soon afterwards music was permitted in places where drink was sold. In 1970 a Royal Commission set up by Premier W. A. C. Bennett rescinded the law banning liquor sales on municipal bye-election days, extended the hours saloons could remain open and permitted the sale of liquor with meals on Sundays.

Prohibition may have been a disaster for Victoria's hotels and saloons, but the introduction of prohibition in the U.S.A. under the Volstead Act (1917-1933) contributed to the fortunes of many local businessmen. The smuggling of liquor to the States became a vast business.

Whiskey was trucked from local warehouses to Spoon Bay in the Uplands, Smugglers' Cove in Gordon Head and other points and shipped from there at night to keep rendezvous with United States receiving vessels. Liquor ships also left Kingston's Wharf and handed over their cargoes to United States ships at lonely Gulf Island spots and sometimes even went as far as San Francisco.

One boat, *The Ark*, was operated by Frank Clark, son of a city policeman. The twin-screw S.S. *Kitniakwa* was operated by Johnny Schnarr and the M.31 by Capt. Boydell. The weekly Alexander boats from San Francisco which docked here, also packed liquor for thirsting United States compatriots. Smuggled liquor was wrapped in burlap and Eli Bean, a local junk dealer, used to sell 3,000 sacks a week to one outlet alone. Liquor was also smuggled in double-bottomed scows which took lime from quarries near Six-Mile House to Seattle.

A whole fleet of liquor ships was owned by Western Freighters who paid wages quadruple those of Canadian Pacific Steamships, namely $250 for a seaman against C.P.S.'s $60 to $65.

Victorians, it will be seen, found a way to circumvent prohibition, but there was no way of circumventing the world-wide depression. The depression was first felt in Victoria towards the end of 1929, a year notable for Winston Churchill's address to the Canadian Club. It reached its greatest depth in 1932 when 12,000 of the area's 40,000 people were on relief and every second worker was out of a job. In Saanich 380 out of 1,500 families were on relief. Douglas, Johnson, Government and Yates Streets were full of beggars. Cars almost disappeared because few could afford gas. Cinemas and restaurants cut prices.

Crime increased. Many houses and business premises were burgled. Even the planks from sidewalks were stolen.

Many school teachers were dismissed as parents could not afford to buy their children school clothing. In 1932 when Canada had 800,000 unemployed, the province's overdraft for unemployment relief was $2,393,600 and the city's relief expenditure $164,143, or 8.5% of the budget. Building permits show the extent of the decline. In 1931 city permits totalled $1,892,262. In 1932 they were only $389,673 — a decrease of 81%. Sawmills closed down, Yarrows, the Victoria Machinery Depot and the Federal drydock cut staffs to the bone; the Empress Hotel staff outnumbered guests.

A relief camp, one of several, was set up at Macaulay Point and paid single men 20 cents a day with board. The city put many unemployed to work at Macdonald Park, paying them $1 a day. The relief dole for a married man was $20 a month.

Retailers and landlords also suffered heavily. People could not meet their obligations for the ordinary necessities of life. Many landlords considered it better to let their tenants live rent free rather than have their property empty and exposed to vandalism.

The city would have liked to help the needy more than it did, but it was itself badly in debt. It had in fact been in financial difficulties long before the depression. By 1937 the city had $16,000,000 in bonded debts and had made two issues, one of $108,000 and one of $500,000 for relief alone. It was able to refinance its obligations, but the effects of this are still felt today in city budgets. Houses sold for tax arrears in 1929 sometimes fetched as little as $900 apiece.

Affairs would have been still worse for Victoria, depending as it does so largely on government employment, if the Kidd report had been adopted by the legislature.

This report recommended a 30 to 50% cut in civil servants and the halving of the salaries of the remainder. The report was partly responsible for the downfall of the Conservative Simon Fraser Tolmie government and for the victory of Liberal "Duff" Patullo, who won the election with the slogan "Work and Wages" — a completely meaningless platform as the depression was world-wide and far beyond the remedial powers of a provincial government.

Things would have been worse too but for the community spirit of Victorians. To help the jobless 600 volunteers canvassed 14,000 homes for an emergency clean-up campaign; Victoria became, as a result, "the neatest depression city in North America," a model of newly-painted houses and trim lawns and gardens.

The Salvation Army as usual was in the forefront of the battle against hardship. It sold booklets of meal tickets to householders, the tickets to be given to needy callers.

Some consequences of the depression were falling birthrates, more marital problems and more hospital (mental depression) cases. But although Victoria had to contend with numerous demonstrations by the unemployed, it never experienced the vicious labour disorders of Vancouver and on the whole people did not feel the depression so much, bad though it was, as other parts of the Dominion. One reason was that it cost money to cross from the Mainland to Victoria and many of those who "rode the rods" from the East to Vancouver could get no farther. Again, most people had gardens and could fish or otherwise supply many of their day-to-day food needs. Many generous owners of orchards had signs erected: "Help yourself. Take all you want."

But the amelioration of some of the worst effects of the depression was due also to the very active community spirit and to the good sense of the better-to-do who not only gave what they could, but curtailed parties, feeling it wrong to be enjoying themselves when so many were in need.

In so doing they showed much greater common sense than the middle classes of Germany, consisting largely of Jews, during the depression. It was the ostentation of these classes while most were in need which aroused the envy and resentment of the German people and helped to provide fuel for the anti-Semitic flames which Hitler later kindled and exploited.

In an effort to dispel the gloom of businessmen during the depression, A. Carmichael addressed the Real Estate Board on January 23, 1931 and urged them to look at the progress the city had made since 1913. He cited the opening of the Crystal Garden in 1925 which had the largest indoor swimming pool in North America, the Empress Hotel, the Kresge Block, Woolworth's (formerly the Vernon Building), Fletcher Bros. Building, the Hudson's Bay Company store and the Bank of Montreal building.

The old livery stables on Broughton Street had been converted into a stage depot for the Vancouver Island Transportation Co., and Victoria had been enriched by the C.P.R. Marine Building, the Memorial Hall and the first unit of Christ Church Cathedral.

"Numerous 'handsome' oil and gas stations have replaced ugly vacant corners," Mr. Carmichael added and electric light users had increased from 12,927 in 1912 to 20,823 in 1930.

He noted also that tourists had increased from 200,000 in 1923 to 360,000 in 1927.

Mr. Carmichael might have mentioned in addition the construction of the Oak Bay Beach Hotel (by Major Merston in 1927), the new Johnson Street bascule span bridge erected at a cost of $918,000 in 1924, the hopes for a movie industry engendered by a film company's construction of a "cow town" in Willows Park and the first flight for paying passengers from Lansdowne Airport on August 3, 1928.

Lansdowne Road, incidentally, was formerly known as Dean's Cross Road, Dean's farm being in the southeast corner of Richmond Road and Dean's Cross Road.

The 30-acre airfield was bounded by Lansdowne, Shelbourne, Richmond and Newton Streets and the owner of the land, Mrs. G. H. Scott, gave B.C. Airways an option to purchase the land for $77,000. Unfortunately B.C. Airways tri-motor Ford disappeared on a flight to Seattle three weeks later.

If Mr. Carmichael's speech had been delivered three years later it would have been better timed. The depth of the depression was reached a year after he spoke. But then the virus which had slowed down the economic pulse of the world began to lose its potency. The patient began to fight back. Britain went off the gold standard, world prices started to recover, confidence to return. It was a slow process. A mill starting up again here, a shop opening there. Then came the Second World War with its demand for lumber, cement, ships, housing.

At the peak of the war effort Victoria Machinery Depot alone had 3,000 workers on three shifts, 24 hours a day and seven days a week, in great contrast with the depths of the depression when the company laid off all but 12 employees and they had work only alternate fortnights.

Chapter 18

VICTORIA IN TRANSITION

IN THE LAST TWO DECADES TO 1970 Victoria has seen changes greater than any in her history. The city has been transformed from a "Sleepy Hollow" to a bustling modern city. The transformation began with new and better buildings. The B.C. Power Commission Building on Blanshard Street broke a construction halt of decades when it was erected in 1951. In the same year the huge block-long Douglas Building went up, providing accommodation for the many hundreds of additional civil servants demanded by the trend to greater bureaucratic control of everyone's life.

These new buildings were followed by the B.C. Electric structure at Pandora and Blanshard Streets, in 1954, a private enterprise corporation which was soon to fall victim to the socialist component of the Social Credit government policy. Heralding the awakening from a lengthy torpor, downtown Victoria got its first office building proper in 40 years with the erection of the Canada Trust headquarters at 650 View Street in 1956. This was followed with the new Law Courts (1962) built at a cost of $2,377,000, Canada Permanent Building, corner of Douglas and Fort Streets in 1963, the Bentall Building in 1964 at 1070 Douglas, replacing McEwen's restaurant which had occupied the site for 10 years, and Executive House in 1965 at the junction of Douglas and Humboldt Streets.

But these buildings were only the beginning. International House went up in 1969 on the site of the former Woodward's stores, the Toronto-Dominion Bank Building at Douglas and Johnson Streets, the Canadian Imperial Bank of Commerce structure at View and Douglas and a new office block at View and Quadra.

Away from downtown the "Murals" — Montreal Trust Building was erected at 1057 Fort and the Alexis Building at Quadra and Fort. These were only two of a large number of new office blocks.

Even greater were the changes outside the city proper. James Bay became largely an apartment complex with the Simcoes, Regent Towers, Beacon Towers and other buildings. The Dallas Road waterfront was transformed in the same way and the 78-suite Camosack Manor erected in 1967 dominated Victoria's skyline by day as the nearby water tower with its "torch" illuminated the night sky. Farther out still, huge, modern shopping centres like the Town & Country, Mayfair, Hillside and Shelbourne Plaza testified to the purchasing power of the rapidly increasing urban population.

With the expansion, Victoria's leisurely way of life disappeared. Downtown Victoria where women in 1950 used to shuffle into Safeway in slippers and haircurlers, became dominated by brisk businessmen. The leisurely arm signals of traffic police were replaced with signs telling pedestrians when they could and couldn't walk and red, yellow and amber lights.

Tremendous parking difficulties were offset only partially by the creation of more and more parkades. Progress demands its price and the price in Victoria's case included the sacrifice of many fine and not-so-fine old homes and landmarks. Old homes, jewels in an emerald setting, gave way often to many smaller jewels crowded together with no setting. These changes took place in the city area mainly in the Vancouver-Cook-Blanshard zone, the latter to make room for a low-cost housing development and increased traffic volume. But the environs also were renewed. The old Oak Bay Boathouse was demolished in 1963 to make way for a large, new Marina. The Willows Hotel at Cadboro Bay and Eastdown Roads was sawn in half and carted away in 1960 to allow the erection of Cranleigh House apartments. Also demolished was the Old Charming Inn at 1420 Beach Drive, where Kipling wrote his ode on a night out in Victoria:

> A gilded mirror and a polished bar
> Myriads of glasses strewn ajar

A kind-faced man all dressed in white
That's my recollection of last night.

The streets were narrow and far too long
Sidewalks slippery, policemen strong
The slamming door, the sea-going hack
That's my recollection of getting back.

A rickety staircase and hard to climb
But I rested often, I'd lots of time
An awkward keyhole and a misplaced chair
Informed my wife that I was there.

Kipling's reference to the rickety staircase recalls the fact that the Old Charming Inn, formerly the Oak Bay Hotel, was built in 1905 in 19 days ... a tempo which gave craftsmen little time to achieve perfection. The last proprietors of the Old Charming Inn were the late Stanley and his widow, Mrs. Morrow, whose charm lived up to the name of the Inn. It was pulled down in 1962 to enable construction of Oak Bay's most prestigious apartment block, the Rudyard Kipling.

Another price demanded by progress was better road communications. The "narrow and far too long" streets of Kipling's day were replaced with highways where cars could travel three and four abreast and where an official speed limit of 30 miles per hour (honoured more in the breach than in the observance) replaced the six miles per hour limit of 60 years ago.

The alleys of the early days — Waddington (lower Yates to Johnson Streets), Duck Alley, Commercial, Poodle Dog, Wilcox, and alongside Hayward's Funeral Chapel, still exist, but excite only a curious glance today. The mud and furtiveness of these dark passages of the pioneer and later years has given way to illuminated cobble- and hard-topped lanes, most of which serve as the rear entrances to warehouses and there is no trace of former life such as the city's first bowling alley, livery stable and commercial baker which once graced Waddington Alley.

But an enlightened city administration and progressive retailers strove to retain the unique atmosphere. Citizens downtown could walk through newly-created secluded passages on Yates, Government and Fort Streets, the more charming because of their novelty.

One passage in the 700 Block Yates Street, had in summer an open air continental-style cafe where the shopper could take coffee beneath gay-coloured sun umbrellas.

The city was indebted mainly to three men for the modernization of downtown Victoria, namely Roderick Clack, former city planner who now has a similar post in Ottawa; former mayor R. B. "Dick" Wilson and Thomas Shanks McPherson.

To Roderick Clack's foresight, energetically backed by Mayor Wilson, Victoria owes the planning of Centennial Square, the model renovation of Bastion Square, the remodelling of the attractive City Hall and the harmonious colouring of downtown buildings.

Downtown buildings were repainted in accordance with a plan pioneered by the City of Norwich in England and brought to the attention of city administrators by architect John Wade.

Thomas Shanks McPherson, after whom the McPherson Theatre (once the Totem Cinema) is named, died in 1962 and left over $3,000,000 to be divided between the City of Victoria, the University of British Columbia and other institutions. It was the greatest legacy in the city's history. McPherson was a bachelor of retiring disposition . . . so much so that the greatest difficulty was encountered in finding a photograph of him after he passed away.

The extent of his fortune was a surprise to his fellow members of the Union Club where he used to add up and initial carefully every bill he incurred. It was even rumoured that in order to save expense he would as winter approached move the desk in his modest office near to the window in order to save switching on the electric light.

But like many people who make money he was careful with it. One could say that most of the big fortunes in Victoria were made as a result of personal sacrifice. For instance David Russell Ker of the great Brackman-Ker milling firm drew only $200 a month when the mills were making thousands of dollars monthly. All profits were reinvested in the business. In this way many of the big businesses the benefits of which we enjoy today were built up.

McPherson operated on the principle that a dime saved was a dime earned. He dealt in real estate and his life interest was to build up his investment portfolio. He came to Canada as a young man from Scotland, ran a general store in Nelson and went to California where he engaged in pottery manufacture. Coming to Victoria he operated in real estate and insurance, one of his biggest ventures being the construction with others of the Central Building on View Street in 1911. During the great depression the Central Building had only one rent-paying tenant, but McPherson survived this. He developed much land in and around the Colwood area, including the Colwood Golf Club itself where he frequently played and was proud of the fact that he achieved a hole-in-one on each of the four par three's.

So wise was McPherson in his investments that his $3,225,000 fortune increased around 50% in the five years between his death and the funds becoming available to the city, university and other beneficiaries. International Nickel and Cominco were in his portfolio.

But the McPherson bequest, generous though it was, would have been of small account without the general expansion of the 1950's and 1960's. The growth was not in Victoria itself, but in the environs.

Between 1951 and 1966 Greater Victoria's population increased from 104,303 to 175,767 — a gain of 75% in 15 years.

The newcomers were mainly the retired, European immigrants and students. The students were the result of the founding in 1963 of the University of Victoria. By 1970 the university was catering to 6,000 students and the total capital investment was estimated at $24,000,000. Numerous imposing buildings and a Centennial Stadium turned a 380-acres Gordon Head area, once the abode of military and skylarks, into an educational conglomerate worthy of the world's largest cities. Still greater were the changes in social strata introduced by the students. Beauty spots like Beacon Hill Park, Centennial Square, Willows Beach and Dallas Road, formerly the preserve of those in the autumn of their lives, were now redolent with serious, polite young men and girls, many of them wearing jeans. Age was offset by youth, mostly well-behaved, impecunious youth, especially in 1970 when so many discovered that university education was no passport to a job. It was a curious paradox that equal higher educational opportunities for all should have coincided with employment opportunities for so few.

The newcomers who were retired people represented another "gold rush," twentieth century style. Increased social security benefits enabled many people from other parts of the province and from Canada as a whole to spend their declining years in a more pleasant environment. It was estimated in 1969 that of the 30,000 retired people living in Victoria 41% came from the prairies and 32% from other parts of British Columbia and that they were bringing $50,000,000 annually into the district, equal to 13% of the total economic intake.

The retired were largely responsible for the tremendous surge in apartment building and a factor in the increased market value of homes from an average of $3,200 in 1941 to $25,000 in 1970.

The immigrants from Europe were mostly Hungarians, Germans, Italians and Dutch who endeavoured in spite of the liquor laws and Anglo-Saxon dull Sundays to introduce a gayer Continental note into social life. Especially successful was the German Edelweiss Club which counted 300 members. These European newcomers helped to counter the increasing Americanization of food outlets through franchised retailers by establishing a large number of delicatessens, the varied food of which appealed to immigrants and natives alike.

Americans also tended to settle in increasing numbers in Victoria where they could find the law and order and absence of racial strife and tension conspicuously absent in many parts of the United States.

Another stimulus to transformation was the tourist trade. The restless, footloose 1960's engendered a tremendous surge in travel. In 1927 the number of visitors to Victoria was 350,000 who came with 18,300 automobiles. In 1969 the corresponding figures were 2,283,000 and 700,093.

Motels and hotels multiplied to cope with the traffic, lining the Gorge, the Old Island Highway and even the Patricia Bay Highway itself. Among the larger new downtown establishments were the Red Lion Inn (1962), the Imperial Inn (1961), the Queen Victoria Inn and the Wilson Inn on Blanshard Street.

At the end of 1970 Victoria had 3,800 rooms to serve tourists.

Simultaneously the introduction of the government ferry service between Swartz Bay and the Mainland shortened the sea journey and resulted in a large increase in traffic.

Victoria's back door became its front door. The overnight visitor instead of viewing on arrival the Parliament Buildings and the Empress Hotel and their lawns encountered 13 miles of black-topped highway leading from Swartz Bay to downtown, the city approaches lined with the showrooms of car dealers and other commercial buildings. But it did not deter visitors from coming, from which one may assume that the final downtown goal was well worth it. Certainly few cities on the North American Continent could boast of Victoria's downtown amenities. The fine new museum and archives complex completed in 1969-70 rivalled the parliament buildings in artistic concept. The Carillon Tower, a centennial gift of the province's Dutch community, and the fountains and displays conveyed an atmosphere of opulence in great and pleasing contrast to the many smaller communities from which many of Victoria's visitors came.

Nowhere was the price of progress felt more keenly than in the business world. The years 1950-70 saw the disappearance of many firms whose names were household words in old-time Victoria and the transfer to Mainland interests of the control of many others.

Among the first to go were J. H. Todd & Sons, Ltd., who moved their offices from 1306 Wharf St. to Vancouver in 1954, extinguishing a connection which had endured since pioneer Jacob Hunter Todd arrived here from the East in the early 1860's. Jacob Todd started as an odd-job man, building a fence for James Douglas on Fairfield Road, and finished up as owner of a fleet of 20 seiners, 300 gillnetters and 40 packers, all of them flying the famous Todd houseflag — a horseshoe on a red background. Like many of the pioneers he owed his fortune primarily to the Cariboo gold rush. He purchased for a song the Victoria interest in the Lightning Creek claim which turned out to be one of the richest claims ever exploited.

The Todd's former "Fairview House" was on the site of what is now McCall's Funeral Chapel on Johnson Street.

Two years after the departure of J. H. Todd & Sons Ltd., Sidney Roofing & Paper, one of Victoria's biggest employers, moved to Vancouver. This company started in Sidney in 1912 making asphalt tiles, moved into town and was sold by its chairman, Robert May-hew, a later ambassador to Japan, in 1948. Their move deprived not only many men of jobs, but the Boy Scouts and the Salvation Army of a profitable market for old newspapers. The Hon. Robert Mayhew is credited with getting the Federal Government to build the new post office building on Government Street, and Fisherman's Wharf.

Other firms no longer with us in name or control include Evans, Coleman & Johnson, with which the later Premier Byron Johnson and his brother "Johnny" — an Oak Bay councillor for over 20 years — were prominently associated; Heaney's Cartage, "Big or Teeny, just call Heaney;" the Northwestern Creamery founded by Francis H. A. Norton in 1911 and now controlled by Silverwood Dairies of Toronto; Shepherd's Dairy; Diggons, successors to Diggon-Hibben and now Willson Stationery; Scott & Peden, now controlled by the Buckerfields of Vancouver, and even the *Chinese Daily News*, formerly published at 640 Cormorant Street.

The penalty for many Victoria businessmen was loss of jobs or transfer to the Mainland and a speeding up of pressure for those who remained. Gone were the old easy-going days. The heart wards of the Royal Jubilee and St. Joseph's hospitals became almost a businessman's club as more and more succumbed to the new stresses imposed on them.

Even Victoria's seagulls were hit by the speeding up. Whereas, fat and lazy, they used to perch on the rails of the Canadian Pacific steamships, unhurriedly awaiting the disposal by stewards of kitchen waste, with the arrival of the British Columbia Government Ferries they found their turn-round time cut by two-thirds.

In the retail field, the take-your-time shopping of 20 years ago gave way to a frantic rush for "sales" and "bargains" caused by the advent of chain and department stores. Woodward's, Eaton's, Woolco and Simpsons-Sears introduced fierce competition not only with small retailers but between themselves.

In the grocery field the competition was still more keenly felt. Piggly-Wiggly, Victoria's original chain grocery, was acquired by Safeway in 1935. In the next three decades came The Red & White

Purity, Super-Valu, Shop Easy, Low Cost and Disco stores which have made this sphere of retailing the most arduous of any.

Just as in the early gold rushes Chinese managed to extract a living from the worked out Fraser pannings when the white miners had abandoned them, so Chinese took over many small grocery stores when the white grocer found the returns too small.

But it has always been an illusion that because Victoria is a seaside and chiefly residential town, life must necessarily be less competitive. In 1925, for instance, with a population of around 40,000, there were in Victoria

- 65 meat markets
- 17 boot and shoe stores
- 13 stationers and booksellers
- 30 cleaners and dyers
- 48 downtown restaurants
- 30 cigar and tobacco stores
- 36 dairies
- 120 confectioners
- 25 drug stores (including A. H. Peacey at 1864

Pandora and now in James Bay, and the Owl Drug store) and, believe it or not, 180 groceries, one-quarter of them Chinese.

The popularity of the large department and chain stores in recent years, most of them owned by outside capital, and their increasing dominance of advertising in newspapers and on radio and television was, in many ways, a regrettable trend. Victoria, when a smaller city, had a way of life so different from that to be found elsewhere, that it could claim to have individuality.

It was largely the British element which provided the well-tended gardens and neat, distinctive individual dwellings which formed the cultural background and earned Victoria the name of "Garden City." As the city and environs succumbed to supermarkets and superhighways it lost something of this distinctiveness.

Victorians at the end of 1970 were questioning more and more many of the aspects of "progress." They questioned the new sodium streetlights which turned many quiet lanes at night into replicas of abandoned sets for a Hollywood spy movie; they questioned the wisdom of widened, hard-topped roads, an enemy of birdlife, and the felling of boulevard trees to enable quicker car travel with consequent more pollution.

They questioned the wisdom of more and more highrise buildings and even the wisdom of expanding populations.

This new social awareness was a hopeful portent that Victoria would continue to be in the future as distinctive a city as it was in the past ... "keeping the best, improving the rest" and thereby making its contribution to British Columbian and to Canadian culture as a whole.

Appendix

LIEUTENANT-GOVERNORS OF BRITISH COLUMBIA
Government House, Victoria

Hon. Sir Joseph William Trutch, 1871-76
Hon. Albert Norton Richards, 1876-81
Hon. Clement Francis Cornwall, 1881-87
Hon. Hugh Nelson, 1887-92
Hon. Edgar Dewdney, 1892-97
Hon. Thomas Robert McInnes, 1897-1900
Hon. Sir Henri Joly de Lotbiniere, 1900-06
Hon. James Dunsmuir, 1906-09
Hon. Thomas Wilson Paterson, 1909-14
Hon. Sir Frank Barnard, 1914-19
Hon. Edward Gawler Prior, 1919-20
Hon. Walter C. Nichol, 1920-26
Hon. R. Randolph Bruce, 1926-31
Hon. J. W. Fordham Johnson, 1931-36
Hon. Eric W. Hamber, 1936-41
Hon. W. C. Woodward, 1941-46
Hon. Charles A. Banks, 1946-50
Hon. Clarence Wallace, 1950-55
Hon. Frank Mackenzie Ross, 1955-60
Hon. George R. Pearkes, V.C., 1960-68

ROYAL GOVERNORS OF COLONIAL DAYS
Appointed by the British Crown

His Excellency Richard Blanshard, Vancouver Island, 1850-51
His Excellency James Douglas, Vancouver Island, 1850-53
His Excellency Arthur Edward Kennedy, Vancouver Island, 1863-66
His Excellency James Douglas, British Columbia, 1858-64
His Excellency Frederick Seymour, British Columbia, 1864-69
His Excellency Anthony Musgrave, 1869-71

In colonial days the Royal Governors were appointed by the British crown. In 1871 the Crown Colony of British Columbia became the Canadian Province of British Columbia, with Lieutenant-Governor and Premier.

Index

In Victoria many businesses, clubs and societies prefixed their title with "Victoria." In order not to make the Victoria section of the index too unwieldy such items have frequently been listed without their Victoria prefix, e.g. Victoria Amateur Club is listed under "A" — Amateur Club. Where such prefixed names occur reference should be sought both under "Victoria" and the name with Victoria omitted.

234

237

242

245